PHILOSOPHICA

TECHNOLOGICAL CULTURE

The Indiana Series in the Philosophy of Technology

Don Ihde, general editor

PHILOSOPHICAL TOOLS FOR TECHNOLOGICAL CULTURE

PUTTING PRAGMATISM TO WORK

LARRY A. HICKMAN

INDIANA UNIVERSITY PRESS

BLOOMINGTON AND INDIANAPOLIS

145953

This book is a publication of
Indiana University Press
601 North Morton Street
Bloomington, IN 47404-3797 USA

http://www.indiana.edu/~iupress

Telephone orders   800-842-6796
Fax orders   812-855-7931
Orders by e-mail   iuporder@indiana.edu

The paper used in this publication meets the minimum requirements of American National
Standard for Information Sciences—Permanence of Paper for Printed Library Materials,
ANSI Z39.48-1984.

Manufactured in the United States of America

Library of Congress Cataloging-in-Publication Data

Hickman, Larry.
Philosophical tools for technological culture : putting pragmatism to work / Larry A. Hickman.
p.   cm. — (The Indiana series in the philosophy of technology)
Includes bibliographical references and index.
ISBN 0-253-33869-7 (cl : alk. paper) — ISBN 0-253-21444-0 (pa : alk. paper)
1. Technology—Philosophy. 2. Pragmatism.   I. Title.   II. Series.

T14 .H45 2001
601—dc21
00-058074

1 2 3 4 5   06 05 04 03 02 01

There is a special service which the study of philosophy may render. Empirically pursued it will not be a study of philosophy but a study, by means of philosophy, of life-experience. But this experience is already overlaid and saturated with the products of the reflection of past generations and by-gone ages. It is filled with interpretations, classifications, due to sophisticated thought, which have become incorporated into what seems to be fresh naïve empirical material. It would take more wisdom than is possessed by the wisest historic scholar to track all of these absorbed borrowings to their original sources. If we may for the moment call these materials prejudices (even if they are true, as long as their source and authority is unknown), then philosophy is a critique of prejudices. These incorporated results of past reflection, welded into the genuine materials of first-hand experience, may become organs of enrichment if they are detected and reflected upon. If they are not detected, they often obfuscate and distort. Clarification and emancipation follow when they are detected and cast out; and one great object of philosophy is to accomplish this task.

An empirical philosophy is in any case a kind of intellectual disrobing. We cannot permanently divest ourselves of the intellectual habits we take on and wear when we assimilate the culture of our own time and place. But intelligent furthering of culture demands that we take some of them off, that we inspect them critically to see what they are made of and what wearing them does to us. We cannot achieve recovery of primitive naïveté. But there is attainable a cultivated naïveté of eye, ear and thought, one that can be acquired only through the discipline of severe thought. If the chapters which follow contribute to an artful innocence and simplicity they will have served their purpose.

—John Dewey, Experience and Nature (LW.1.40)

CONTENTS

ACKNOWLEDGMENTS

THIS BOOK IS an attempt to rethink and refine some of the central arguments that I advanced a little more than a decade ago in *John Dewey's Pragmatic Technology* (Indiana University Press, 1990). Seven of its nine chapters are revisions of essays published separately during the 1990s. Here, together, they invite consideration of some of the pivotal problems and prospects of our technological culture.

I am grateful to Barbara Levine and Diane Meierkort of the Center for Dewey Studies for the care that they lavished on the preparation of the manuscript. Diane's keen eye for the typo and Barb's for stylistic infelicities averted more than one disaster. Warm thanks are also due to Donald Koch for the numerous critical comments that helped me get a better sense of what John Dewey was up to, especially during the early years of his long career. And for many years of marvelous advice and assistance whose description would certainly require more pages than this book contains, I am grateful to Ignacio Angelelli, Douglas Browning, Paul Durbin, Michael Eldridge, Don Ihde, John Lachs, John J. McDermott, Carl Mitcham, Herman Saatkamp, the late Ralph Sleeper, and (most of all) Elizabeth Porter.

Chapter 1, "Tuning Up Technology," began life as the 1994 Berry Lecture, presented at Vanderbilt University.

Chapter 2, "Technology and Community Life," appeared in an earlier version in *Classical American Pragmatism: Its Contemporary Vitality,* edited by Sandra B. Rosenthal, Carl R. Hausman, and Douglas R. Anderson (University of Illinois Press, 1999).

Chapter 3, "Productive Pragmatism, Critical Theory, and *Agape,*" is a revision of "Pragmatism, Technology and Scientism: Are the Methods of the Scientific-Technical Disciplines Relevant to Social Problems?" which appeared in *Pragma-*

tism: From Progressivism to Postmodernism, edited by Robert Hollinger and David Depew (Westport, Conn.: Praeger, 1995). Praeger is an imprint of Greenwood Publishing Group, Inc., Westport, Connecticut.

Chapter 4, "Art, Technoscience, and Social Action," is adapted from "Liberal Irony and Social Reform" in *Philosophy and the Reconstruction of Culture: Pragmatic Essays After Dewey,* by John Stuhr (Ed.) (SUNY Press, 1993) by permission of the State University of New York Press. © 1993 State University of New York. All Rights Reserved

Chapter 5, "Technoscience Education for a Lifelong Curriculum," is a revision of "Science Education for a Life Curriculum," published in *Studies in Philosophy and Education,* Volume 13, and reprinted in *The New Scholarship on Dewey,* edited by James Garrison (Kluwer Academic Publishers, 1995).

Chapter 6, "Literacy, Mediacy, and Technological Determinism," is based on an essay of the same name that appeared in *Lifeworld and Technology,* edited by Timothy Casey and Lester Embree (Center for Advanced Research in Phenomenology and University Press of America, 1990). It also includes a portion of a review of Albert Borgmann's *Holding On to Reality* (University of Chicago Press, 1999), published in *Knowledge, Technology, and Policy,* 12, no.1 (Spring 1999): 93–94.

Chapter 7, "Populism and the Cult of the Expert," appeared in an earlier version under the same title in *Democracy in a Technological Society,* edited by Langdon Winner (Kluwer Academic Publishers, 1992).

Chapter 8, "Hope, Salvation, and Responsibility," appeared in an earlier form as "Creación de mitos tecnológicos: Ellul, Heidegger, Dewey," published in *El Nuevo Mundo de la Filosofía y la Technolgía,* edited by Carl Mitcham and Margarita M. Peña, and Jim Ward (STS Press, 1990).

Chapter 9, "The Next Technological Revolution," is based in part on my 1995 presidential address to the Society for Philosophy and Technology, which was published as "Technē and Politeia Revisited: Pragmatic Paths to Technological Revolution" in *The Quarterly Electronic Journal of the Society for Philosophy and Technology* (Spring 1996), <http://scholar.lib.vt.edu/ejournals/SPT/v1n3n4/Hickman.html>.

The standard references to John Dewey's work employed in this volume are to the critical edition *The Collected Works of John Dewey, 1882–1953,* edited by Jo Ann Boydston (Southern Illinois University Press, 1969–1991), and published as *The Early Works* (EW), *The Middle Works* (MW), and *The Later Works* (LW). These designations are followed by volume and page number. The epigraph for this volume, for example, is from *The Later Works,* volume 1, page 40 (LW.1.40). In order to insure uniformity of citation, the electronic edition, edited by Larry A. Hickman (InteLex Corporation, 1996), preserves the line and page breaks of the print edition.

PHILOSOPHICAL TOOLS FOR TECHNOLOGICAL CULTURE

❖ INTRODUCTION ❖

PHILOSOPHY IN A HIGH-TECH WORLD

IT IS BY NOW a commonplace that the characteristic traits of our culture are pervasively and irrevocably technological. Each of us pays tribute to this fact in innumerable ways during each day of our lives. No longer does any aspect of the food we eat, the clothes we wear, the goods and services we produce, the means by which we travel and communicate with one another, or the ways in which we organize ourselves socially and politically, remain untouched by complex technological factors.

We cannot know how historians a thousand years hence will characterize their own time, but given the factors just mentioned we can be reasonably confident that the late twentieth century, especially that of North America, Europe, and the Asian Pacific Rim, will be remembered as having been permeated by the tools and methods of highly sophisticated technologies just as surely as the culture of the Latin West of the late tenth century was suffused by the tools and techniques of religious forms of life. Techniques have been a part of human life at least since *Homo habilis,* some two million years ago. But advanced technology, as the deliberate and systematic study of tools and techniques, stamps our own milieu as unique.

It is no less a commonplace that our technological culture, because of its size and complexity, and above all because of the many paradoxes it presents, resists easy analysis. The very techniques and technologies that disburden men and women of the backbreaking and mind-numbing work performed by previous generations—and still performed by men, women, and children in developing countries—also present challenges that many perceive as threatening. The same techniques and technologies that bring the exhilaration of rapid change are perceived in some quarters as diminishing the quality of life. One of the most basic paradoxes of our technological milieu is that techniques and technologies ostensibly developed as means of control are now viewed by many individuals as spinning out of control, or at the very least as operating beyond their personal control.

What, if anything, can philosophy contribute toward clarification of this complex situation and rectification of its defects? It has become fashionable in some quarters to dismiss philosophy as moribund, if not already long since dead and buried, and therefore as incapable of any meaningful contribution to the problems faced by contemporary men and women. Some deconstructionist literary critics, for example, and some neo-pragmatist philosophers as well, have told us that the long career of Western philosophy is now finally at an end and that philosophy, especially conceived as an attempt to take account of cultural experience in a holistic fashion, is just another version of the now discredited fallacy of the totalizing "master narrative." Since the complexity of the contemporary milieu is in any event well beyond the understanding of any one person or discipline, they have urged us to abandon all hope of flourishing and to remain content with merely "coping." Since the post-modern condition has left us without polestar or compass, they tell us, effective and confident navigation through the troubled seas of our personal and public lives is consequently no longer possible. The situation that they depict is one in which we are condemned to drift on a sea of endless textual reinterpretations, literary "redescriptions," and private conversations, none of which has any particular privilege over any other. At least that is the way their argument runs.

For reasons that I will explore in detail in the chapters that follow, I view this characterization of the role of philosophy in our technological culture as both feckless and unproductive. It is not that I am nostalgic for the kind of grand philosophical system-building that was fashionable during earlier centuries, nor even that I dream of some future culture in which philosopher-kings will have the last word. It is rather that I find ample evidence that philosophy is alive and well precisely *because* it has finally turned its attention to technical and technological themes.

Philosophers have finally begun to warm to their roles as critics and reformers of some of the most troubled areas within our technological culture. After several decades during which they seemed content to keep to themselves, to write primarily for one another, and to develop vocabularies that few outside their narrowly articulated discipline could comprehend, let alone put to any beneficial use, philosophers of a younger generation have begun to direct their attention outward toward a wide range of vital issues that are both well defined and of pressing common interest. These include controversies in areas as diverse as medical practice, biotechnology, agriculture, engineering, communications, business, and the environment.

I am greatly encouraged, then, that philosophers are at long last testing the idea that they can function as cultural critics and facilitators of cultural reforms, even if some of their criticisms and some of their suggestions for reform operate within circumscribed areas such as the ones just mentioned. And I am delighted that after an extended period of self-imposed exile from the domain of public discourse, philosophers are once again developing some of the tools that will be necessary if we—"we" being all of us who live out our lives on the stage of developing technologies—are to "tune up" our technology, and thereby also to tune up our public and private lives.

Each of the areas of philosophical inquiry just mentioned—medical practice, biotechnology, agriculture, communications, engineering, business, the environment—exhibits its own unique set of philosophically important issues. But there are also more general philosophical considerations that transcend the boundaries of these disciplines. Studies of risk assessment, for example, are applicable to fields such as medical ethics, engineering ethics, and environmental ethics. And studies of sustainability provide important information to agricultural ethicists as well as environmental ethicists.

Beyond these specific disciplines, however, and even beyond the more general cross-boundary studies, there are even larger issues that require the attention of philosophers. It is apparent to anyone who reads a good newspaper on a regular basis that there are public debates that involve perceptions of technology in its widest and most comprehensive sense, which is to say *technology as our culture.* To acknowledge this concern with technology writ large, however, it is not necessary to capitulate to those who hold fast to the old-fashioned notion that technology is a "thing" with an "essence." It is rather to honor the observable fact that technoscience as taught in the schools, as presented in films and on television programs, as the subject of science reporting, and as it relates to the planning and implementation of public projects both large and small helps to shape the ways in which we view ourselves and our communities, and consequently the direction that our individual, community, and corporate activities will take.

So even if it is accepted that philosophers have a role to play in agricultural ethics or engineering ethics, for example, or as participants in broader debates such as those that concern risk assessment or sustainability, it still seems necessary to confront the claims of the "end-of-philosophy" critics at this more comprehensive level. Their claims require us to ask ourselves whether it is any longer possible to address the problems of "technology as culture." Their challenge is that we provide reasons for rejecting their pessimism—their claim that splintered and cloistered specialism is the best we can do, and that the ideal of a holistic philosophy—of philosophy as an attempt to see how things hang together—must once and for all be declared vain and vacuous. Their challenge is that those of us who propose ways of thinking about technology in the broadest senses of the term—technology as culture—explain how such programs are possible at the same time that we avoid appeals to a master narrative.

The central theme of this volume is that technology as culture—as *our* culture —is a legitimate concern of philosophers, and that philosophers can be cultural critics and reformers in the broadest of senses. This theme, and the essays that attempt to work out some of its consequences, draw their inspiration from the work of John Dewey, who regarded himself as a critic and reformer in precisely the sense just described. (See, for example, his characterization of culture in LW.1.363.) I do not claim that a philosopher, or for that matter anyone else, is capable of viewing our technological culture from the outside or with crystal-clear objectivity. I contend only that there are good reasons, and excellent prospects, for improving our understanding of the ways in which the various aspects of our technological milieu are related to one another. I also contend that philosophical tools and methods can contribute to that improved understanding.

The first two chapters are devoted to the broadest of themes within the philosophy of technology. Chapter 1, "Tuning Up Technology," sets the agenda. I attempt to sharpen some of the terms that will be employed in the remaining essays and propose that technology should be naturalized, that is, located within both the evolutionary history and the quotidian activities of humankind. Then I introduce what I call the "productive pragmatism" of John Dewey as a theme that will leaven the entire volume and against which several alternative approaches will be measured. I begin to locate Dewey's work within the context of the history of Western philosophy and examine some of the tools that he recommended for coming to terms with the problems of our technological culture.

Chapter 2, "Technology and Community Life," continues this line of inquiry. Its central claim is that Dewey's version of pragmatism presents a powerful set of tools for reconstructing community life in the age of electronic communication. Those tools include strong accounts of: (a) the relations between what is existential and what is abstract, (b) the objectivity of technoscientific knowledge, and (c) the interdependence of individual and community.

Although chapters 3 through 7 are devoted to topics that are more specific, they nevertheless exhibit broad implications for a philosophical critique of technology. Chapter 3, "Productive Pragmatism, Critical Theory, and *Agape*," examines Dewey's methods in the light of objections advanced by two of his most ardent critics that his program is too weak. The first is the claim of critical theorist Max Horkheimer that Dewey's version of pragmatism is nothing more than an apology for vulgar instrumentalism, and that it is therefore unable to account for what he termed "objective truth." The second is the claim of liberal theologian Reinhold Niebuhr that Dewey's productive pragmatism cannot lead to cultural reform because any such reform must be built on a foundation of an absolutizing moral principle such as Niebuhr's own candidate *agape,* or Christian love.

If Horkheimer and Niebuhr thought Dewey's productive pragmatism too weak, then neo-pragmatist Richard Rorty has seemed to argue that it was too strong. Chapter 4, "Art, Technoscience, and Social Action," addresses Rorty's claim that public platforms for the reconstruction of technology are no longer available, in part because the distinctions between the arts and the sciences have been "rubbed out," and therefore that the best we can do is "work out our own private salvations." By way of countering his claim, I follow Dewey's lead: I provide specific examples of cases in which the technosciences and the arts have made their own unique contributions to effective social reform, and in which they have accomplished more by working together than either could have by working alone.

Chapter 5, "Technoscience Education for a Lifelong Curriculum," takes the measure of some recent retreats from the methods and content of the technosciences and presents a prescription for the low esteem in which technoscientific thinking now appears to be held by the general public. I examine three antiscientific factors, including supervening economic interest, the resurgence of various types of religious fundamentalism, Islamic as well as Christian, and the splintering effects of contemporary specialism. I then present Dewey's three-point program for remediating such factors by developing a robust program for technoscientific education.

Chapter 6 takes up issues that are at once more specific and more personal, but that at the same time involve interests and values that are widely shared. "Literacy, Mediacy, and Technological Determinism" argues that attempts to make hard-and-fast distinctions between print-based media and media based on audio, video, CD, and film tend to frustrate rather than advance fruitful inquiry. I examine the work of neo-Heideggerian Albert Borgmann, who mounts some of the best-wrought arguments available for what I term "text-type determinism."

Chapter 7, "Populism and the Cult of the Expert," draws on examples and arguments from the Vietnam War era as a part of an examination of the role of the expert in technoscientific societies. I carry this theme forward well into the 1990s, a decade that saw both the abolition of the Congressional Office of Technology Assessment under the Speakership of Newt Gingrich and the work of neighborhood organizers such as San Francisco's Randy Shaw. Again following Dewey's lead, I claim that the role of the expert in democratic societies is not to make policy or to tell people what to think, but to alert people to possible ways in which their thinking about matters of importance may be improved. The role of the expert is thus educative: it is to provide fresh ideas based on the pushes and pulls of concrete experiences so that people can determine whether their long-held cherished values are in fact appropriate to their changed and changing circumstances. But the activities of the expert must be balanced by other factors that include both responsible policy-making bodies and publics that are well educated and involved. Above all, philosophers and educators should not shy away from their role as experts, since they are in Dewey's view able to bring tools of critical reflection to bear on outlooks that would otherwise remain habitual at best and prejudicial at worst.

Chapter 8, "Hope, Salvation, and Responsibility," compactly contrasts Dewey's critique of technological culture with those of Jacques Ellul and Martin Heidegger. Its central claim is that the stories told by Ellul and the later Heidegger are covert religious stories whose structure is more or less that of a classic three-point sermon. Whereas Ellul calls for an ungrounded hope in the face of the silence of the Christian God, and whereas the later Heidegger admonishes us that we must prepare for salvation through an epiphany of what he terms "Being," Dewey's secular program—productive pragmatism—presents a clear call for informed and responsible action that is measured by its ability to promote amelioration and growth.

In chapter 9 I expand the account begun in the previous chapter by asking what would count as "The Next Technological Revolution," or more properly, as an effective reform of technological culture. I call attention to the fact that Anglo-American analytic philosophy has not spawned anything that could be termed a philosophy of technology in the robust sense in which I have developed the term. Then I consider proposals for technological reform advanced by several representative figures within "praxis" philosophy: (a) early critical theorists Max Horkheimer, Herbert Marcuse, and Walter Benjamin; (b) later critical theorists Jürgen Habermas, Langdon Winner, and Andrew Feenberg; and (c) phenomenologists Martin Heidegger and Maurice Merleau-Ponty. I suggest that none of these philosophers, despite their forceful critiques of enlightenment rationality, their brilliant phenomenological investigations, their vigorous attempts at political involvement, or their investigations of the grounds of unhindered democratic discourse, has developed anything as coherent or comprehensive as Dewey's program for a "political technology." Nevertheless, there is hope. Feenberg, for example, as a part of his attempt to "update" critical theory and supplant the essentialism of Heidegger, has moved perceptibly in the direction of Dewey's productive pragmatism.

Finally, I suggest that one of the key steps to the effective reform of techno-logical culture will be reconstruction of the time-honored antagonism between theory and practice. Those traditional rivals must be de-hypostatized and viewed in a new light—as phases of inquiry and as partners in the production of new and more intelligent outcomes. And above all, there must be new initiatives in an area in which none of the representative philosophers discussed has made a major con-tribution, but which was the centerpiece of Dewey's life work: education.

Taken together, these chapters are offered as suggestions for tuning up our technological culture. Their premise is twofold. First, we do not need a master narrative, since as Donald Koch has put the matter, what we really want to do is control our present narrative in the near and foreseeable future. And second, we can do more than simply cope with change and uncertainty. Their claim is that the current cultural milieu offers unprecedented opportunities for the growth of individuals and communities alike, and that the productive pragmatism of John Dewey provides tools with which we can capitalize on those opportunities.

1

TUNING UP TECHNOLOGY

> "Technology" signifies all the intelligent techniques by which the energies of
> nature and man are directed and used in satisfaction of human needs; it can-
> not be limited to a few outer and comparatively mechanical forms. In the
> face of its possibilities, the traditional conception of experience is obsolete.
> —John Dewey, "What I Believe" (LW.5.270)

I. Parsing "Technology"

Since it is one of the "ology" words, along with others such as "geology" and "biology," we might reasonably expect "technology" to denote some sort of inquiry or study. But if geology is the study of the materials of the earth's crust, and biology is the study of living things, then what about technology? Surely it must be the study of what the Greeks called *technē*, that is, techniques or productive skills together with the tools and artifacts that are required for their expression. So it would seem that we should understand "technology" as inquiry into techniques, tools, and artifacts.

As reasonable as this suggestion might sound to etymologists and historians, however, it doesn't quite square with the ways we speakers of English tend to use the word. In fact we use the term to designate all sorts of things, from vague to precise. It seems to function as a kind of conceptual junk drawer—a place to keep miscellaneous things that don't fit anywhere else.

To be sure, we do sometimes use the term in its etymologically correct sense. "Report Finds Girls Lagging Behind Boys in Technology," announced an October 1998 *New York Times* headline.[1] The reporter interviewed Janice Weinman, executive director of the American Association of University Women: "What we've learned through the studies is that girls feel much less comfortable with technology than boys, that they see computers primarily as a matter of word processing rather than as an opportunity for a different kind of problem solving." Ms. Weinman seemed to be concerned that girls use computers in unimaginative and uncreative ways, simply as tools for accomplishing routine, predetermined tasks. They don't seem to be pushing the envelope of computer technology. In her opinion they don't get involved in the cognitive aspects of computing. In short, the girls she had in mind were mastering computing *techniques,* but they didn't seem to be interested in computing *technology.* They were typing, but they were not programming.

One of the most common uses of "technology" appears in this full-page advertisement, also from the *New York Times.* "Cash in on Canon. The latest technology. The greatest deal. Up to $50 Rebate. Hurry, offer ends soon." Canon's advertising agency knows well enough that most readers of the *Times* will understand "the latest technology" to mean "the latest boxes that contain silicon chips and software," but not to mean "the latest *inquiry* into boxes that contain silicon chips and software." Even more to the point, Canon wants you to know that "the latest technology" means that using their product doesn't require much thought. It's "plug and play." Take it out of the box, plug it in, turn it on, and watch it work. The subtext, of course, is: "It's turnkey. We did the technology so you don't have to."

The same week that the *Times* printed these two items, the inside cover of the *New York Review of Books* contained an advertisement by Johns Hopkins University Press. One of the featured books was *The Technology of Orgasm: "Hysteria," the Vibrator, and Women's Sexual Satisfaction,* by Rachel P. Maines. In her discussion of mechanical vibration of female genitalia as a nineteenth-century treatment of the now-discredited "disease" then known as "hysteria," Maines tells us that "like many husbands, doctors were reluctant to inconvenience themselves in performing what was, after all, a routine chore."[2]

Despite their many significant differences, including their respective ends-in-view, Canon's latest printer technology and the technology of the mechanically aided orgasm turn out to be remarkably similar. Although technology may have been at one time a part of their development, neither the printer nor the vibrator is any longer technology in the strict sense of the term. For the most part, both cases involve routine techniques and the tools and artifacts that are required for their expression.

The situation is not significantly different in the growth industry we call "technology transfer." Given the increased emphasis on globalization, the transfer of technology is rapidly establishing a position at the center of the world economic order. But what does it mean to transfer technology? Most commonly it means the transfer of techniques, tools, and artifacts—but not the transfer of *inquiry* into such things.

This may be one of the reasons why technology transfer, especially the transfer of military hardware and other big-ticket items such as hydroelectric projects, sometimes turns out to have consequences that are both unanticipated and undesirable. The history of technology transfer, from steel axes to the "green revolution," is replete with cases in which the transfer of techniques, tools, and artifacts from one culture to another without regard for the context in which they were developed, that is, without the "ology" that went into their development and continues to be important in their use, has destroyed the fabric of the recipient culture.[3]

These cultural contexts, or what sociologists and anthropologists call "systems," recall yet another of the common meanings of technology. Vague complaints about the complexity and autonomy of technology—that "things" are moving too fast or that "things" are getting out of control—are frequently directed against the structural aspects of a cultural or social system rather than against specific techniques, tools, and artifacts that support the system. The title of Jacques Ellul's influential sociological study *The Technological Society,* published in English translation in 1964 (and still in print as I write), employed the term "technology" in precisely this way.[4] The target of his many complaints was the "technological" system and the technocrats who keep its engines running. Popular films such as *Armageddon* and popular writers such as Michael Crichton and Jeremy Rifkin have elaborated on Ellul's theme.[5]

There is more. Judging from what my students tell me and what I read in newspapers, the most widely held notion of technology is probably something like the one enshrined in the *American Heritage Dictionary.*[6] According to its editors, technology is "the application of science, especially to industrial or commercial objectives." The Alfred P. Sloan Foundation, which publishes a series of books about technology, apparently subscribes to this view. "Technology," the series editor writes, "is the application of science, engineering, and industrial organization to create a human-built world."[7]

This popular notion carries with it the implication—which it will be the task of the essays in this book to challenge—that technology is chronologically later than, and even ontologically inferior to science, and this because science is theoretical and technology is "merely" practical. The intuition behind this common usage is that theory takes both temporal and ontological precedence over practice. It is apparently what people have in mind when they contrast technology to the "pure (could they possibly mean non-technological?) research" that they think takes place in scientific laboratories. I shall contend that nothing of the sort exists.

This deeply rooted idea has a long pedigree. For reasons that reflected their social structure, for example, the Athenian Greeks created a hierarchy of types of human endeavor in which theory (abstract sciences such as mathematics) took top honors while practice (concrete activities such as politics) took second place. Coming in a distant third, near the bottom of the social pyramid just above the labor of slaves, was production, or the work of the artisan. Perhaps because they viewed their social arrangement as reflecting the natural order of things, the Greeks failed to develop technology in the sense of a deliberate and systematic study of *technē*. In other words, the low esteem in which they held the work of even the most creative of their artisans—their practitioners of *technē*—led them to conclude that *technē* neither had nor warranted a systematic study, that is, a *logos*.

As for the relation between technology and science in more recent times, it is now apparent that the scientific revolution of the seventeenth century would have been impossible without the major technological advances that produced glass beakers, the telescope, the microscope, the air pump, and many other types of instruments. So much for chronological priority. And if someone is tempted to retort that science was indeed the "ideas" or "pure research" that engendered these crucial instruments, then there is an easy reply. Historically, they were invented and underwent development in a relationship of continual feedback with the thought-experiments that expanded their use.

The crucial point about the scientific revolution of the seventeenth century is that what had been an empirical/observational proto-science, because it lacked an instrumental component, became aware of itself as a technological activity in at least two senses.[8] First, it became aware of itself as a systematic activity of production of new consequences. And second, it became aware of itself as profoundly and irrevocably instrumental.

We speakers and writers of English, then, seem to be able to tolerate a high level of ambiguity with respect to our use of the term "technology." We use it to designate, among other things, (a) techniques, tools, and artifacts (means of production, instruments, products, skills, and even documentation); (b) systems that exhibit and depend on such things; (c) the application of scientific theories; and (d) less commonly but more accurately from an etymological standpoint, inquiry or even systematic inquiry into such things.

It almost seems as if we have allowed "technique," meaning "habitualized skills together with their tools and artifacts," to be absorbed by "technology," meaning "systematic inquiry into technique." Or perhaps it is the other way around. Perhaps the habitualized practice of techniques has led us to neglect systematic inquiry into such practices.

In either case, the confusion is no small matter. It is as if our language itself now commits us to two incompatible propositions: first, that the proper employment of a technical skill requires a systematic study of that technical skill, and second, that it does not.

Behind this apparent paradox, however, lies a not-insubstantial truth. It is that the functional relationship between technique and technology is rooted in our most basic organic rhythms: excitation and consummation; disturbance and equilibrium; doubt and resolution. Technology, in its role as inquiry into techniques and their respective tools and artifacts, occupies a middle position between the polar phases of these rhythms.

Ordinarily, technical skills tend to function well enough on their own. But when they break down, for whatever reason, then technology is called for. When technology has done its work, however, new techniques are secured and equilibrium is restored. Techniques are a part of the equilibrium that makes life orderly and predictable. They are, as William James reminded us, the mainsprings and the flywheels of life. They are the stable platforms on which we live our lives. But it is technology that we use to tune up and renew our techniques.

Technology in its most robust sense, then, involves the *invention, development, and cognitive deployment of tools and other artifacts, brought to bear on raw materials and intermediate stock parts, with a view to the resolution of perceived problems.*[9] Technology in this sense is what establishes and maintains the stable technical platforms—the habitualized tools, artifacts, and skills—that allow us to continue to function and flourish.

We have come a long way, linguistically as well as in terms of non-linguistic practice, from the platform that José Ortega y Gasset termed "the technology of the craftsman," or that historical milieu in which well-articulated and narrowly demarcated skills were transmitted from one generation to the next without significant modification. In other words, the "technology" of the craftsman was in fact much more technical than technological; it was much more habitual and routine than cognitive and innovative. Where doubt does not occur, technology—the inquiry that leads to the production of new techniques—does not intervene within technical practice.

None of this is meant to deny that there is something wonderful about observing a skilled craftsman at work. Nor is it meant to deny that there were intermittent technical advances even before the technoscientific revolution of the seventeenth century. The development of coinage more than 600 years B.C.E.; the stirrup in the fifth century of our era; button and buttonhole (the term was originally "buttonhold") in the thirteenth century:[10] each of these developments constituted a major innovation that contained the seeds of far-reaching results. There have been flashes of brilliance, such as those exhibited by Leonardo da Vinci, and there have even been periods of relatively steady improvement of certain artifacts such as the warships that plied the Mediterranean during the period of the Greek and Roman empires.[11]

Ortega wished to deny neither the existence nor the importance of such innovations. His point was rather that during the period of "the technology of the craftsman" there was little or no inquiry into techniques *as such*. There have been specific techniques as long as there have been human beings, and there have been piecemeal attempts at improvement as long as there have been specific techniques. But technology in the robust sense of systematic inquiry into techniques, that is, into the methods of innovation—*technology as such*—did not come into its own until the scientific revolution of the seventeenth century.

Ortega went on to characterize our present milieu as one in which what he termed "the technology of the technician," or systematic cognitive interaction with technical skills, tools, and artifacts, plays an increasingly important role. "In the paleolithic age or in the Middle Ages," Ortega wrote, "technology, that is invention, could not have been a profession because man was ignorant of his own inventive power. Today the engineer embraces as one of the most normal and firmly established forms of activity the occupation of inventor. . . . The engineer need not wait for chances and favorable odds; he is sure to make discoveries."[12]

Nevertheless, something of Ortega's "technology of the craftsman" remains, and it remains by design. One of the goals of innovation is to standardize and automate technological innovations, that is, to turn them into techniques so that they can (a) be performed with a minimum of effort and (b) provide stable platforms from which further innovation can be launched.

Two of the great inventions of the late nineteenth and early twentieth centuries, interchangeable parts and the assembly line, emphasized the first of these two ideas. Standardization and automation were taken so seriously that attempts were made by efficiency experts such as Frederick Winslow Taylor to standardize and automate even the workers who installed the interchangeable parts on the assembly lines. Innovation became the exclusive domain of managers and engineers. The crafts went into eclipse.

Recently, however, emphasis has begun to shift to the second of these ideas. Progressive managers and engineers have begun to think of production-line workers as sources of insight into improved techniques. Though still far from ubiquitous, important new feedback relations have begun to be established between routinized technical platforms and the cognitive assessment of those platforms.

So it now seems more appropriate than ever to understand the relationship between *technology*, which is for the most part active, reflective, and creative, and *technique*, which is for the most part passive, non-reflective, and automatic.

David Pye, a professor of furniture design at the Royal College of Art in London, fine-tuned this picture—and complicated it somewhat as well—in his 1968 book *The Nature and Art of Workmanship*. He distinguished between the two modes of craftsmanship that he termed "the workmanship of risk" and "the workmanship of certainty." Writing with pen and ink, for example, involves a certain risk. Printing from a computer file involves an outcome that is all but certain. Typing is an intermediate form of work, since it involves a small to moderate amount of risk.[13]

His observations have the unexpected effect of appearing to invert what is normally referred to as "high-tech" and "low-tech," since unique handcrafts involve the "high technology" of risk whereas identical mass-produced items involve the "low technology" of certainty. In back of this analysis of the crafts versus the machine, however, lies the recondite fact that there is also risk in the invention and production of the machines and machine tools that make the identical mass-produced items possible. His account recalls the fact that even during the periods that Ortega termed the technology of chance and the technology of the craftsman, there was cognition and innovation. But Ortega's account reminds us that cognition and innovation during these periods were not systematic, that is, not experimental, as they were to become later, during the seventeenth century.

In this matter, as well as others, Ortega was prescient. He thought that the chasm between the activities of worker and thinker that had opened up during the early phases of "the technology of the technician" would eventually have to be bridged. He thought that whenever communication between these two groups is diminished, there is the danger that human beings will become deracinated from nature before they have completed the construction of their new "technological" home. Workers will have to be thinkers, and thinkers will have to expand their notion of work to include that important insight.

Shoshana Zuboff's study of workers in the bleach plant of a pulp mill further illuminates this relation of shifting emphasis between technology and technique.[14] The plant she chose for her study had been redesigned and its operators had been moved away from its caustic environs into computerized control rooms that were both clean and safe. But the workers were ambivalent about their new situation. They found ways to override the air lock between the control room and the fume-filled plant floor. They were, of course, fearful of the chemicals used to bleach the wood pulp and they wanted to be protected from them. But they also resented the new structure because it seemed to diminish the importance of the standardized techniques—the "know-how" that they had incorporated through long practice.

Zuboff's study richly illustrates the ways in which our rapidly changing electronic environment demands that technology continually review and reconfigure techniques, tools, and artifacts. An obvious advantage of this situation is that increased emphasis on technology as systematic inquiry into techniques, tools, and artifacts leads to workplaces that are cleaner, safer, and more efficient. A disadvantage for many workers, as Zuboff points out, is that techniques that have traditionally involved adaptive skills developed within an embodied life-world are increasingly displaced by ones that involve the manipulation of abstract symbols.

This phenomenon is not restricted to factory floors such as the one that Zuboff studied. As I write, there is news that the Chicago Board of Trade will introduce computerized trading as a supplement to the sweat and shouts and gestures of its traditional trading floor. Commodity trading will be cheaper, but traders have already begun to complain about the innovation. The physical interaction of the floor is a valued part of their life-world. They have spent time and energy incorporating physical skills that will no longer be needed.

Because the pace of this change has sped up so dramatically during the past fifty years, simple retraining will no longer suffice. As traditional technical skills give way to skills that require ever-higher levels of symbol manipulation, manager and worker alike will have to increase their commitment to lifelong education. Narrow training will have to be replaced by a context-rich, lifelong curriculum.

II. Naturalizing Technology

In one of its common meanings, then, "technology" as systematic inquiry tends to absorb technique, or habitualized practice. In this sense it includes the store of tools, methods, and even stock parts that have been incorporated into the lives of those who have employed them in ways that have made those things merely "practical" or "mechanical." Even though there might at one time have been a great deal of creativity involved in the invention and development of such things, they have come to be used in ways that are habitual. Like dead metaphors, they have become transparent in use. They have come to be used unconsciously, at hand when needed and used without much thought. At the level of quotidian or everyday life, these are the basic techniques involved in activities such as driving a car, cooking a casserole, or typing an e-mail note.

But basic techniques also play an important role in highly specialized fields such as engineering. When a structural engineer looks up the formulae for calculating load factors, for example, or when an airplane mechanic uses a torque wrench to apply the proper force to a fastener, he or she is applying a basic technique that does not have to be reinvented each time it is used. Whether it is operative in quotidian life or in the work of the specialist, then, the use of basic techniques proceeds regularly, freely, and without much consideration. For better or worse, it is habitual.

Such activities deserve to be called "technical" in the sense that they involve skilled, instrumental engagement with something artifactual. At the same time, however, they involve qualities that are more immediate than reflective. The fact that they have such qualities is hardly accidental. They tend to be the result of deliberate, reflective learning that is undertaken expressly for the purpose of habituating or routinizing them. When they form complexes, they function as more or less stable technical platforms that specialists and non-specialists alike use as the basis for the more active, reflective (and incessant) work of reconstructing such platforms or creating new ones.

Although the details of his thesis remain controversial, it is probably fair to say that what Thomas Kuhn termed "normal science" constitutes an example of a technical platform in precisely this sense.[15] Normal science operates on the basis of certain routinized conclusions that have come to be treated as assumptions, and that are therefore largely unquestioned. Like other platforms, however, normal science tends to undergo periodic renovation. Even the most serviceable platforms sometimes deteriorate to the extent that they can no longer be renovated. They have to be demolished and new ones have to be built. In the example just provided, what was at one time normal science falls into desuetude as a new normal science is constructed.

To take another example, the stages of the history of techniques elaborated by Lewis Mumford—the eotechnic phase of wind, water, and wood; the paleotechnic phase of steam, coal, and steel; and the neotechnic phase of electricity, synthetics, and now silicon chips—are also technical platforms.[16] Each of these historical eras exhibited innovations that differentiated it from a previous era. Once they were incorporated as standard technical practice, many of those erstwhile innovations tended to ossify in ways that impeded further technical progress.

The reconstruction of technical platforms requires reflection or cognition, and consequently inquiry into existing techniques, tools, and artifacts. It is therefore best termed "techn*ology.*" If the term "technology" were used in its etymologically correct sense, it would refer to (and characterize, as well) experiences in which breakdown of transparency or immediacy occurs and in which tools and methods of reconstruction intervene. In short, technology would be said to involve cognitive intervention into the technical, that is, inquiry concerning the skillful use of tools and artifacts. Technology would thus be the study of technique, since it is only with the intervention of systematic inquiry that *technē* comes to have a *logos* of its own.

My theme in this section is naturalizing technology—locating technology within the evolutionary history of human development. It is also, incidentally, an attempt to clear up some misunderstandings that were occasioned by my treatment of technology in *John Dewey's Pragmatic Technology*.[17] Carl Mitcham, for example, took my claim to be that all activity is in some sense technological. He responded that "if virtually all knowing, and indeed all human activity, is or ought to be at its core technological, this raises the specter of reductionism." He quite reasonably concluded that "if all life is technological then the concept of technology becomes vacuous."[18]

A responsible reply to his objection calls for a brief account of four interrelated but functionally separate types or phases of human activity, and this in order to demonstrate that in fact vast areas of human activity lie outside the domain of what I have characterized as technological.

Some activity, for example, involves the use of tools and artifacts and some does not. Activity that *does* involve the use of tools and artifacts can be divided into two types. What is *technological* involves cognitive or deliberate inferential activity,[19] whereas what is merely *technical* is generally and for the most part habitual. It is non-cognitive or non-inferential. Activity that *does not* involve tools and artifacts may likewise be divided into two types. First, there is activity that is *non-instrumental but at least minimally cognitive*. Second, there is activity that is *non-instrumental as well as non-cognitive*. Activity of this last type usually involves little more than immediate perception or habitual "knee-jerk" responses.

Activities that are *technological* include much of what engineers, computer programmers, musicians, architects, and historians do, as well as what each of us does when we utilize tools and artifacts, whether they be concrete or abstract, to address some perceived problem. Such activities are characterized by organized and deliberate transformations of existing situations in ways that generate new outcomes, or products.

In certain cases of this type of activity we may wish to distinguish concrete or tangible tools from those that are abstract or intangible. When such a distinction is made, however, it is itself a tool used within a particular sequence of inquiry.

There is, for example, a difference between the work of an architect and the work of a novelist, or between the work of an engineer and the work of a politician, or even between the work of a sculptor and a person who is planning a vacation. In each of these pairs, the first project emphasizes the material and tangible over the abstract and intangible. The second project in each pair emphasizes the abstract and intangible over the material and tangible. A sculptor is likely to use a mallet and chisel, acquired woodworking skills, a block of oak, and perhaps even some previously constructed ornamental detail that she has in her workshop. A person planning a vacation might use a computer, skill at using the Internet, a list of schedules and fares she finds there, and perhaps an address or phone number of a restaurant or hotel that she has in her files or remembers from a previous trip.

In terms of basic activities, however, each of these examples involves a basic pattern of cognition, or productive problem-solving. Considered in terms of the pattern of inquiry involved, the question of whether the tools involved are tangible or intangible simply dissolves into the background. In the event that such activities were examined from another angle, however, such as how much work space is required to accomplish a task, the distinction between tangible and intangible might well return to the foreground. A sculptor, for example, usually requires more work space than a person planning a vacation.

In the case of a mathematician, hardly any space is required. Nevertheless we must count her tools and artifacts, such as pi and the square root of minus one, as more or less on the same footing as the tools and artifacts of any other profession. This is a point that Dewey made and elaborated in his 1916 essay "Logical Objects" (MW.10.89–97).

Examples of merely *technical* activities include most of what assembly line workers do, what carpenters do when they drive nails, what most of us (except student drivers) do when driving a car, what engineers do when they look up data for load factors, and in fact what most of us do most of the time when we employ tools and artifacts, regardless of whether such tools be counted as tangible or intangible. If this category of behavior were not very large, creativity and innovation that is a part of technological activity would be stifled. We would drown in a sea of details.

If the technical activity of driving a car were not for the most part habitual, for example, then it would not leave room for the cognitive work that must also be done while driving. To take another example, if the technical activities of airline pilots did not involve standardized, habitualized, practical skills, there would be no space left in which to deal with in-flight anomalies or emergencies that demand immediate creative—technological—attention.

The category of *non-instrumental cognitive* activities is extremely difficult to characterize. In cases of this sort a need is identified and then satisfied by the use of something non-artifactual that is immediately at hand—perhaps even by the hand itself. This might involve deciding that the water in a mountain stream is safe, and then cupping a hand and drinking. Or it might involve deciding that a wild animal constitutes a threat and then running away. Simply deciding to pick a flower and enjoy its scent is an uncomplicated example of this type of experience. Since we do not normally talk of hands and feet as tools, it does not seem quite right to identify these activities as instrumental. But there is cognition at a very low level. Each of the examples involves the solution of a fairly simple problem.

What makes these examples so slippery is that in an extended or analogous sense each of them might be said to involve tool-use because it involves low-level inference. This is because inference generally involves the use of conclusions that have proven to be of value in the past and that have become the inferential stock parts we term "premises," as well as the type of tools that we call "transformation rules," when they reach the level of conscious and deliberate use. William James, John Dewey, and Marshall McLuhan, among others, had some of the same difficulties with this category of activity that I am now experiencing as a part of my attempt to characterize it. To call it technological without qualification would be to create confusion with activities that are unambiguously instrumental and cognitive. But not to recognize that there is at least a low level of cognition present would be to deny the obvious.

A part of the problem is attributable to certain vestigial structures that continue to affect—one might even say *infect*—our language. It is almost impossible, for example, to ignore the influence of mind-body dualism on linguistic usage. Some major industries even have a vested interest in maintaining these linguistic fossils. If the mind and body are separate, for example, insurance companies can continue to offer health plans for "physical" diseases but avoid paying for "mental" ones. Of course I have avoided talk of minds and bodies altogether because such talk relies on assumptions that are empirically suspect. I have instead talked about the empirically obvious fact that human beings are biological organisms with an evolutionary history and multiple ways of interacting with their environments. It is in this context that it is possible to point to the existence of a grey or fuzzy area between "tools" that are extra-organic and those that are intra-organic. The difference between what is not cognitive in the activities of non-human animals and what is cognitive in the activities of human beings is a matter of degree.

Activities that are *non-instrumental and non-cognitive* include immediate perceptions and unconscious habitual responses. They include the immediate delight associated with viewing a sunrise or walking on the beach, and the immediate pain involved in stubbing a toe or straining a muscle. They also include the expression of organic habits such as particular ways of smiling, standing, or walking. If there is any inference at all, it is usually below the level of consciousness.

Two things stand out about this class of activities. First, it is extremely large. Most of our activities are of this type. The very size and importance of this category should provide an antidote to Mitcham's objection that my account "raises the specter of reductionism," that "if all life is technological then the concept of technology becomes vacuous." What I term *technological*, because it involves both artifacts and cognition, in fact constitutes but a small part of the lives of most people. What is merely *technical*, because it involves artifacts but little or no cognition, plays an increasingly large role in life. The type of activities that are *non-instrumental and minimally cognitive*—the one that is the most difficult of the four types to describe—is also a major part of non-technological life. And the greatest part of life is what is immediate and habitual, that is, *non-instrumental and non-cognitive*. It is this type of experience, however, that provides much of the raw material for technological activity.

Second, activities that are *non-instrumental and non-cognitive* are real enough in their own terms. They are just what they are experienced as. Experienced on their own terms, they are neither true nor false, since they do not involve judgment.

Philosophers, especially since the time of Descartes, have spent an inordinate amount of time and energy attempting to deal with experiences that are non-instrumental and non-cognitive, but by and large they have not been very successful. They have debated the status of things such as hallucinations, mirages, sticks that appear bent in water, and so on, as if there were matters of deep metaphysical importance at stake. Most of these debates could probably have been cut short, however, if it had been recognized that experiences of this type do not have any role whatsoever in inquiry unless they are called upon to serve some representative function, that is, unless they are required to point beyond themselves as a result of their being involved in some doubtful situation that requires inquiry.

This is a point that Dewey made in his 1927 essay "Appearing and Appearance" (LW.3.55–72). His account inverted the standard epistemological story. Knowing, he argued, is not the sole and only legitimate method of experiencing, nor is it the criteria of experience. Most of our experiences are not anything cognized, but they do offer a possibility of being an occasion for cognitive activity.

More needs to be said about what Dewey told us about this type of experience, since his account helps to clarify what my analysis of these four types of activity has to do with the theme of this section, namely "naturalizing technology."

In his 1938 *Logic,* Dewey devoted a section to what he called "common sense and scientific inquiry." He began by calling attention to what he termed a "situation." A situation is a contextual whole that is experienced as prior to any object or event or set of objects or events that might eventually be found in it or abstracted from it. A situation, then, is some part of an environing experienced world that has a certain dominant character or quality. A singular object or event may stand out from the complex whole or situation, however, when the situation presents what Dewey called "some problem of use or enjoyment" (LW.12.72). The object or event is then abstracted or isolated with a view to determining the nature of the problem at hand and carrying forward some course of action that will lead to its satisfactory reconstruction.

It is at this point that the cognitive enters in. "When the act and object of perception are isolated from their place and function in promoting and directing a successful course of activities in behalf of use-enjoyment, they are taken to be exclusively *cognitive*" (LW.12.73). To be cognitive in this sense means that what has been isolated from a situation will be used to prolong enjoyment or avoid suffering. In short, the cognitive alters the environing situation of the organism. The new situation is artifactual and a product of the type of manufacture we term cognitive. It is the product of an activity that is best termed technological.

At this point I need to recur to what I said earlier about the purpose of offering this fourfold analysis of human activity. *Its aim is to naturalize technology, that is, to locate technology as a cognitive activity within the evolutionary history of complex organisms.* Once this has been done, I hope that it will be apparent that my account does not advance the unsupportable claim that "all life is technological."

This evolutionary history can be fleshed out by saying something more about the relations between and among the four types of activities I have just described. Immediate perception and habitual non-instrumental response are just that: immediate. Upon reflection, however, elements that are found in such experiences or abstracted from them may be analyzed as either something to be avoided or something to be sustained.

Humans, and even less complex organisms, tend to intervene in such situations —either to adapt themselves to the situation or to alter it in some way. Some animals, for example, such as rabbits, adapt passively to perceived danger by freezing in their tracks or hiding. Other animals are more active; they alter their environing situation. An alarmed squid, for example, alters the visibility of the water in its vicinity. Taken together, processes of adaptation and alteration constitute what Dewey calls "adjustment."

The adjustive activities of humans, when they reach a certain level of organizational complexity, may be called "cognitive" or "inferential." As I use these terms, they refer to choice that is purposive, deliberate, and productive of new outcomes designed to resolve perceived problems.

Charles Sanders Peirce and Alfred North Whitehead argued that there seems to be choice, or in the case of inorganic materials, at least valence, all the way down to the most basic known particles of physics. In any event, given the obvious fact that there is at least some level of choice among non-human animals, some philosophers and anthropologists—especially those who work with higher primates or cetaceans—have attempted to determine at just what point choice becomes deliberate and aware of itself, or what we term "cognitive."

Peirce took up this matter in his essay "Concerning Certain Faculties Claimed for Man." After some discussion of whether there can be a "first" cognition, he concluded that "cognition arises by a *process* of beginning, as any other change comes to pass."[20] The implication of this remark, supported by Peirce's view of evolution, is that there is choice and, indeed, inference, in the non-human world.

Although Dewey did not address the matter of the intelligence of non-human animals in any detail, he was quite interested in the issue that Peirce had raised. "From [a] biological point of view," he wrote, "deliberate or conscious behavior is just a way of doing more effectively and economically what unconscious life adaptations do in a relatively wasteful and uncontrolled way, namely, modifying the environment so as to make it a more varied and more stable or secure stimulus for the exercise of functions" (MW.6.439).

Unconscious "inference" may thus be said to utilize "tools" such as "premises" in a sense that is parasitic on tools such as premises that are used in conscious inference. But such a characterization is analogical at best. It can be made only by conscious inference and only in retrospect. By placing the issue in the context of "behavior," Dewey was able to bridge the gap between what is unconscious and what is conscious in much the same way that Peirce had done. Both Peirce and Dewey emphasized the continuity of processes.

In any event, at least since *Homo habilis* some two million years ago, conscious choice or cognition has involved the augmentation of organic responses by the use of tools and artifacts. In addition to the voluminous anthropological literature, a considerable philosophical literature is also dedicated to this subject. John Dewey, Martin Heidegger, Maurice Merleau-Ponty, Marshall McLuhan, Don Ihde, among others, have discussed the interface between organic responses, such as those involving arms, legs, and fingers, and extra-organic tools by means of which arms, legs, and fingers are extended. Merleau-Ponty, for example, discussed cases in which the use of a blind person's cane becomes an extension of arms and fingers. McLuhan wrote about extensions as different as money and automobiles. Ihde has written a phenomenology of dental picks.

Do we then call the cane and the dental pick "organic," or not? Is the voice of a singer or actor her "instrument"? It is indisputable that the blind person feels the sidewalk with her cane and that the dentist feels the tooth with his dental pick in ways that extend their respective central nervous systems. It is also indisputable that the singer or actor trains her voice as if it were a finely wrought tool. As McLuhan put it, media are the extensions of man. The many examples offered by Merleau-Ponty and Ihde support the view, which had been adumbrated some years earlier by Dewey, that the dividing line between body and not-body, between intra-organic and extra-organic, is both vague and shifting. Moreover, it is a boundary that is probably capable of being determined only on a case-by-case basis. There are thus borderline examples, such as the one I just mentioned, that might be counted as either *technological* or *cognitive-intra-organic*, and there are habitual responses that might be counted as either *technical* or *immediately experienced*. Our decision would depend on the precise question being asked and the assumptions involved. When language doubles back on itself, such decisions become even more interesting.

The fact that the boundaries between such cases are fuzzy, however, hardly constitutes an adequate reason to reject the picture I am presenting. On the contrary, it serves to underscore my general point that techniques and technology are evolutionary products. They have evolved from non-instrumental, non-artifactual behavior in ways that appear continuous when seen in retrospect, even though there were probably cases of saltation along the way.

Cognition that involves the use of tools and artifacts that are relatively external to the organism is what I have termed "technology." But once technological work has been done, that is, once problematic situations have been resolved with the help of those tools and artifacts, their solutions tend to be habitualized or routinized. Techniques are then stored as habits and used as needed. When habitualized techniques are applied to problematic situations but fail to resolve them, then more technology—more deliberate inquiry into techniques—is called for.

In the world in which most of us live there is continual reciprocal movement between the technical and the technological. In other words, the technical and the technological are *phases* of our experience. Technology is what we use to tune up the way we experience the world, and the way we experience the world is increasingly technical.

III. The Role of Philosophy

If technology in the sense of deliberate, cognitive deployment of tools and artifacts is what we use to tune up the (increasingly technical) world of our experience, to operate upon situations that are not what we wish them to be, then how do we go about tuning up technology? Perhaps such activities are the proper concern of engineers or systems analysts, or even political scientists (but not philosophers). Perhaps philosophy should restrict itself to analyzing and tuning up skills associated with natural and artificial languages, as some have suggested. Perhaps it has no business with other types of skills. This is a view that has been advanced by many philosophers within the Anglo-American analytic tradition. It is a view that I will discuss in more detail in chapters 2, 3, and 4.

For the present, however, I am suggesting that such a view amounts to a gratuitous impoverishment of philosophy. A far better response, I would argue, is that philosophy has a unique role in reconstructing, or tuning up, technology in the robust sense in which I have characterized it.

In the broadest of senses, philosophy is the bearer of this responsibility because it includes as one of its disciplines logic, or the theory of inquiry. But inquiry, or deliberation, enters into every area of human experience where there is a pressing problem to be solved or difficulty to be overcome. This is no less true in the fabrication of shoes than in the construction of space shuttles. Of course these tasks can be performed either poorly or well. Shoes can be made in the same mechanical way over many decades, or they can continually be redesigned and refined to provide greater cushion and support. And aerospace engineers can make "mechanical" decisions about O-rings that result in lift-off disasters, or they can perform the kind of inventive work that has allowed disabled spacecrafts to return safely to Earth.

Nevertheless, because the scope of inquiry, properly understood, also includes a criticism of inquiry itself, it is important to understand that logic, or the theory of inquiry, is a self-analyzing and self-correcting enterprise. Logic, in this broad sense, comprises the best set of tools so far developed for an ongoing critique of inquiry, and its tools can be utilized to refine themselves and to generate further tools that are instrumental to its self-criticism. What has come to be known as formal or symbolic logic is one of these tools, informal logic is another, and what is loosely called the scientific method is yet another.

In a narrower sense, of course, it also falls to philosophy to deal with the specific problems engendered by the use and development of specific techniques.

Medical ethics, agricultural ethics, and environmental ethics are just a few of the locations where these specific inquiries are conducted.

The role of the philosopher in these contexts is of course not to tell physicians, farmers, environmentalists, and others what to think, but to alert them to possible ways in which their thinking about matters of importance to their own endeavors may be improved. The role of the philosopher is to provide fresh ideas so that specialists in these fields can determine whether their cherished ideas and values are in fact appropriate to their changed and changing circumstances.

Somewhere between these broad and narrow philosophical tasks—the theory of inquiry on one side and technical field-specific studies on the other—there lies yet another area of activity, uniquely philosophical but at the same time intimately associated with anthropology, sociology, history, and other disciplines, such as economics. This is the field known generally as the philosophy of technology, or the philosophy of technological culture.

IV. John Dewey as a Philosopher of Technology

The reigning historian of the philosophy of technology, Carl Mitcham, has written that the first publication in the field was Friedrich Dessauer's *Philosophie der Technik,* published in 1927.[21] That year also marked the appearance of Martin Heidegger's *Sein und Zeit (Being and Time),* which is widely accepted as the first major contribution to the field. Works on the subject by Ernst Juenger in 1932 and by José Ortega y Gasset in 1939 quickly followed.

Until recently, however, no one seemed to notice that American philosophy, or more specifically classical American pragmatism, had also made a solid contribution to the field.[22] I have argued that John Dewey's treatments of education, aesthetics, social and political philosophy, logic, and the philosophy of nature should also be read as contributions to a cultural critique of technology.[23] Some twenty years prior to the publication of the works of Dessauer and Heidegger, Dewey was already writing about a whole range of topics that today are considered central concerns within the philosophy of technology. Later, Dewey's books *Essays in Experimental Logic* (1916), *Experience and Nature* (1925), and *Art as Experience* (1934) all contained incisive critiques of technological culture.

To put this matter in perspective, it may help to recall that Dewey was born in 1859, the year of America's first successful oil well in Titusville, Pennsylvania, and the publication of Darwin's *Origin of Species*. He died in 1952, the year of the first hydrogen bomb test and the first mass marketing of the birth control pill. Dewey's ninety-two years thus spanned two major technological revolutions in

America. At the time of his birth, America's economy was based to a great extent on wind, water, and wood. As he grew to maturity, he observed the shift to an economy of steel, coal, and steam. At the time of his death, America had entered the age of synthetics, electronics, and nuclear energy. The post-industrial society in which we now live was already present in rudimentary form.

I draw attention to these details because Dewey's work as philosopher of technology is of more than just historical interest. His analysis of human experience as transactional with, and within, its various overlapping contexts holds the promise of stimulating new ways of thinking about many of the concerns—especially the ones that involve our environment—that have only recently received the attention of professional philosophers.

The key to understanding Dewey's work as a contribution to the philosophy of technology is, I suggest, an appreciation of his contention that all inquiry or deliberation that involves tools and artifacts, whether those tools and artifacts be abstract or concrete, tangible or intangible, should be viewed as instrumental: in other words, as a form of technology. In short, he understood that technology involves more than just tangible tools, machines, and factories. It also involves the abstract thought and cultural practices that provide the contexts for such things and make them possible. His view of this matter was based upon his broad characterization of technology, which served as the basis for the functional taxonomy of types of activity that I developed earlier in this essay, and that may also be formulated as the *invention, development, and cognitive deployment of tools and other artifacts, brought to bear on raw materials and intermediate stock parts, with a view to the resolution of perceived problems.*[24]

This is my gloss on thousands of words that Dewey devoted to his characterization of technology. It is also quite close to his statement, provided as the epigraph to this chapter, that " 'Technology' signifies all the intelligent techniques by which the energies of nature and man are directed and used in satisfaction of human needs; it cannot be limited to a few outer and comparatively mechanical forms. In the face of its possibilities, the traditional conception of experience is obsolete" (LW.5.270).

It might be objected that this characterization begs the question by identifying technology with "intelligent techniques." But what Dewey in fact accomplished by putting matters as he did was the very distinction between technology and technique that I attempted to work out earlier in this chapter. He was also distinguishing between cases in which it appears that technology is being done but in which in fact something else, such as economic self-interest, has intervened. On this radical view, when such interventions occur, it is intelligence itself that suffers. In chapter 5 I shall discuss the factors that led to the resurgence of rubella as a public health problem in the 1980s as an example of just such a failure of intelligence.

Dewey's view of these matters constitutes a radical departure from the epistemology of the modern period of philosophy. At least since Descartes it had been generally accepted that the central problem of epistemology was the problem of skepticism: how is it that we can have certain or reliable knowledge of the world? Although the story of modern epistemology is long and complex, certain of its features stand out in high profile. As Descartes and other modern philosophers attempted to move out from under the influence of medieval scholastic thought, they faced the difficulty of constructing a foundation for science that offered the same level of certitude that scholasticism had claimed. Since their move was toward naturalism, however, they were obligated to locate certitude within nature, as opposed to the supernatural.

The best recourse seemed to Descartes and others to treat certainty as knowledge possessed by an *individual thinking mind*. Modern theories of knowledge and belief were thus designed to find ways of depicting states of affairs in a world that was assumed to exist separately from a thinking mind, and this in a way that would ensure that such depictions were reliable.

Like the late-nineteenth-century photographers who attempted to get ever better emulsions for ever more accurate photographs of a world outside and independent of their cameras, these epistemologists were attempting to get ever more accurate mental representations of a world that they thought was outside and independent of their minds. They characterized that world not just as independent of mind, but also as whatever it was without respect to whether or not it would ever be known by an individual mind. Now, some 350 years later, some epistemologists and philosophers of science are still doing this.

Dewey thought that this "picture theory" or "spectator theory" of knowledge was deeply flawed. He reasoned that knowing is not just the capturing of a picture or impression, but an active and experimental involvement of an entire organism (not just a "thinking substance" or even a brain) with the raw materials of its experience in such a manner that tools—including habits and concepts, for example—are brought to bear on those materials and new products are formed. And he thought that the point of making these new products was not to take a more accurate picture representation of what was or had been the case (an external "state of affairs"), but rather to deal with felt problems and difficulties in ways that effected their resolution. He thought that inquiry is always launched for the sake of resolving some specific felt difficulty. When inquiry is successful, he argued, it produces a new product—a new outcome.

For Dewey there is no such thing as knowledge in general, but the production of new knowledge in specific cases, ranging from the most quotidian to the most abstract, involves technology just as surely as cases of problem-solving in chemical engineering. This is because we live forward in time in a world that is perilous at best and in continual need of being "tuned up." We have to keep turning out new knowledge-products, including new tools and methods, if we are to convert conditions that range all the way from what is merely irritating to what is life-threatening into situations that are stable, harmonious, and more nearly what we wish them to be.

For Dewey, therefore, one of the most important concerns of philosophy was not so much epistemology, or the attempt to deal with the problem of skepticism, but logic, or the theory of inquiry. Inquiry, he once wrote, is not so much a matter of "grasping antecedently given sureties" as it is a matter of experimentation, or "making sure" (LW.1.123).

Unlike modernist epistemology, Dewey's notion of inquiry emphasizes the use of raw materials and the tools that have been designed for the refinement of those materials. It also involves other tools whose purpose it is to refine and reconstruct tools that already exist, but that are simpler and more primitive. Inquiry also requires the production and stockpiling of intermediate parts, among which are relatively secure concepts and objects. The end or goal of inquiry is products that can be said to be finished in a relative sense of that term, that is, satisfactory until they are challenged by further experience and demonstrated to be in need of reworking or reconstruction.

It was by means of this view of the instrumental or productive role and function of inquiry in human experience that Dewey avoided the problems that had vitiated the work of many of his predecessors. His view avoids the problems of the empiricism advanced by John Locke, for example, since the central place that his instrumentalism gives to production allows it to undercut both the sensory atomism and the associationism on which such empiricism depends. The problem with putative sensory atoms, Dewey argued, is that they are not primitive at all. They are the products of reflection. And the problem with associationism is that its associations tend to be arbitrary if they are based on nothing more than an arrangement of sensory atoms.

His view avoids the difficulties of Cartesian rationalism, moreover, by treating productive inquiry as a public, observable enterprise that takes place within a community, and not as something that takes place within private, non-extended, albeit reified mind. Dewey called inquiry "an outdoor fact," and thought it no less natural and observable than activities such as chewing or walking.

It also avoids the pitfalls generated by the Kantian treatment of knowledge, especially the view that perceptual and conceptual contents have different origins, by treating perceptual and conceptual materials as functional aspects of ongoing inquiry, even as different portions or aspects of judgments. In Dewey's view, the perceptual is concerned with marking out and locating a problem in inquiry, whereas the conceptual is concerned with setting out possible methods of solution. That both types of materials function correlatively within organized inquiry is apparent from the structure of judgments, whose subjects, Dewey pointed out, tend to be perceptual and whose predicates tend to be conceptual.

Dewey worked out his extended technological metaphor for inquiry at great length in the introduction to his 1916 *Essays in Experimental Logic.* That essay is pervaded by technological figures. Here is a typical example:

> Hence, while all meanings are derived from things which antedate suggestion or thinking or "consciousness"—not all qualities are equally fitted to be meanings of a wide efficiency, and it is a work of art to select the proper qualities for doing the work. This corresponds to the working over of raw material into an effective tool. A spade or a watch-spring is made out of antecedent material, but does not pre-exist as a ready-made tool; and, the more delicate and complicated the work which it has to do, the more art intervenes. (MW.10.354)

In the same essay Dewey asserted that "there is no problem of why and how the plow fits, or applies to, the garden, or the watch-spring to time-keeping. They were made for those respective purposes; the question is how well they do their work, and how they can be reshaped to do it better" (MW.10.354–55).

This passage contains several points that are important to the issue at hand, namely the relevance of philosophy as a tool for tuning up technological culture.

First, Dewey wanted to demystify those entities traditionally called "logical objects," "essences," and "ideals," by taking them out of the psychical or metaphysical realms they had occupied in the works of Plato and Frege, for example, and by treating them as so many tools in a toolbox. These tools include logical connectives and numbers, abstract terms such as "democracy," and essences such as "the family."[25] When it is understood that these entities are tools and the products of tools, then it will also be understood that they are open to reconstruction and reconfiguration. They will not be honored as essences that are deemed to be fixed and finished for all time.

Since Dewey's program is radical, its application would involve certain casualties. Among the big losers, to name just a few examples, would be Platonism in mathematics and the doctrine of original intent in constitutional law. This is because each of these positions, as it is usually articulated, depends upon the premise that its respective essence or ideal is absolute and fixed, and not instrumental and consequently in need of continuing reconstruction as circumstances dictate.

So Dewey argued that essences and ideals should be treated not as absolute and fixed, but instead as just more artifacts, constructed not so much *by* inquiry as arising *from* inquiry. They are not found within a chain of inference, but are instead the by-products of inference. In this way they are like agricultural implements that are developed and improved not as a direct consequence of farming but incidentally, as the by-products of tilling, planting, and harvesting.

In all this Dewey was developing a metaphor that would allow him to bring the various types of inquiry we term "successful" under one general formula. He worked out what was already implicit in the work of his fellow pragmatists Charles Sanders Peirce and William James. For those philosophers, all successful inquiry is productive of new outcomes that are more secure than the situations that occasioned the inquiry that produced them. This is true in the sciences, in the arts, in engineering, in agriculture, and in quotidian or everyday enterprises as well.

As Dewey argued in his 1938 *Logic,* the subject matter and the specific tactical methods of inquiry may be, and most likely are, different from one of these enterprises to the next; but each enterprise nevertheless participates within a more general strategic form of inquiry that he called the "general method of intelligence." Because his root metaphor was technological, however, Dewey was able to do explicitly what Peirce and James had done only implicitly. He was able, for example, to reconstruct the important categories of human activity traditionally termed "theory," "practice," and "production."

He did this by reconstructing the Aristotelian hierarchy of types of knowledge. Aristotle had lived in a world in which science was still only empirical and not yet experimental. In other words, Aristotle's science was observational, and not yet instrumental. Instrumentation was not yet viewed as an essential ingredient in science, nor as a source of insights into the pattern of successful inquiry. Aristotle therefore held theory, or contemplation, to be the highest form of knowledge and as such he regarded it as superior to practice, which he in turn regarded superior to production.

But because Dewey's emphasis was on the production of successful outcomes as the end of inquiry, he treated theory and practice as component parts within inquiry and as instruments for further production. He did not completely invert the Aristotelian schema, however, since he regarded theory and practice as phases of inquiry, whose outcome is the production of something new. In Dewey's view, theory and practice must cooperate if there is to be success in the production of new knowledge. I shall have more to say about this matter in chapter 9.

V. Three Objections

In talking to people about Dewey's program for tuning up our technological culture as I have sought to articulate it, several objections have been raised. I believe that they are based on misunderstandings not just of Dewey's critique of technology, but also of the problems and possibilities of our technological culture.

1. Some have claimed that it is an exaggeration to say that philosophical inquiry *is* a form of technology—an instrumentality—for the transformation of our technological culture. This objection seems to reflect the traditional view that philosophy has its own areas of interest, that technology has its own concrete areas of interest, and that despite some occasional areas of overlap, the two activities are fundamentally separate. What has philosophy got to do with the space program or the construction of bridges? The former has to do with human values, and the latter has to do with instrumental rationality.

A version of this view has been advanced by Jürgen Habermas, for example, who has tended to drive a wedge between what he has called the "knowledge constitutive interests" of science and technology on the one hand and the "communicative" and "emancipatory" interests of the human sciences on the other. Put more simply, this is the old "fact-value" split that was lamented by C. P. Snow in *The Two Cultures.*[26]

There are three things I want to say in response to this. First, one of Dewey's great insights was that philosophy has a special kind of productive function, since philosophy is a kind of general "liaison officer," as he put it, "making reciprocally intelligible voices speaking provincial tongues, and thereby enlarging as well as rectifying the meanings with which they are charged" (LW.1.306). In other words, philosophy can serve as a kind of translator that helps the various arts, sciences, engineering, and agriculture continue their discussions with one another. Just as philosophers of science help scientists within different disciplines talk to one another and learn from one another's methods, philosophers as critics of technological culture are in a position to perform this function on a more inclusive scale.

There are several very good reasons why it is up to philosophy to perform this task. As I have already indicated, philosophy contains as one of its parts logic, or the theory of the most general patterns of inquiry. And whereas inquiry within computer aesthetics and inquiry within materials science have different subject matters and different tactical methods, each contributes to and in turn receives the contributions of more general strategic methods of inquiry. Logic, as the theory of this general method of inquiry, serves as a facilitator.

Second, philosophy also involves metaphysics, which Dewey reconstructed as "a statement of the generic traits manifested by existences of all kinds without regard to their differentiation into physical and mental" (LW.1.308). "Any theory," he wrote, "that detects and defines these traits is therefore but a ground-map of the province of criticism, establishing base lines to be employed in more intricate triangulations" (LW.1.309). For Dewey, metaphysics is anything but arcane: it has a connection to the objective world. The importance of the generic traits, he wrote, "lies in their application in the conduct of life: that is, in their *moral* bearing provided *moral* be taken in its basic broad human sense" (LW.16.389). In short, philosophers at their best are not only involved in a criticism of culture, but, because the process is self-correcting, they are also involved in a criticism of criticisms of culture as well.

The material just quoted comes from well-known passages from Dewey's great book *Experience and Nature.* I therefore find it remarkable that several generations of philosophers could have read them without grasping their implications for technological culture.

Third, as I have already indicated, philosophy as a critique of technology does not honor the traditional dualisms of body and mind, tangible and intangible, concrete and abstract, except as they are required as tools of inquiry. The general pattern of inquiry, as laid out by Dewey in his numerous books and essays on logic, is a technological enterprise precisely because it utilizes raw materials upon which tools are brought to bear in a cognitive fashion in order to produce novel artifacts, namely situations that are determined to be more desirable than the ones with which it started.

But this general pattern applies to inquiry of all types, whether the primary focus is that part of our experience we call tangible or that other portion we call the intangible. In other words, this general pattern of inquiry fits cases that involve what we would call hardware, and it also fits cases that are patently conceptual. It applies to descriptions of how manufacturers proceed from iron ore and coal to intermediate and finished steel products, and it applies to descriptions of how writers move from the raw materials of their experiences and research interests to working drafts and thence to finished works of fiction and nonfiction. It applies to the construction of logical and mathematical proofs, and it applies in social and political inquiry.

This concern with the means and ends involved in the production of novel artifacts seems to me to be one of the most important of Dewey's insights about technology. Whenever and wherever techniques of production and construction are utilized, no matter whether the sphere is conceptual or material, there is, in Dewey's view, productive work being done. This is why Dewey regarded the public, or better yet, the many publics that make up what we normally call "the public," as products. They are created as responses to issues of common interest, and their members seek to secure the ends-in-view that they hold in common. It is hardly a secret that billions of dollars are spent each year, from Madison Avenue to Pennsylvania Avenue, to create, manage, and reconstruct such publics precisely as artifacts.

2. A second objection comes from people who are interested in the arts. A colleague once objected that it is a mistake to say that a writer at work on a novel is doing anything "technological." There is in back of this second objection, I think, just the same confusion of terms that plagued Dewey during his long career. When I call writing a novel a problem-solving or technological activity I mean only that there is inquiry going forward and that it is technological because just as in other types of inquiry there are raw materials, there are tools that are deliberately or cognitively deployed and further refined for tasks at hand, there are artifacts produced, and those artifacts are the responses to perceived goals as those goals are themselves developed and refined during the course of inquiry.

Applied to the work of the novelist the pattern is clear. The raw materials are the experiences of the novelist and the experiences of others that she has at second hand. But the novelist doesn't utilize *all* her experiences, and so there is involved a process of abstraction, selection, and reconfiguration. Dewey thought that this happens in all types of inquiry. As a goal or procedure is set up to solve some problem, in this case the writing of a novel, some things are taken as the facts of the case. Then they are weighed, tested, tried, and refined, all with respect to the task at hand. During this process, the task itself is usually modified. This calls for a reevaluation of what have been taken as the facts of the case. Some formerly pertinent data are discarded; other data are seen for the first time to be relevant.

In the case of writing a novel, characters emerge and are developed, plots thicken and then thin again, and there is the production of a new artifact: a novel. (Beyond that, the novel takes its place as an artifact that is used in the construction of further products or artifacts: various publics that will be motivated to purchase the novel, as well as the lives that will be altered as a consequence of reading it.)

Although there is a confusion of terms present in this objection, I believe that there is something else as well. The objection betrays a concern that the "fine" arts be held in higher esteem—or at least a different kind of esteem—than those that are "merely technological." But to treat the fine arts in this manner is to cut short their full reach as instrumental to an enhanced appreciation of the materials with which they are concerned.

Another variety of this type of objection might take the following form: if writing a novel in fact falls under the definition of technology as it has been advanced (namely, *the invention, development, and cognitive deployment of tools and artifacts brought to bear on raw materials and intermediate stock parts, with a view to the resolution of perceived problems*), then why shouldn't the editors of a journal of automotive engineering accept for publication an essay on literary criticism? Writing novels and designing automobiles are, after all, both forms of technology.

This objection misses the point on two counts. First, even if we were to employ the popular and uncritical notion of technology as having exclusively to do with material culture, we still would not expect the editors of the journal of automotive engineering to publish essays on hydrology or coal research. Although both disciplines fit the common definition of technology, their practitioners have different interests and ends-in-view. Second, it might in fact be appropriate under certain circumstances for the editors of the automotive engineering journal to publish a literary essay that explores some aspect of automobiled life in a way that would inform and expand the horizon of automotive engineers. To deny this would be to honor the "fact-value" split about which Dewey continually complained, and which has retarded the resolution of many of our most pressing social problems.

Dewey took a significant risk when he reconstructed the term "technology" in the way that I have described. He took the risk that he would be labeled an uncritical follower of what some have termed "Enlightenment rationality." He also took the risk that he would be thought to have attempted a reduction of all human cognitive activity to one grey, amorphous discipline. (Both of these risks will be discussed in more detail in the next chapter.) But he seems to have thought the risk worth taking since the perceived benefits were so great. Repairing the old fact-value, technology-culture split was one such benefit. And naturalizing technology was another.

3. A third and related objection is that if we treat technology as inclusive of

conceptual tools and artifacts as well as those that are tangible and material, then we have just taken technology so broadly that *everything* is included. This is the objection that I discussed in the section on naturalizing technology. Drawing the net of this objection somewhat more tightly than Carl Mitcham's articulation of it, however, the intuition is that we must reserve the term technology for operations with hardware, or perhaps also for the kind of software that can be held in the hand, or put on a bookshelf, or loaded in a computer, so that we can differentiate what happens in those regions from what happens in religion or poetry, for example. The idea behind this objection is that religion and poetry are "spiritual," whereas technology is not.

As I hope to have demonstrated, what is strictly technological—what involves inquiry into technique, tools, and artifacts—constitutes but a small part of the experience of most people. That portion or phase of experience that I called "technical" is a much larger part, to be sure; but the most prevalent feature of experience is what is immediate, that is *non-cognitive and non-instrumental* organic. This is a far cry from "just turning everything into technology."[27] But because the misunderstanding has been so profound, perhaps more needs to be said.

First, I believe that this objection rests on an explicit ontological dualism that is itself untenable. If what is "spiritual" is of value, then it would seem worthwhile to find ways of allowing it to penetrate all of our experiences. And if "technology" fails to be "spiritual," then its development has somehow been cut short. Dewey rejected dualities of this type because he thought that they "formulated recognition of an impasse in life; an impotence in interaction, inability to make effective transition, limitation of power to regulate and thereby to understand" (LW.1.186).

Second, we cannot identify the technological with the cognitive *as such*, since there is cognitive work that does not involve tools except in a highly attenuated and analogous sense of the term. In retrospect, anthropologists may wish to speak metaphorically of the opposed thumb as a tool that the higher primates used to make the transition from savanna to forest. But the notion of an organic structure as tool is parasitic on the notion of extra-organic structure as tool. To reverse the relation would be anachronistic.

Nevertheless, once we begin to reflect on the ways in which tools are invented, developed, and utilized, it is possible to read the script forward in such a way that mathematical and logical objects, for example, are accepted as legitimate cases of tools. When this occurs, then the last nail goes into the coffin of Platonism. These are more or less the conclusions that Dewey reached during his decade at the University of Chicago, 1894–1904, and that formed the core of his productive pragmatism.[28]

Third, whether or not we use the term "spiritual" to designate religious practice, the undeniable fact is that religions, too, utilize tools, instruments, and artifacts of various types to effect their chosen ends. The leaders of the Roman Catholic Church long ago understood the importance of relics, the bread and wine of the Eucharist, incense, gilded altars, and other material artifacts, together with certain techniques such as the confession, as tools that could be used for the maintenance and enlargement of a believing public. Moreover, the cases in which the Church has retarded or rejected the advances of science in the name of what is "spiritual" have represented some of its greatest embarrassments. The case of Galileo, who was finally pardoned in 1992, some 359 years after being condemned as a heretic, is but one example of this phenomenon.

VI. Four Advantages

I believe that there are several advantages of thinking about philosophy in the sense in which Dewey understood it, and as I have tried to expand upon that understanding, that is, as a tool for tuning up technology. I shall discuss four of these advantages. The first is what I shall call the *felicities of genetic analysis;* the second is the enormous *ecological power* gained by treating human technological activity as continuous with other natural activities; the third is that we get *off the foundationalist hook;* and the fourth is that we are able to generate *stable platforms for social action.*

1. First, this broad view of philosophy as criticism of technology opens up a whole new area of inquiry, namely the genetic analysis of conceptual tools. Just as there is a vestige in the modern plow of the bent stick, there is a vestige in the square root of minus one of the marks made on the wall of an ancient shepherd's fold in order to compare the number of outgoing sheep in the morning to the number of incoming sheep in the evening. And it is hardly surprising that organisms with ten fingers, counting thumbs, would operate in much of the world with number systems of base ten.[29]

This genetic approach to technology rejects the claims of scientific realism, namely that there is a prefigured reality "out there" waiting to be discovered, just as it is, in and of itself, apart from any contribution on the part of inquiry. It argues instead that the conceptual tools of science, including those we call scientific laws, are constructed, but not that they are constructed out of nothing. When they are sophisticated and complex, they are constructed out of tools and intermediate stock parts that are already on hand. In some cases, such as in mathematics, they are primarily relations of relations, or abstractions of abstractions. And the most primitive of such tools are constructed out of the rawest of raw empirical materials, namely, felt needs and desires and flashes of insight or accident.

Why is this felicitous? Because it helps get philosophy out of the box it has often found itself in during its long career and out into the world of human affairs where it can do the work of criticism and reconstruction. It helps philosophy to link up with disciplines such as sociology, anthropology, archeology, and paleontology and thereby to focus its considerable energies upon real problems. It is also felicitous because it helps us get out from under the positivist-scientistic burden, the one that claims that the methods of the physical sciences provide "master narratives" that are somehow independent of such histories.

2. A second advantage of the view I am advancing is that it leads us to look for continuities between the adjustive activities of human beings and the adjustive activities of other natural organisms. This has profound consequences for environmental philosophy. Technology "naturalized" as I have described it, as inquiry into the techniques that human beings utilize to accommodate themselves to their environments and to alter those environments to their needs, functions as a kind of linkage or bridge to similar activities undertaken by higher primates, and even by "lower" non-human animals. It is not something above or apart from nature, but rather the cutting edge of evolutionary development.

I wish I could report that this last point is a minor one and that it has little import for the future of technoscientific education. James Moore, one of the team that worked with Martin Marty and R. Scott Appleby on the "Fundamentalisms" project, reported that by 1984 the Institute for Creation Research had a mailing list of some 75,000, an annual budget of $1.2 million, and a publication list of some fifty-five books that together had sold over one million copies.[30] As late as 1993, one of the largest technical universities in the United States, on whose faculty I was employed for two decades, still had engineering faculty who publicly defended "creation science," thus denying the type of continuity thesis that I have just put forward. In its place they argued for a strong version of supernaturalism that cuts technology off from its roots in the evolution of non-human nature. It is difficult to determine how successful these engineers were in moving their students to accept their arguments, but when the campus newspaper polled students regarding which one book they would choose to have with them in the event of a major disaster that destroyed their civilization, the majority of those polled chose the Bible over other presumably more practical tomes such as *The Foxfire Book*.[31]

This point directly addresses a different sort of objection, namely that if we treat philosophy as a tool for tuning up technological culture, as Dewey recommended that we do, then we have thereby become too preoccupied with one kind of philosophical activity, namely the type that is designed to alter the physical environment, at the expense of another kind of philosophical activity, namely the one by means of which we accommodate ourselves to our environments by means of certain "spiritual" exercises. This is similar to a charge that was brought against Dewey by first-generation critical theorists and others during his lifetime, and it is a charge that is still advanced against him during our own time. Put succinctly, it is that Dewey was a latter-day proponent of "Enlightenment rationality" who urged the domination of nature, and who ignored "spiritual" values or thought them nothing more than impediments to greater levels of efficiency.

It is correct to say that an awareness of this split between what have been called "technologies of environmental domination" and what some have called "technologies of the self" is important for understanding the history of technology, as well as the history of the philosophy of technology. But this is also a point on which Dewey's critics have profoundly misunderstood his work.

The fact is that we can identify two poles or dimensions *within* human experience. One is concerned with the alteration of circumstances that are relatively external to us, organically speaking. Another is the pole that is primarily concerned with the accommodation of ourselves as organisms to such circumstances. Although the first of these poles has sometimes been characterized as the domination of nature, it has also been characterized in some technophobic circles as "technology" *simpliciter*. Because Dewey lived in the wake of Darwin, however, and because he was interested in constructing a new form of naturalism that would take into account continuities within nature, he looked for a way to define technology with sufficient breadth that it could include this second pole of experience. This second pole has been the concern of thinkers such as Max Scheler and Michel Foucault, and it has been advanced in some strains of Buddhism. It also had an important place in Dewey's thinking.

In the first few pages of his 1934 book, *A Common Faith*, Dewey made this point clear. It is significant that such a clear statement of the matter appears in Dewey's only book on the philosophy of religious experience. Here is Dewey's remark:

> While the words "accommodation," "adaptation," and "adjustment" are frequently employed as synonyms, attitudes exist that are so different that for the sake of clear thought they should be discriminated. There are conditions we meet that cannot be changed. If they are particular and limited, we modify our own particular attitudes in accordance with them. Thus we accommodate ourselves to changes in weather, to alterations in income when we have no other recourse.

When the external conditions are lasting we become inured, habituated. . . . The two main traits of this attitude, which I should like to call accommodation, are that it affects *particular* modes of conduct, not the entire self, and that the process is mainly *passive*. It may, however, become general and then it becomes fatalistic resignation or submission. There are other attitudes toward the environment that are also particular but that are more active. . . . Instead of accommodating ourselves to conditions, we modify conditions so that they will be accommodated to our wants and purposes. This process may be called adaptation.

Now both of these processes are often called by the more general name of adjustment. But there are also changes in ourselves in relation to the world in which we live that are much more inclusive and deep seated. They relate not to this and that want in relation to this and that condition of our surroundings, but pertain to our being in its entirety. Because of their scope, this modification of ourselves is enduring. . . . It is a change *of* will conceived as the organic plenitude of our being, rather than any special change *in* will. (LW.9.12–13)

In this passage Dewey deftly undercuts the traditional philosophical problem of the inner and the outer, the mental and the physical, by locating it in the context of his critique of technology. Viewed as a part of a larger picture, habits are tools of adjustment. A habit is something that has a certain generality of application. It is something that has been tried out and found to be capable of serving certain purposes. Viewed from this perspective, as habits of a sort, hammers and saws become continuous with the other habits developed over millennia by higher order primates, for example, in their attempts to adjust to changing environmental conditions. Viewed in this perspective, to say that human beings are uniquely technological animals is not to place them outside and above nature, but within nature and a part of it. Our activities differ from those of our non-human relatives and ancestors not in kind, but only in level of complexity.

Habits are found throughout nature, but only human beings have reached the level of complexity that allows such a high level of self-control with respect to their deliberate formation, development, retention, and modification. It is for this reason—our ability to engage in the self-controlled manipulation of habits—that we human beings are able to reach very high levels of efficiency. We not only accommodate ourselves to environing conditions, but we also adapt environing conditions to our needs. These two activities taken together Dewey calls *adjustment* or *growth,* and he identifies the inquiry that is involved with such adjustment with technology in his broad sense of the term.

3. Here is a third advantage of Dewey's view of philosophy as a tool for tuning up technology. If knowing is a technological activity, then we are off the foundationalist hook. "Certainty" becomes an honorific term that is restricted to narrow

non-existential domains. The laws of mathematical addition and subtraction are "certain" in this honorific sense not because they correspond to "the furniture of the world," to use Bertrand Russell's infelicitous phrase, but because a great deal of work has been focused on a very narrow area of inquiry, that is, one that is so narrow as to exclude actual existence. As for the remaining domains of inquiry, which constitute the vast majority of the locations where technoscientific work is done, reconstruction continues to be done on the assumption that further improvements can be made in existential affairs and in the laws that are developed and employed to characterize them. "Fallibilism" and "probability" replace "certainty" as key operational terms.

4. Fourth, this view has the advantage of providing secure and steady platforms for the improvement of situations that are not as we wish them to be. It is not that we "look for" solutions in the sense of keeping our eyes open, or even that we wait for them to appear, as Heidegger told us that a *"Holzweg"* or clearing in a forest might just appear. If we are to flourish, we must construct hypotheses in a deliberate and intelligent fashion. Knowing is not so much a matter of "finding out" as it is a matter of "making sure." On this view, the kind of inquiry that leads to greater control of problematic social and political situations is also a type of technological undertaking, since it involves an active construction of desirable outcomes through the use of the tools and artifacts that are proper to that domain of knowledge-getting. Not only science itself, but the philosophy, sociology, and politics of science become important technological undertakings.

It is instructive to note the ways in which Dewey's view on this matter contrasts with that of Heidegger. Heidegger writes of a waiting readiness for a clearing to appear in the forest. Dewey writes of sharpening our tools in order to engage conditions that are not what we wish them to be. In one case we get a kind of watchfulness before the incomprehensibility of Being. In the other we get active management of problematic situations.

Critics of technology, such as Heidegger and his followers, have often said that it is technology that constitutes the major human problem. But what they have usually meant is that there are too many techniques, tools, and artifacts and that those things prevent our involvement in more proper occupations such as those that are religious, or "spiritual" in a broad sense, that is, that are concerned with what Heidegger termed "the shepherding of Being." I believe that Dewey would have agreed that technology constitutes the major human problem, but for reasons that are radically different from the ones just given. He thought of technology as inquiry into techniques, tools, and artifacts. And he thought that techniques are among the habits that are necessary to the continuance and growth of human life. He therefore thought that the major human problem was improving intelligence, which he identified with technology. And this means no more or less than developing better and more productive methods of inquiry into our techniques, our tools, and our artifacts.

Following Dewey's lead, I have characterized technology as *the invention, development, and cognitive deployment of tools and other artifacts, brought to bear on raw materials and intermediate stock parts, to resolve perceived problems.* I have also argued that philosophy is one of the most effective tools we have for tuning up technology. This is a theme that will pervade the essays that follow.

In addition, I have argued that what are commonly called the "theoretical sciences" such as chemistry and biology are no less cases of this type of activity than what are commonly called "material technologies" such as mechanical engineering and crop science. Theoretical knowing, such as that involved in mathematics, is no less a case of technological activity than is the type of knowing that is involved with concrete, practical outcomes such as building bridges. Because the theoretical is also artifactual, even what is sometimes called "pure research" is a type of technology.

So whereas the narrow characterizations of technology often tend to draw a line between material artifacts and everything else, which is commonly called science or even culture, and whereas some phenomenological accounts often tend to draw a line between what is practical and what is theoretical, I want to draw a line between what is involved in and a conscious result of intelligent, reconstructive activity, on the one side, and what is merely passive, rote, and uncritically accepted on the other. It seems to me that by dividing things up as I have, we achieve a kind of continuity within the domain of human enterprises that increases our power to effect meaningful adaptive change, that we are able to develop a wider appreciation for the ways that human beings function in and as a part of nature, and that we are able to see the relevance and make more sense out of genetic or historical studies.

If the program that I have outlined is a viable one, then philosophy is indeed an important and effective instrument for tuning up our technological culture. In the chapters that follow, this program will be examined in more detail.

VII. Addendum: "Technoscience"

One more thing. The cumbersome term "technoscience" is now employed in a variety of ways by philosophers, sociologists, and historians who write about technology, science, and technical artifacts. In his book *Postphenomenology,* for example, Don Ihde writes that "[t]he claim of technoscience—as it is now increasingly called—put in phenomenological terms, is that it reveals a world which, perceptually identified, is both a microworld and a macroworld which could not be experienced except through the mediations of instruments."[32] Raphael Sassower even uses the term in the title of his book *Technoscientific Angst.*[33] After citing a text in which Jean-François Lyotard employs the term,[34] he informs us that he will use the term to denote "a dynamic relationship among instruments and people within a cultural context that brings about conceptual and practical changes." He further tells us that technoscience is "the constellation of science, technology, and engineering."[35]

In general, I applaud the manner in which Ihde, Lyotard, or Sassower use this term. Even though I will not use it as freely as they do, I nevertheless need to triangulate it within the context of the distinctions I have attempted to draw in this chapter and that will be the basis of the ones that follow.

As I have indicated, I shall use the term "technology" to mean *the invention, development, and cognitive deployment of tools and other artifacts, brought to bear on raw materials and intermediate stock parts, with a view to the resolution of perceived problems.* Prior to the seventeenth century, technology was intermittent. Since that time, it has been increasingly systematic. As such, technology is more or less inter-definable with what Dewey meant by "inquiry" in his *Logic: The Theory of Inquiry* (1938) and by what he meant by "the general method of intelligence." It is thus a general term under which fall various disciplines that employ their own particular inquirential tools and methods, such as the physical sciences, engineering, the arts, the humanities, jurisprudence, and so on. But as I have indicated, it *excludes* the other categories of activity that I explicated in this chapter. Given the objections raised by some of the critics of this definition of technology that it is reductionist, or that it is so vague that it becomes vapid, this is a crucial point.

Some of the disciplines I just mentioned—the physical sciences, engineering, the arts, and so on, can of course be grouped in various ways, just as they themselves can be used to group various sub-disciplines. It is in this sense that "the humanities," for example, is a term that we can use to group philosophy and historiography. I shall use the term "technoscience" to refer to disciplines that include the natural sciences, the various types of engineering, agriculture, and so on. In addition to the other uses that I have described, I shall use the adjective "technological" to refer to our milieu—a milieu that is characterized (but not yet quite dominated) by the methods and products of technology in the sense in which I have characterized it in much the same manner that the milieu we call "medieval" was characterized (though also not quite dominated) by institutionalized religion.

The term "technology" looks backward to the broad activities of making and doing once designated by the term "*technē,*" including the observational science of Aristotle as well as the magnificent work of the Greek shipbuilders and architects. The term "technoscience" signals the fact that the "scientific revolution" of the seventeenth century initiated the systematic use of instrumentation for experimental purposes, thus forever conflating putatively "pure" theory and putatively "applied" instrumental practice. In the seventeenth century, science transcended its role as "knowledge" and became forever "technoscience" or *instrumentally experimental* knowledge. It is in this sense that the history of the craftsmen, builders, and architects of antiquity is a chapter in the history of technology, as is the history of technoscience.

The order in which I have placed the parts "techno" and "science" in "technoscience" is therefore not accidental. It indicates my view, which follows the lead provided by Dewey, that what we now call science is in fact a type or branch of technology since it involves *the invention, development, and cognitive deployment of tools and other artifacts, brought to bear on raw materials and intermediate stock parts, to resolve perceived problems.*

2

TECHNOLOGY AND COMMUNITY LIFE

> When the machine age has thus perfected its machinery it will be a means
> of life and not its despotic master. Democracy will come into its own, for
> democracy is a name for a life of free and enriching communion. It had its
> seer in Walt Whitman. It will have its consummation when free social in-
> quiry is indissolubly wedded to the art of full and moving communication.
> —John Dewey, *The Public and Its Problems* (LW.2.350)

I. Dewey's Productive Pragmatism in Context

One of the central lessons of the history of technology is that change generally
entails displacement and conflict. At the level of community life, new institutions
and methods compete with older ones for public acceptance. Familiar jobs and
occupations disappear and are replaced by others that require new skills. Geo-
graphic migrations occur. Forms of social organization and practice that seemed
satisfactory for parents and grandparents no longer seem appropriate or even
possible.

From early in his life, Dewey was impressed with the effects of rapid technological change upon community life. During a visit to his father, who was then
in the Union army in Virginia, the seven-year-old Dewey witnessed the devastation that had been brought about by the new technologies and techniques of
the American Civil War. As he began his academic career, his world exploded
with new inventions. During his decade at the University of Michigan (1884–94),
Americans received news of the first steam turbine engine, the first single-cylinder
automobile engine, the first pneumatic tire, and the first wireless telegraph. The
following decade, which Dewey spent at the University of Chicago, was a time of
even more rapid technological innovation. The cinema, X rays, magnetic recording of sound, radio transmission, airplane flight, and many other inventions contributed to a period of breathtaking change. Chicago was irrevocably altered by
changing technological factors. During his decade there, Dewey's city absorbed

massive waves of immigration from Europe and migration from the southern United States. It was also the site of bloody confrontations between workers and industrialists.

Dewey's association with the Hull House experiments of social reformer Jane Addams provided him with an important vantage point from which to view these phenomena. He became acutely aware that technological change not only produces the difficulties of displacement, but also offers opportunities for new forms of cooperation and communication. Even more important, he developed the view that philosophy could play a positive role in the transformation of American culture. In 1925, two decades after he left Chicago for New York and Columbia University, he would write that the "proper task" of philosophy is the liberation and clarification of meanings, including those that have been generated and propagated by advances made in scientific technology (LW.1.307).

In Dewey's time, as in our own, many philosophers have argued that their discipline should be above the fray of ordinary, everyday concerns. These arguments have taken two principal forms. The first, espoused by some of the heirs of the logical positivism of the Vienna Circle tradition, has been that philosophy should be modeled after the theoretical sciences,[1] and that its proper focus should thus be limited to what is narrowly empirical or rigorously abstract. The second, most recently espoused by some "post-modern" philosophers and even by some neo-pragmatists,[2] has been that philosophy is primarily an imaginative or literary art, and that its focus should thus be limited to exploration of the aesthetic dimensions of experience. Although these two approaches appear to have little else in common, they do share the view that philosophy has little or no role to play in the public sphere with respect to the reform of technological culture.

It was Dewey's position that both of these views are defective as they are usually articulated, but that each nevertheless contains an element of truth. He thought that any philosophical activity worthy of the name aims at transforming inchoate or confused human experiences by helping to generate the conditions and implements necessary for their enlargement and clarification. Consequently, it is a part of the task of philosophy to facilitate the construction and use of abstract entities insofar as such entities can function as tools of inquiry. But Dewey also thought that a central aim of philosophy is criticism of received values, or, as he put it, the promotion of "a heightened consciousness of deficiencies and corruptions in the scheme and distribution of values that obtains at any period" (LW.1.308). Consequently, it is a part of the task of philosophy to promote active and refined aesthetic appreciation as a tool for the development of critical consciousness.

An important source of Dewey's activism with respect to the reform of technological culture in general, and his own American culture in particular, was his commitment to what has been termed "evolutionary naturalism." As I described it in the last chapter, this is the view that humans are biological organisms who live their lives interacting with and evolving within the rest of nature. As such, we humans are not ontologically separate from nature, nor can we ever fully escape the existential pushes and pulls of its facilities and constraints. We are, however, able to enhance some of those facilities and mitigate some of those constraints through the use of tools. As Dewey wrote in his lecture notes during 1926, "[t]ools are the expression of the man/environment interaction; by their way means and consequences of action are adapted to each other."[3]

As I also indicated in the last chapter, when Dewey used the term "tools" he was referring to more than just tangible objects such as hammers or computers. He thought that other tools, such as personal habits, shared ideas, and even social institutions, are not any less involved in what is technical and technological just because they are abstract or intangible. He argued that the traditional separation of what is concrete from what is abstract, with its tendency to award the abstract a place of special honor above the concrete, has been the source of considerable confusion and a brake to social progress.

It is by means of the use of many sorts of tools—tangible as well as intangible, and concrete as well as abstract—that human beings are able both to alter their environing conditions and to accommodate themselves to those conditions. This adjustment occurs as a result of inquiry that enables human beings to project themselves forward in time beyond the preoccupations of the present moment in ways that are unavailable to less complex organisms. In populations of such organisms, adjustment occurs as a result of multiple factors that include sexual selection, genetic mutations, and the demise of individuals that are not fitted to changing conditions. Adjustment within human populations also occurs in these ways, but humans are also able to enhance their adjustment by means of an ongoing invention, development, and use of tools of all sorts. The most important tool that humans have at their disposal is language, which Dewey called "the tool of tools" (LW.1.134).

Unlike many current philosophers of language, however, Dewey thought that the domain of language is much wider than spoken or written expression. He argued that the many varieties of expression in the plastic and visual arts, for example, not to mention music, are also instances of communication or language. They are among the tools that human beings use to assess the meanings of their experience and to effect ongoing adjustment within their changing environments.

Dewey thought that knowledge itself—in the arts as well as in the sciences—is both a technologically[4] produced artifact and a tool that human beings use in order to make other artifacts.

In the last chapter I explicated some of the meanings of "technology" along Deweyan lines. In terms that are more specific to the philosophical movement of which he was one of the founding members, however, Dewey's productive version of pragmatism is committed to the use of tools of all sorts within experimental situations in order to effect forward-looking adjustment to environing conditions by means of consideration of practical effects. As he put it in his well-known (1925) essay "The Development of American Pragmatism," productive pragmatism, or what he called "instrumentalism," involves "an attempt to establish a precise logical theory of concepts, of judgments and inferences in their various forms, by considering primarily how thought functions in the experimental determinations of future consequences. . . . It aims to constitute a theory of the general forms of conception and reasoning, and not of this or that particular judgment or concept related to its own content, or to its particular implications" (LW. 2.14).

Implicit in these remarks is the claim that "forms of conception" and "reasoning" take place not just "in the mind," but as features of a fully fleshed out involvement of the organism within its environment. In Dewey's view, reasoning takes place in the literary and plastic arts, in engineering, in jurisprudence, in the writing of history, in agriculture, in music, in the culinary and vintner's arts, and wherever else systematic, self-conscious, creative, forward-looking adjustment occurs.

Dewey's productive pragmatism has been sharply attacked from two fronts. From one side it has been dismissed as being too weak to provide adequate guidance for difficult decisions.[5] Some of these critics, such as the partisans of fundamentalist Christianity, have argued on the basis of their personal or institutional religious commitments that decisions must be grounded on absolute truths that are revealed by God and applicable to all times and places.[6] Other critics, such as some of the first generation of the Frankfurt School, have argued on more strictly philosophical grounds that truth is much more than a tool of action.[7] In their view it is the absolute, unshakable bedrock of certainty in an otherwise uncertain and dangerous world.

From the other side, the position advanced as a part of Dewey's productive pragmatism has been assailed by those who think its claims too strong. Some of these critics have objected to the claim that there are grounds for assessing one judgment or form of life as better than another.[8] Others have argued that productive pragmatism cannot be a participant in community life as long as it holds that its own method is superior to all others.[9] For these critics, truth remains tightly bound to the context of cultural or individual behavior in ways that render objective assessments of such forms of behavior impossible.

Dewey met both of these attacks head on. First, he recognized that a major feature of the history of philosophy has been what he called its "quest for certainty." Ever since Plato, he noted, philosophers have attempted to discover ideals or rules that could serve humankind as foundations, or absolutes. The quest for certainty has also been a dominant feature of most institutional religious thought. But productive pragmatism breaks with this long tradition. It treats ideals and rules as artifacts, and it holds that neither artifacts nor the tools that are used to produce them are absolute. Productive pragmatism rejects the idea that there are absolutes in two of the leading senses of the word.

First, if the term "absolute" means "unmoved or unconditioned by anything else," in the sense in which some theologians have held that Christian God is absolute, then even if there were anything of that sort it would not be possible to know it. This is because whatever is known comes by that very fact to be related to whomever knows it. More specifically, it is related to the interests and attitudes of the knower. As Dewey argued in his classic essay "The Reflex Arc Concept in Psychology" (EW.5.96–109), it is the interests and attitudes of the knower that lead to the selection of data from an indefinitely large field of possible experience, and it is also interests and attitudes that contribute to the reworking and reconfiguration of that data into objects of knowledge. "The fact is," Dewey wrote, "that stimulus and response are not distinctions of existence, but teleological distinctions, that is, distinctions of function, or part played, with reference to reaching or maintaining an end" (EW.5.104). Knowing is thus constructed by relating data to other data on the basis of context and interest. Knowing invokes comparison, contrast, measurement, and assessment of one thing in relation to another. In short, it involves experimentation that results in the alteration of something relative to something else.

Knowing is also relative in the sense that it involves connections to other knowers. Knowing is sharpened and extended by taking the stances or viewpoints of others within a community of inquiry, that is, by considering a problem from as many different perspectives as possible. Thinking, language, and knowledge are all community enterprises, both in terms of their historical development and in terms of their ongoing function of construction and reconstruction.

Second, Dewey rejected the notion of an "absolute" in the related sense of "absolutely certain or immutable knowledge." Because we live forward in time and can never be sure what the future will bring, there is nothing in our experience that is totally impervious to change. Physics textbooks, for example, have tended to treat the speed of light as fixed and certain. That may be true in a perfect vacuum, but in the existential world where perfect vacuums do not exist, the speed of light is anything but fixed and certain. Harvard physicist Lene Vestergaard Hau and her team, for example, were able to slow a beam of laser light to just thirty-eight miles per hour. They transmitted laser light through a cloud of ultra-cold sodium atoms, thus reducing its speed to what one report termed "a pace slower than her bicycle."[10]

The commitment of Dewey and the other pragmatists to experimentalism—and thus experiments of this sort—led them to develop the view that they termed "fallibilism"—the view that knowing is a project that is open to continual review and revision, and that knowing advances by means of such adjustments.

It might be objected that some statements (even if they are not the ones that report the speed of light) are beyond revision, and therefore that Dewey's version of fallibilism suffers from fatal difficulties. The statement "2 + 2 = 4," it might be argued, could never prove to be false and so must count as an example of absolutely certain knowledge. If anything is certain, it would seem, then this equation must be.

Dewey took up this difficult issue in his 1938 *Logic: The Theory of Inquiry*. In mathematical propositions such as "2 + 2 = 4," he argued, "the interpretation to be put upon the contents is irrelevant to any material considerations whatever" (LW.12.395). It is this feature that distinguishes mathematical propositions from the laws of physics. Physical laws require what Dewey called "preferred or privileged interpretation," such as "operating in a perfect vacuum." On the other hand,

> the contents of a mathematical proposition, *qua* mathematical, are free from the conditions that require any limited interpretation. They have no meaning or interpretation save that which is formally imposed by the need of satisfying the condition of transformability within the system, with no extra-systemic reference whatever. In the sense which "meaning" bears in any conception having even indirect existential reference, the terms have no meaning—a fact which accounts, probably, for the view that mathematical subject-matter is simply a string of arbitrary marks. But in the wider logical sense, they have a meaning constituted exclusively and wholly by their relations to one another as determined by satisfaction of the condition of transformability. (LW. 12.395–96)

The question that Dewey considered in this passage is "what do we know when we know that 2 + 2 = 4"? His answer is that we know the "meaning" of a mathematical proposition, insofar as it has a meaning, relative to, or as a function of, its role in a mathematical system, which is itself a construct.

Further, insofar as the proposition "2 + 2 = 4" may be said to be "true" or "false," it refers to an existential situation. Our knowledge in this sense is not absolute either, but dependent upon the existential facts of the case. If we place two apples beside two other apples at a certain point in time on a table, then we can have empirical knowledge that there are exactly four apples on the table. If, on the other hand, we add two cups of milk to a beaker containing two cups of popped popcorn, then we can have empirical knowledge that at that moment the beaker contains two cups of soggy popcorn. (This is one of several examples provided in *The Mathematical Experience* by Philip J. Davis and Reuben Hersh.)[11] In one case, it is true that 2 + 2 = 4. In the other, it is false that 2 + 2 = 4. Here is another example, one that involves division. If I divide 100 by 3, I get 3.333. . . . The string of 3's on the right side of the decimal, of course, goes on indefinitely. But if I go to the grocery store to buy one of the cans of tomato sauce that cost three for a dollar, how much do I pay? I pay 34 cents. It will do me no good to inform the clerk that it is false that 100 divided by 3 is 34. In a world in which I get my food from grocery stores, which is the existential world in which I live, 100 divided by 3 is sometimes 34.

Put another way, Dewey distinguished between a proposition that refers "to *each and every individual* [that] has certain characteristics . . . and a proposition that refers in its own content to *no* individual" (LW.12.256). If we take "2 + 2 = 4" as an example of the former type of proposition, then the matter is an empirical one, that is, it requires that we examine the objects being added together in order to determine whether they have such characteristics that when two of them are taken together with two others, the sum will be four. As is obvious from the examples just given, sometimes this is the case, and sometimes it is not. If we take "2 + 2 = 4" as an example of the latter type of proposition, however, then it refers to *no* individual, but functions merely as a part of a system that has been constructed in order to effect certain types of transformations among abstract objects of knowledge. Knowledge of the meaning of this type of proposition is not absolute, but only relative to its restricted domain.

Even though Dewey viewed knowledge as relative, however, he rejected the type of relativism advanced by some "deconstructionist" philosophers who claim that there is no way to decide between "alternative readings of a text," whether that "text" be a written one, a "text" of nature, or the information that we have about our artifactual world. This position holds that conflicting views about a particular matter do not really prove to be better or worse, but are just expressions of different cultural biases (cultural relativism) or individual preferences or emotions (subjectivism or emotivism) that exist on an equal footing because there is no independent or context-free basis on which to decide among them.

Dewey thought this family of views faulty for several reasons. First, he thought it possible to articulate a general method of intelligence that takes into account successful inquiry in many different areas of human activity, such as the various sciences, the arts, politics, and jurisprudence. He thought that this method undergoes continual revision as it takes new cases into account, and that it has proven the best method so far devised for making decisions. And although technoscience has made major contributions to the development of this general method of intelligence, it is only one of the many sources that continue to nourish that general method and to help it evolve. In this way Dewey avoided the charge that he had accepted "scientism," or the view that the methods of the sciences should be the paradigm for all other forms of inquiry.

Second, Dewey believed that there have been numerous areas of technological and social life in which it is possible to point to examples of objective progress. In the domain of astronomy, for example, the geocentric model of the solar system that was accepted before the Copernican heliocentric model has been shown to be false. Among biologists, the pre-Darwinian view that all living things were created simultaneously is now regarded as quaint. Even though it is true that some individuals, and even some cultures, still hold these discredited views, it is an objective technological fact that such views have been tested and found to be inferior to the views that replaced them.

Dewey thought that objectivity is a function of experimentation within a community of candid and committed inquiry. Not all hypotheses carry equal weight within such communities of inquiry: some of them have been shown to be of little or no value as starting points for getting further knowledge. Others have even proven to be a barrier to getting further knowledge.

Of course there are also social hypotheses that were at one time widely held but that have since proven false. There was a time, for example, when attempts were made on "Biblical" grounds to justify the idea that one race is inferior to another. The same was true of the view that armed combat is the best method of solving disputes about cultural superiority. But both of these hypotheses have been shown to be faulty. Examples of social hypotheses that have proven to be true, in Dewey's sense of enhancing adjustment through what he called "warranted assertibility," include women's suffrage, universal public education, and social security for the elderly.

But it might be objected that this claim, that certain hypotheses should be privileged above others, violates the principle of fallibilism, that is, the principle that holds that our knowledge is never finished and certain. In fact, Dewey would have agreed that our current models of the solar system and the origin of plant and animal species are open to revision. This is true because these are matters that involve abstraction from concrete experience, transformation at the level of abstraction, and then application and reconstruction with respect to existential situations. In other words, these are matters that are subject to ongoing experience. It is conceivable that current models of the solar system or evolutionary biology might someday be replaced by other views, but it is also highly unlikely that they will be subject to substantial correction. The same might be said of women's suffrage, universal education, and social security. In Dewey's view, these hypotheses have been tested and have proven to be "true," that is, to constitute relatively stable platforms for further action.

Dewey's position with respect to these matters might be termed "objective relativism."[12] His position is objective because of his belief that when individual interests and goals are subjected to public, objective, falsifiable experimentation, then they can and do yield concrete results that can become broadly accepted and utilized within communities that take seriously the methods and results of experimentation.

Another way of putting this is to say that Dewey's productive pragmatism involves a moderate form of relativism that is based on the observation that intelligent action takes into account the different legitimate interests of the various groups that make up larger communities of discourse. It is also based on the observation that action tends to be unintelligent when it is based upon private or subjective viewpoints that have not been adequately tested. He thought that subjective viewpoints are appropriate places for inquiry to begin, but that they are not very good places for it to end. He thought that the history of human progress is a history of men and women coming together to form communities of discussion, inquiry, and activity and then constructing new tools: new ideas and new habits of action that are based on careful experimentation and held in common. When this fails to occur, parties to disagreement tend to remain intransigent with respect to received ideas. The development of new tools and new options is cut short.

It was evident to Dewey that cultural, political, and religious differences may sometimes be the sources of sharp disagreement. But a part of his faith in the methods of science and democracy was his belief that even the most serious disagreements could be transcended if subjected to the application of the proper tools.

Dewey therefore rejected the version of what has come to be known as the "incommensurability thesis,"[13] which states that there are unbridgeable chasms of understanding between different cultures or between different cultural groups within complex societies. He thought such a view unsatisfactory on two counts. First, the incommensurability thesis prejudices the very issue it purports to investigate. The assumption that cross-cultural communication is ineffective tends to be an instrument of its own validation.

Dewey's second objection rests on his view of human communication and the role of philosophy within human communities. Even though it is an observable fact that cultural and religious misunderstandings occur, and even that the practitioners of the various scientific-technical disciplines utilize different conceptual models and sometimes fail to understand one another, it is also an observable fact that properly controlled inquiry has been capable of bridging even the most profoundly recalcitrant differences between competing interest groups by identifying common interests and generating common goals.

Dewey regarded communication as one of the most wonderful of human activities, and he thought that wherever enhanced communication is held honestly as a goal and an ideal, then new areas of agreement can be constructed and community life rendered more satisfactory for all concerned.

But what does productive pragmatism have to say to those who hold the general method of intelligence and democratic ideals in contempt? What support can productive pragmatism offer for its claim that its method is superior to the methods of religious or political dogmatism? The answer to dogmatists of these sorts is that the methods of productive pragmatism have proven themselves to be the best methods so far devised for settling disputes and enhancing cooperation between conflicting factions. To privilege these methods is just to recognize that they are the only methods that have proven capable of avoiding the intransigence of absolutism on one side, and the drift of radical relativism, subjectivism, and emotivism on the other. And to opt for either intransigence or drift is to return to methods that have been tried and have failed. Productive pragmatism thus neither appeals to absolute values nor admits that there are no grounds for decision. At the same time, however, it treats its own ideals of inquiry and democracy as tools that are in need of continuing refinement. In other words, it is not just that its methods are the best so far devised, but, more importantly, that they are the best hope for settling future difficulties.

Dewey's rejection of these extremes—absolutism on one side and unqualified relativism on the other—led him to reject some of the most persistent dogmas of the history of philosophy.

He rejected Plato's ideal, perfect, immutable Forms and sought to supplant them with ideals and goals that are artifacts and therefore temporary, provisional, and in need of periodic tune-ups. He also rejected Aristotle's view that there is a fixed order of nature and that we can know natural kinds by making copies of them in our own minds. The model of nature advanced by productive pragmatism is based instead on multiple taxonomies that interact with one another and that are based on an awareness that the kind of information we get from natural events depends on the types of questions we ask and the types of tools we employ.

In fact, productive pragmatism doesn't treat nature as a "thing" at all, but as a human social artifact constructed from many different received ideas, interests, test results, points of view, and working hypotheses. Dewey thought that one of the most serious difficulties associated with Aristotle's view of nature was that he had treated natural science as an empirical activity rather than as an experimental one. The principal difference between the "empirical" and the "experimental" in this context is that the latter involves the intervention of technical and technological artifacts as tools to enhance and extend knowing, whereas the former is primarily a matter of observation and single-model classification. Dewey thought that the great advances in human knowledge since the seventeenth century have been the result of the experimental methods of technoscience. Or put another way, science as we now know it would have proven impossible without the application of instrumentation to the selection and testing of what is observed, as data of experimentation.

Dewey's productive pragmatism also rejected Descartes's idea that thinking substance (mind) and extended substance (matter) are experienced as the most basic ontological categories of things. It holds instead that we experience neither "mind" nor "matter" directly or in the absence of the other, and that both "mind" and "matter" are concepts or tools that we use to divide up our gross, immediate experiences, to operate on them, and to render them more manageable.

Consequently, productive pragmatism holds that the uniqueness of human beings is not attributable to a non-empirical "spirit" or "soul" that is qualitatively different from the rest of the animal world.[14] Human uniqueness is instead the result of an extremely high order of complexity that enables us to take control of the ways by which we form our own habits and therefore to take charge of our own development as individuals and our own evolution as a species. Productive pragmatism regards "mind" and "body" as different focal points within experience, or as different phases in the act of getting knowledge and adjusting to changing environmental conditions. In Dewey's book, "mind" and "body" are not natural ontological entities, but instead important functional tools of knowing.

All of this means that Dewey took a very broad view of what counts as technology. As I indicated in chapter 1, he held that technology is the *invention, development, and cognitive deployment of tools and other artifacts, brought to bear on raw materials and intermediate stock parts, to resolve perceived problems.* This means that tractors and televisions count as technological artifacts, but so do individual habits, the social habits that we call institutions, and even working hypotheses. Sports skills, universities, political parties, and pi are as much technological artifacts as is a hammer. This is so because neither individual habits, nor social institutions, nor shared concepts, are just "given" to us by a god or by nature. They are instead artifacts that are constructed in much the same way that hardware is constructed—not out of nothing, but out of various raw materials and previously constructed artifacts. And since it holds that goals and plans are also technological constructs, productive pragmatism takes very seriously individual and collective responsibility for the future. Unlike less complex animals, we human beings construct our own futures; they are among the artifacts that we continually build and rebuild.

In "The Development of American Pragmatism," Dewey summed up his view of productive pragmatism, or "instrumentalism." "It is therefore not the origin of a concept, it is its application which becomes the criterion of its value. . . . The function of intelligence is therefore not that of copying the objects of the environment, but rather of taking account of the way in which more effective and more profitable relations with these objects may be established in the future" (LW.2.16–17).

II. The Individual, Publics, and Community Life

Because of its view of the ways in which human beings interact with their environments, continually adjusting and readjusting with respect to them, the term "community life" takes on great significance for productive pragmatism.

Dewey thought that both of the principal ways in which social philosophers since the seventeenth century have conceived of community life have proven faulty. The first view is what has generally been known as "classical liberalism" and is now termed "conservatism." This was the view of thinkers such as John Locke, Jeremy Bentham, and John Stuart Mill. This view holds that each of us is born and develops as an individual in the strict sense of the word, that is, as a more or less complete social atom. At some point in prehistory, according to some versions of this thesis, individuals joined together with other more or less equally independent and complete individuals by agreeing among themselves to the terms of some version of a "social contract."

Now Dewey did not object to the claim of the conservatives that social groups are purposely and consciously formed, since he thought that such groups are technological artifacts just as surely as are hammers and saws. But he thought it absurd that anyone would think that individuality and self-conscious personhood could arise in the absence of social interaction. He thought that it is only by means of communication and shared experiences that human beings can become self-conscious individuals in the first place. He consequently regarded education as one of the most important human activities: it is the means by which children are enabled to develop their own talents and interests in ways that take into account environing social conditions.

Dewey also thought that most versions of the "social contract" worked out by political and social philosophers were faulty. Some proponents of this view argued that there had been an actual historical moment in which individuals must have come together to form such a contract. But Dewey pointed out that no such historical moment had ever been demonstrated. Still others attempted to support their view by listing the specific rules that must have been agreed upon and then followed by all the parties to the new social contract. But Dewey thought that such lists of rules were fiction at best. He thought that lists of rules are just as often abstractions from actual living human communities, and not historically prior to them. Human communities develop rules on the basis of practice, and their practice is developed on the basis of rules as those rules indicate and serve as solutions to common difficulties.

It was Dewey's view that a second group of social and political philosophers have also misunderstood community life. These philosophers hold that the individual is *only* or *primarily* a function of his or her society, and that the needs of the community should always take precedence over the needs of its constituents. This view was popular in the Soviet Union during most of its history. It was also a feature of European fascism during the 1930s, and in our own time it is the guiding principle of some "theocratic" states, such as certain Islamic republics, and some religious groups as well. The adjectives "totalitarian" and "authoritarian" are often used to refer to such social arrangements because of their failure to take into account relevant differences between human beings.

Dewey thought this view of community life faulty for several reasons. First, it tended to stifle human growth and development. Each of us has unique interests, talents, and outlooks that can be focused and developed through well-thought-out and carefully articulated educational practice. But when indoctrination is substituted for education, as is usually the case in closed societies, then development is cut short. Second, closed societies also cut short the open discussion and social experimentation that are necessary for determining the nature of common problems and seeking solutions to them. As a consequence, such societies tend to stagnate and eventually to decay.

The major source of invention and insight, in Dewey's view, lies with individuals as they strive to overcome some experienced difficulty. "Every *new* idea," he wrote, "every conception of things differing from that authorized by current belief, must have its origin in an individual" (MW.9.305). Wherever individuals are not free to articulate problems and to attack them experimentally, then growth within the society is greatly diminished. At the same time, however, problems exist within social and cultural contexts, and they are best articulated and refined by means of discourse within communities.

Underlying his critique of these two extreme views of community life was Dewey's contention that both of them had failed to realize that the concepts "individual" and "society" are just abstractions, or tools to be used, and not absolutes. Dewey thought that the problems of community life would not be solved by deciding whether individual or society should have priority over the other, but by recasting the discussion in terms of the relation between what was properly private and what was properly public. What is private, he argued, does not have consequences beyond the boundaries of narrow actions and associations. What is public has wider applicability, and should therefore be a matter of common involvement and oversight.

The real problems in community life are thus for Dewey not the consequences of conflicts between individuals and society, or even conflicts between individuals. Instead, he thought that the problems of community life are due to conflicts within two broad and vague areas: one of them takes place where the public encounters the private, and the other is where various publics encounter one another. In the first of these areas, space must be scrupulously maintained for private activities that have little or no public consequence. Sexual interaction between consenting adults, for example, including the choice of partner and means of contraception, would normally constitute just such a domain of private action.

In the second area of potential conflict, ways must be found to arbitrate and adjudicate between legitimate but conflicting interests of various publics. Dewey thought that both of these areas of discourse can be made more manageable and productive through active planning undertaken at the level of the comprehensive public we call "the state." Dewey thus saw the state as more than just referee or traffic cop that ensures that the rules of the road are observed by all. The state must be more than simply neutral. He thought that because the state is the most comprehensive of publics in which most of us participate, it is also the most comprehensive means available for developing common interests and directing energies toward change that results in the growth of individuals and communities.

At the same time, however, Dewey did not think that action by the state should be a substitute for concrete action within the various publics that it comprehends. The proper role of the state is to aid the liberation of individual talents and resources and to enable and empower various interacting groups so that they can develop new goals and ideals and thus make their best case within a meritocracy of ideas.

In all this Dewey urged us not to forget that publics are technological products. There is no such thing as a "natural" public. Publics are artifacts created and maintained by human effort. One of the primary tools utilized to create publics is the dissemination of information. Books, newspapers, television, and electronic networks are among the tools by means of which publics are formed and held together for common purposes. But disinformation and propaganda, as well as information that is warranted and useful, are also among the tools by which publics are formed. And although there is no place within a free society for the censorship of even what a majority perceives as disinformation, it is also important that public education should foster the development of the tools of critical intelligence by which information of all types can be evaluated.

III. Technological Design for Community Life

Productive pragmatism rejects technological determinism. Unlike Marx, Dewey did not think that forms of technological artifacts uniquely determine social arrangements. In one of his more famous statements, for example, Marx had pronounced that the hand mill produces a society with the feudal lord, whereas the steam mill produces a society with the industrial capitalist. For Dewey, however, tools do not have the last say. Instead, technological innovations tend to rearrange existing alliances, tip balances of power, render some forms of community life obsolete, and encourage the development of others.

Dewey did argue, however, that we can learn from the past. The history of technological innovation teaches us that after initial periods of invention, experimentation, and decentralization, new forms of technology tend to become centralized and monopolized as economic interests are reorganized and consolidated. And the danger of centralization and monopoly is that those publics that are the most vulnerable tend to be ignored and thus to become politically marginalized. In our own time, children, the mentally ill, and the homeless have been excellent candidates for marginalization, and this because they do not have deep-pocket lobbyists and they are either unable to vote or not qualified to do so.

A part of Dewey's rejection of technological determinism was his view that new forms of technoscience do not carry a single value on their faces. He thought that new techniques and technologies are multi-valent, that is, that they offer all sorts of new possibilities and that it is the obligation of those who use them to choose the best of those possibilities and then to rework them in order to render them more valuable. Electronic technology, for example, produces artifacts that are inherently neither pro-nor anti-democratic. They are both—and neither. They are what their users will, and can, make of them.

If Dewey were alive today, he would surely realize that the phase of the electronic revolution that we are now entering will radically alter the ways in which publics are formed and the means by which they interact with one another. Because productive pragmatism is democratic at its core, and because it is experimental in the sense that the technological disciplines are experimental, it always asks whether new forms of technology will tend to support or undercut democratic procedures and institutions.

The much-discussed "information superhighway" offers an excellent case by which to test whether the tools of productive pragmatism can play an effective role in social reconstruction. The first thing to notice about this new form of technology is that it is still in an incipient stage of development. Although its bases such as the Internet have been in existence for some time, they have only recently begun to be available beyond relatively narrow educational, research, military, and corporate circles. As the general public has expressed increasing interest in computer-to-computer communication, however, its use has begun to experience enormous growth. As a consequence, various commercial and public interest groups have begun to recognize its potential and to compete with one another to define its parameters for their own benefit.

What would be the results of applying Dewey's productive pragmatism to the problems associated with the configuration and use of this new public medium?

First, because productive pragmatism is a form of evolutionary naturalism, it takes into account the genetic development of tools as well as organic structures. In pragmatic terms, then, a successful design strategy would take into account the fact that new forms of technological methods and artifacts tend to incorporate elements of older techniques and artifacts as their content. New technologies do not arise out of nothing, but are built on the basis of more or less viable institutions, customs, and habits. Nevertheless, painful discontinuities and displacements sometimes occur when accepted institutional practice is altered. One of the goals of intelligent design should be to mitigate the pain of such displacements. What kinds of displacement might the information superhighway involve, and how could they be taken into account at the design stage?

One form of displacement involves what has been called the "electronic sweat-shop." Once work becomes decentralized, for example, there is a tendency to return to the outmoded practice of piecework. Because laptops can be used at home and on trips away from the office, even salaried workers are beginning to find themselves working longer hours than they did when most of their work was done at centralized locations.

A second form of displacement involves the de facto exclusion of various segments of the population from participation in the electronic network because they lack the skills or the resources with which to access it. Children who attend schools with inadequate computer facilities or instruction, for example, suffer a profound disadvantage with respect to peers whose education affords computerized instruction. A study released by the U.S. Department of Commerce in July of 1999, for example, indicated that 47 percent of whites own computers, whereas only 19 percent of blacks do. Even worse, it found that a child in a white low-income family was three times more likely than a child in a black low-income family to have Internet access.[15]

A third form of displacement is the result of novel stresses experienced by individuals accustomed to "hands-on" work, but who have been reassigned to work with more abstract tools such as computers. In the previous chapter I recalled Shoshana Zuboff's detailed study of just such a situation in the bleach plant of a pulp mill. Zuboff has argued that the transition from "action-centered" to "intellective" job skills not only requires massive retraining, but can be the source of high levels of job-related stress.[16]

A fourth form of displacement results from the facility with which specialized, interest-specific communities develop within "information space." Will the point-to-point communication features of the information superhighway contribute to a splintering of comprehensive community life into smaller and smaller communities that reinforce their own eccentricities and insulate themselves from the methods and forces that serve to promote the coherence of the wider community?

In its own unique fashion, each of these forms of displacement harbors potential threats to community life.

How would intelligent design based on Dewey's productive pragmatism deal with these potential problems? First, it would seek to avoid the techniques of "technology assessment" that were popular in the United States during the 1950s and early 1960s. This usually involved top-down, expert-based assessments of the features of proposed technologies, and there was a tendency to take into account narrow "technical" considerations or to engage in behind-the-scenes social engineering. At the same time, input from the publics most affected by the proposed changes was usually ignored. The massive "urban renewal" and public housing programs of that era continue to serve as reminders of the limitations of such approaches.

Because productive pragmatism exhibits a core belief in the methods of democracy, its methods dictate that all affected parties be heard from not only during the planning stages of significant public projects, but during the stages of their implementation as well. As Dewey put it, productive pragmatism calls not so much for a "planned" society as for one that is continually "planning." The role of the "expert" within productive pragmatism is thus to draw on the energies and sources of information within affected publics and to formulate scenarios for action, but not to exercise ultimate decisions regarding the determination and execution of public policy.

Dewey was well aware that not every affected party or public has the ability to appreciate or articulate its own best interests. It was for this reason that he thought that the interaction between "expert" and affected publics should be a "transaction" that would serve to educate experts with respect to the needs of publics, as well as to educate publics with respect to the assessment and articulation of their own needs and goals. This issue will receive an extended discussion in chapter 6, "Populism and the Cult of the Expert."

On the pragmatic model, then, existing forms of mass and point-to-point communication would be examined for strengths and weaknesses in the performance of their various roles such as entertainment, communication, and education. Media theorists and media historians would be commissioned to address the strengths and weaknesses of broadcast radio and television, cable, the Internet in its current form, and even the telephone, so that past mistakes could be avoided and past successes could be used as models for new developmental strategies. The results of their research would most likely have important consequences for ownership of media, public access, and other regulatory matters.

As new forms of communication alter the nature of work, new agreements would need to be forged among government, industry, and workers in order to avoid new patterns of exploitation. As I write, for example, negotiations of this type are being demanded of the World Trade Organization by members of various non-governmental organizations (NGOs) such as environmental groups and critics of child labor. More equitable income distribution (through more progressive forms of taxation and other means such as raising the minimum wage) would probably be required to ensure that no segment of the larger society—such as the low-income black children just mentioned—is excluded from participation in what promises to become the new social and cultural "central nervous system." Public access to the new information superhighway might be modeled on the successes of rural electrification during the 1930s and the network of interstate highways constructed during the years immediately after World War II.

Government, business, industry, workers' groups, and private foundations would need to enter into new cooperative ventures in order to ensure that every member of the community has access to basic information services. This would in turn require that a realistic accessibility baseline be established and reevaluated on a periodic basis. Historically, new forms of technology have required significant realignments of existing social structures. Whenever this has occurred in a haphazard way and without intelligent planning, the results have usually been disastrous for those publics that are the most fragile.

Second, there would need to be a continuing commitment to the methods of the technosciences and the methods of democracy that have proven in the past to be highly effective tools for the improvement of community life. One of the pillars of the experimental method is fallibilism, and one of the pillars of democracy is its rejection of the intransigence of absolutism, at one extreme, and the drift of radical relativism, subjectivism, and emotivism, at the other. What this means in practical terms is that the information superhighway would need to be designed so as to leave open as many parallel paths of development as are practicable, so that if one path were to prove undesirable or unworkable, another could be taken up and pursued. Fallibilism dictates strategies of design and implementation that remain flexible by maximizing options and creating redundancies wherever possible. Objective relativism, in its turn, takes into account the unique perspectives of the various groups that have a legitimate interest in the development of the new technology. At the same time, however, democratic processes such as negotiation and third-party arbitration would need to be employed, and their techniques continually improved, in order to ascertain the extent to which the actions of a particular public should be judged unreasonably obstructionist to the good of other publics and to the wider community.

Third, because one of the central tenets of productive pragmatism is its belief in the importance of education, one of the central aims of the information superhighway would be to increase educational options. Dewey argued that education is neither indoctrination nor unregulated change. Instead, he suggested, it is a process by which a teacher enters into a transaction with a learner with the aim of developing the learner's talents and interests and enhancing transaction between the learner and the institutional features of his or her society. Good teachers are capable of appreciating the wide range of talents and interests that they find among learners. They also understand that education is a source of personal development for teacher and learner alike, as well as a source of novel ideas about the ways in which social problems can be articulated and addressed.

One of the most interesting features of the emerging information environment is the rapidity with which new tools are becoming available. As a consequence of this, education is already becoming much less age-graded. Younger people often find themselves educating their elders in the use of new electronic tools and techniques. At the same time, however, older and more mature individuals are able to offer the young insights developed during a lifetime of learning to work within the context of complex relationships. Design and implementation of the educational dimension of the information superhighway would thus call for a reconstruction of educational practice that would take these factors into account with a view to establishing new patterns of interaction between teacher and learner. In short, new types of conversation will need to be constructed to take into account these new units of discourse.

Finally, if cultural splintering is to be avoided, educators will need to reevaluate their methods for leading children to an appreciation of the historical and cultural contexts of the wider society in which they will live and work as adults. Dewey argued that educators have a double task in this regard: it is their task to help children develop their interests and talents in ways that enable them to be individuals in the best sense of the word, and it is also their task to help children find a place within the broader society and to envision their own role in its reform.[17]

Productive pragmatism offers many more tools for the design and implementation of new forms of technology and the reconstruction of community life than I have been able to detail in this chapter. In the chapters that follow, I shall also discuss its applicability to some of the aesthetic dimensions of community life and its treatment of religious issues.

The methods of productive pragmatism are by no means uncontroversial. Some of its critics have charged that its commitment to democratic inclusiveness runs the risk of undermining the very democratic processes and institutions that it holds so dear. Critics of another sort have argued that productive pragmatism is uncritically technophilic and elitist, and that it is therefore incapable of taking into account cultural values that have emerged outside of what they regard as its own liberal-democratic circle. A third group of critics has argued that productive pragmatism is overly sanguine about the prospects for progress; that it does not take into sufficient account the darker, dysfunctional aspects of human life.

It was with the first type of critic in mind that I have suggested some of the ways in which democratic inclusiveness can continue to strengthen community life. And it was in response to the second type of critic that I have argued that technology comprehends more than just the tangible implements that occupy the spaces of human life. It also involves the methods and ideals by which men and women can organize themselves into mutually beneficial overlapping publics and thereby enhance the life of the wider community. To the third group of critics it must be admitted that human methods and institutions are unlikely to reach perfection; that it appears that there will continue to be serious constraints on human progress; and that pathologies sometimes deflect the best-intentioned attempts to build community life.

In the face of all this, however, the productive pragmatist continues to exhibit faith in the methods of democracy and technology because she is convinced that they offer the best alternative so far devised for overcoming what is mean, debilitating, and even pathological in human life.

PRODUCTIVE PRAGMATISM, CRITICAL THEORY, AND *AGAPE*

Science through its physical technological consequences is now determining the relations which human beings, severally and in groups, sustain to one another. If it is incapable of developing moral techniques which will also determine these relations, the split in modern culture goes so deep that not only democracy but all civilized values are doomed. Such at least is the problem. A culture which permits science to destroy traditional values but which distrusts its power to create new ones is a culture which is destroying itself.
—John Dewey, *Freedom and Culture* (LW.13.172)

I. Productive Pragmatism and the Retreat from the Technosciences

As a part of a more general retreat from the optimism that accompanied the successes of Enlightenment science and the industrial revolutions of the last several centuries, serious doubts have been registered in some quarters regarding the applicability of the methods of the technoscientific disciplines to the solution of social problems.[1]

These doubts have taken several forms. They have ranged from arguments that the technoscientific disciplines in fact exhibit no coherent method, all the way to claims that such methods are coherent within their own sphere but inapplicable to social problems. Claims of the latter type have at times amounted to charges that attempts to apply the methods of the sciences to social problems amount to "scientism," or the apotheosis of science. At other times such claims have amounted to assaults on what some have called "the cult of expertise" in industrial democracies, a matter that I shall discuss at length in chapter 7.

Dewey's productive pragmatism affords an important source of insight into these matters. Dewey sought to develop a rigorous characterization of the methods of the technoscientific disciplines and to demonstrate their relation to the methods of other productive disciplines including the arts, the practice of law, and the writing of history. He also sought to relate these highly productive methods of inquiry to other methods that he regarded as less productive, such as magic and religion. In all this, one of his principal goals was to call attention to ways in which the methods that have proven inquirentially valuable, such as those utilized in the technoscientific fields, could be applied toward the resolution of pressing social ills.

An important element of Dewey's reconstruction of this material was his argument that the debates that take place as a part of experimental inquiry within the technosciences should be distinguished from two further classes of debates. They differ from those that take place between the partisans and the critics of science, and they also differ from those that take place completely outside of technoscientific communities, that is, without the benefit of experimental techniques.

Differences of opinion between two paleontologists, for example, regarding whether evolution is characterized better by gradualist or by punctuationalist accounts, are radically different from debates between scientists (such as paleontologists) and non-scientists (such as creationists).[2] This is so because in the former case both sides of the debate are committed in principle to experimental methods, whereas the participants in the second type of debate do not share that commitment. Debates between two non-experimentalist camps, as for example those between the proponents of two radically different religious or political ideologies, are different still.

Dewey never tired of pointing out that disagreements within the context of technoscientific inquiry admit of techniques of analytical evidence-gathering and experimental testing that are notably absent in some other, more popular and more commonly utilized forms of inquiry. The successes of the technoscientific disciplines have, he argued, been based upon methods of "discriminating and arranging data that evoke and test correlated ideas." Those ideas are in turn "employed as *hypotheses,* and are . . . of a form to prescribe . . . determinations of facts" (LW.12.485).

Present in this remark is the germ of Dewey's characterization of the ways in which means and ends interact, not just as a part of inquiry within the technoscientific disciplines, but within any inquiry that is systematically productive. Data are employed as the means of eliciting and extracting new ideas in a particular instance of inquiry. Ideas, in their role as hypotheses, serve as the means for further isolation and selection of the facts of the particular case under review. Neither ends nor means are privileged, and conclusions reached are always susceptible to further inquiry in the event that new doubts should arise, as does, in fact, frequently occur.

But it is important to note Dewey's contention that technoscientific fields are not the only locations of successful inquiry. Dewey claimed the same special place for debates between and among individuals who undertake critical and productive work in the arts. It was Dewey's view that although the arts and the sciences address different questions and perform different types of services, they nevertheless share a common method of inquiry, which he often called the "method of intelligence." Put another way, even though the arts and the sciences utilize different tools and operate with different types of materials, they nevertheless exhibit common logical or inquirential strategies insofar as they bring problematic situations within their respective fields to a fruitful conclusion. The point here is that both types of activity—the arts as well as the technosciences—are capable of producing novel ways of adjusting unsettled or problematic situations.

The arts, Dewey suggested, "express" meanings, whereas the sciences "state" them. Nevertheless, both types of enterprise, when successful, are bound to criteria by means of which the elements and facts of their selected problem areas are subjected to critical appraisal, to honesty with respect to materials, to evaluations within a peer group or community of inquiry, and to relevance with respect to cultural-historical contexts.

In addition to tactical inquiry in the technoscientific disciplines, the arts, jurisprudence, historiography, and elsewhere, there is thus in Dewey's view also an overarching strategic method of inquiry in operation. Further, this general method undergoes continual refinement as it transacts business with its more tactically oriented tributary disciplines. This is what Dewey called the general pattern of inquiry or the method of intelligence. It is also what I, following his lead, have termed technology.

Dewey's characterization of this overarching method—technology—is itself an idea, a complex hypothesis about the general features of inquiries that have proven successful. As an idea about the general pattern of inquiry, it has been elicited from data that include elements of the history of the technosciences, the histories of the arts, and even the histories of the proto-sciences that preceded the development of technoscience during the seventeenth century and the trial-and-error techniques that reach into the distant past of humankind. As a hypothesis about the characteristics of successful inquiry, it serves as a guide to the further determination of the facts of that case. Moreover, refinement of the relevant facts leads to further improvement of the hypothesis, which in this particular case involves the methods according to which a general theory of successful inquiry may be characterized in an ever more precise manner.

One of the principal differences between inquiry that is successful and inquiry that is not is that unsuccessful methods of fixing belief tend to terminate prematurely the give-and-take between the means and ends of a particular process of inquiry. Unsuccessful methods tend to avoid or dismiss experimentally based challenges to their received doctrines. Facts are selected because of their support for conclusions accepted in advance and often without qualification; new data are consequently denied or ignored and improved hypotheses are stillborn. In broad terms, this is one of the crucial differences between technoscience and ideology.

It is for this reason that even though less productive methods such as religion and magic have had some remarkable successes (defined in terms of their ability to produce satisfactory adjustment to changing conditions and to control situations that are perceived as undesirable), they have nevertheless historically proven less likely to produce such reliable results over the long haul.

Dewey was by no means the first to advance the general outlines of this theory of inquiry. He was, in fact, following up on the suggestions laid out in Charles Sanders Peirce's 1877 essay "The Fixation of Belief" and in William James's "The Will to Believe," published in 1896. Peirce had argued that the alternatives to the scientific method, among which he included the methods of tenacity, authority, and intuitive plausibility (or what he termed *a priori* reasoning), were all less reliable than the method utilized by scientific inquiry. Peirce was quick to admit, however, that some non-scientific methods, such as authority, have proven to be more dependable than others, such as tenacity.[3]

For his part, James had taken a different tack to reach a similar conclusion. He had argued that the primary virtue of the method of science resides in its techniques, its methods of experimental testing. Even though the "truth of truths" might come its way as hunch, revelation, flash of insight, or dream content, James argued, science "would decline to touch it. Such truth as that, she might [say], would be stolen in defiance of her duty to mankind."[4]

Like Peirce and James, then, Dewey had high praise for the methods of the technoscientific disciplines, and he thought that their methods operate as a kind of exemplar for arriving at the truth of a matter.[5] As had his two predecessors, Dewey argued for the extension of this method into other areas of human inquiry, including the social sciences, that have thus far proved resistant to its application.

But Dewey went further to suggest that when generally successful methods of inquiry are enumerated and examined, tactical methods such as those utilized in the arts, in law, and in historiography (to take three of his examples) obviously stand as essential partners alongside those utilized by the technoscientific disciplines. Each of these bodies of tactical method provides material for a more generally applicable pattern or strategy of inquiry, and each is in turn tested by the more general pattern. As I have indicated, Dewey identified this general strategic pattern of inquiry as the method of intelligence, or technology, and he thought that logic was the means by which we assess and improve it.

As James had, Dewey recognized well enough that even received methods of inquiry that do not take full advantage of the method of intelligence are often nevertheless the source of enormous energy, and that they frequently issue products that serve as stimuli that broaden and deepen discourse in the technoscientific fields, in the arts, and elsewhere. This is particularly true when, as James put it, options are live, forced, and momentous, and when acceptable evidence for or against a particular viewpoint or course of action is scant or absent. This is arguably the main thesis of James's essay "The Will to Believe," and it is a theme that Dewey developed in dozens of books and essays.

But Dewey also argued that the products of such methods, because their claims are usually premised on luck, tradition, economic interests, or intuitions of various sorts, nevertheless inevitably require for their sustained success the enhanced focus and refinement that can only be brought about by the application of the method of intelligence. He was particularly critical of social theory and practice based on overly generalized goals or ends that are themselves assumed to be exempt from analytical inquiry.[6]

II. Technology—The General Method of Inquiry

This argument of Dewey's—that many social problems are remediable by the application of the type of inquiry that has proven successful in the technoscientific disciplines, the arts, and law—has been both broadly and profoundly misunderstood. Before turning to the arguments of some of Dewey's critics, however, and before attempting to determine whether or not it is possible or desirable to apply the methods of the technoscientific disciplines to social problems, it will be helpful to examine a bit more closely Dewey's general method of inquiry, especially as it functions in the technoscientific disciplines.

First, a central feature of Dewey's method of inquiry is his rejection of realism, whether of the metaphysical or the scientific variety. One variety of scientific realism, for example, advanced by Albert Borgmann, holds that science reveals the "lawful fine structure of reality," and that reality is just the "final structures" of the world.[7] Borgmann's views will be discussed at length in chapters 6 and 9.

Dewey's alternative to scientific realism was his productive pragmatism or instrumentalism, which holds that technoscience works in a piecemeal fashion with interlocking sets of problems, fashioning and improving upon tools as required. Proffered solutions are not so much reflective of a preexisting reality as they are tools for the resolution and reconstruction of the difficulties encountered in previously reconstructed solutions that have subsequently proved unreliable or untenable. What counts as the facts for a particular sequence of inquiry is determined in the course of that very sequence of inquiry. In other words, in the course of inquiry some data recede into the background at the same time that others become more prominent. In Dewey's view, there are no absolute or free-floating facts; facts are always facts-of-a-case.

In a related move, Dewey reserved the term "object" to refer, as he put it, to "subject-matter so far as it has been produced and ordered in settled form by means of inquiry; proleptically, objects are the *objectives* of inquiry" (LW.12.122). Nevertheless, it is not necessary for each inquirer to begin *ab ovo;* there exists prior to any particular sequence of inquiry a rich storehouse of objects, that is, a base line constituted by things that "have been previously determined as outcomes of inquiries" (LW.12.122).

Second, as I have already suggested, the activities of the technoscientific disciplines utilize a family of tactical methods that operate in a relation of transaction or feedback with a more general pattern of strategic inquiry that I have termed technology. In the broad sense of the term, Dewey characterized "inquiry" as *"the controlled or directed transformation of an indeterminate situation into one that is so determinate in its constituent distinctions and relations as to convert the elements of the original situation into a unified whole"* (LW.12.108; emphasis in original). This statement characterizes successful inquiry wherever it occurs, whether in technoscientific disciplines, in the arts, in the practice of law, in the writing of history, or in inquiry into social problems. If the technoscientific disciplines have exhibited greater success in the utilization of this method than have other disciplines, then that success is not due to any special or privileged place occupied by them. It is due instead to the fact that their material has tended to be less complex and more manageable than that of other disciplines.

In other words, although the methods developed and utilized successfully in the technoscientific disciplines have contributed greatly to the refinement of the pattern of inquiry, their methods are only contained in it as a part, and are not exhaustive of it. The continuing refinement of the methods utilized by the general pattern of inquiry, the method of intelligence, technology, is also affected by advances in the methods of the other areas of inquiry just enumerated.

The pattern exhibited by the general method of intelligence, now taken to be inclusive of the technoscientific and other disciplines, is itself a logical tool, an abstraction that has been constructed on the basis of past outcomes that have proven successful. But this pattern is generated as a by-product of inquiry, not as a direct result of it. Just as in agricultural practice, the aim of a particular sequence of inquiry is the resolution and reconstruction of a particular problem. And just as in the case of agriculture, when tools appropriate to a problem are invented or improved, they are the by-products, not the direct goal, of the relevant practice.

Third, the methods of inquiry utilized in technoscientific disciplines undergo constant change. They may evolve, as they have since the seventeenth century, or they may devolve, as they did during the period that was marked by the breakup of the Roman Empire and the onset of the early Middle Ages. Methods utilized by the technoscientific disciplines may even evolve at the same time that the methods utilized in social inquiry devolve. There is ample evidence to conclude that this situation occurred during the early stages of the first industrial revolution, that is, the revolution that introduced industrial machinery first into Great Britain and later into other countries that we now know as industrialized.

Technoscientific methods are in constant need of corrective feedback that can be secured only by involvement with actual cases of successful technoscientific practice and at the same time by means of transaction with the general method of inquiry. The general method of inquiry, technology, like the methods of those disciplines tributary to it, is a general characterization made at a specific time. It is itself a tool that is open to continuing improvement, just as are the tools of carpentry. It is in this sense that the method of intelligence is said to be "self-corrective." (It should be obvious that the present account of this process is itself fallible, that is, open to continuing revision. The publication of this account is in that sense, therefore, just a snapshot of an ongoing inquiry.)

Fourth, as I attempted to demonstrate in chapter 1, there are vast areas of human activity within which the method of intelligence does little or no work, but from which it may receive interesting and important raw materials for its eventual use. The contents of dreams, the insights of religious mystics, folk tales and folk remedies, and even the most vile crimes committed by one human being against another:[8] all these and myriad other elements of human experience may serve as materially important within inquirential situations.

Fifth, emphasis within inquiry is not upon the origin of material to be tested, but rather upon the analysis and ordering of that material, upon the selection from it of elements that are appropriate to the problem at hand, and upon the checks and tests utilized within a community of inquiry in order to maintain standards of evidence, relative disinterestedness, and honesty.

III. Critical Theory: Max Horkheimer

As I have indicated, Dewey's position with respect to these matters has been profoundly misunderstood. His critics have tended to grasp neither the import of his general theory of inquiry, nor his view concerning the ways in which methods that have proven successful within the technoscientific and other disciplines may be applied to social problems.

Some of Dewey's harshest critics were members of the "first generation" of Frankfurt School critical theory such as Max Horkheimer. In the 1990s, W. A. Paringer revived and reasserted some of their criticisms. Horkheimer accused Dewey of reliance on what he called "instrumental reason," which he identified as an outdated Enlightenment positivism or scientism coupled with an uncritical faith in the institutions and goals of industrial technology.[9] Since these misunderstandings and misrepresentations of Dewey's work are even at this late date still the stock-in-trade of some educational theorists, I shall address them at some length. As I shall demonstrate in chapter 8, however, some of the heirs of the original critical theorists have in fact moved toward positions that are key components of productive pragmatism.

Horkheimer accused Dewey and the other pragmatists of preoccupation with means at the expense of ends;[10] of emphasizing practice to the detriment of theory;[11] and of attempting to abolish philosophical thought altogether in favor of an apology for crass commercial and industrial experimentalism.[12] "Pragmatism," wrote Horkheimer, "in trying to turn experimental physics into a prototype of all science and to model all spheres of intellectual life after the techniques of the laboratory, is the counterpart of modern industrialism, for which the factory is the prototype of human existence, and which models all branches of culture after production on the conveyor belt, or after the rationalized front office."[13]

Horkheimer was, in short, charging Dewey with espousing what Langdon Winner has called "straight-line" instrumentalism. As Winner crisply characterizes it, straight-line instrumentalism "begins with a preconceived end in mind. Then one decides upon an appropriate instrument or organization of instruments to achieve that end, usually weighing the advantages of two or more alternative methods. Next comes the actual *use* of the instrument in the way established for its successful exercise. Finally, one achieves certain results which are judged according to the original end."[14] As I shall argue in chapter 6, this procedure is often confused with its opposite. In the tragic American involvement in Southeast Asia during the 1960s and 1970s, for example, there seemed to be no clear end, preconceived or otherwise. In that case, it was apparently the means that were predetermined, and then sent in search of an appropriate end.

When judged in terms of the general remarks on Dewey's theory of inquiry that I presented a few pages back, Horkheimer's criticism appears to be badly misdirected. My aim in the next few paragraphs is not to demean Horkheimer, however, but to utilize his criticism as a tool for constructing an enhanced understanding of Dewey's position.

First, straight-line instrumentalism depends upon some sort of scientific or metaphysical realism to provide its inflexible goals. But such realism is more apparent in Horkheimer's own view than in that of Dewey. Horkheimer contended that "objective truth" should be "pursued for its own sake" as a "concept of an order or hierarchy, of static or dynamic structure, that would do full justice to things and nature."[15] Dewey viewed matters quite differently. He held that such generalizations as "absolute truth" and "essential structures"[16] usually serve only to short-circuit inquiry, and that the legitimate role for metaphysics lies in its provisional generalizations about the generic features of existence.

Second, Dewey did not seek to measure all experience by technoscientific analysis, as Horkheimer claimed. He did not even think that technoscientific inquiry should serve as the pattern for all forms of inquiry. Rather, it was his view that much of human experience, especially within the domain of simple aesthetic delight, has no need of inquiry because it is not problematic. Further, even where inquiry is called for, the methods of the technoscientific disciplines constitute only one important source of insight among others (including but not limited to the methods of the various arts and legal practice) into ways of understanding and improving upon a pattern of inquiry that is more general than that employed in the technoscientific disciplines. His theory of inquiry, or what I have identified as technology, is thus considerably broader than his theory about the methods of the technosciences.

Third, it is simply not true that Dewey disregarded "any speculative capacity of reason as distinct from existing science," as Horkheimer claimed.[17] But speculation was for Dewey not the same as contemplation, which he regarded as for the most part static and passive. Speculation functioned for Dewey as an important means of the determination of further facts of a case and of the setting out of refined hypotheses. Speculation, unlike contemplation, was in Dewey's view both experimental and productive.

Finally, Horkheimer's charge that Dewey's method of inquiry was irremediably subjective is also misdirected. He took particular offense at Dewey's suggestion that intelligence effects a "projection of the desirable in the present," and an invention of "the instrumentalities of its realization."[18] Horkheimer claimed to see only two possible interpretations of this remark: either that it accepts in an uncritical way the desires of people just as they are, or that it accepts some notion of objective desirability, an alternative that would of course have been foreign to what he viewed as Dewey's subjectivist approach. In the former event, philosophy would be reduced to popularity polls. In the second, the pragmatists would have abandoned the subjectivity that he thought they had championed elsewhere and would have thus taken the first step on the road of critical thought, a road on which he, Horkheimer, regarded himself as an experienced traveler. But it is clear that Horkheimer did not think of himself and Dewey as traveling the same road.

Dewey's account of inquiry was in fact not subjectivistic. He argued that successful inquiry always takes place within a community because it is only within such venues that adequate checks and tests can be performed. This argument lies at the heart of the extended discussion of the difference between what is (subjectively) "desired" and what is (objectively) "desirable" that Dewey developed in the tenth chapter of *The Quest for Certainty* (LW.4.203–28), a work that appeared almost two decades before Horkheimer published his remarks.

IV. A Brief Excursion Regarding Scientism

The charge made by some of Dewey's critics that he was a proponent of a naive Enlightenment scientism calls for further elaboration by means of a brief excursion from the main lines of this chapter. I take scientism to have at least three important components: the view that the methods of the natural sciences are paradigmatic for all other areas of experience, the view that the conclusions of the natural sciences are universally applicable to all other areas of experience, and the view that the natural sciences are objective or "value free."

There is widespread agreement among philosophers of science that one of the most radical critics of scientism has been Paul Feyerabend. In assessing the extent to which Dewey's views are scientistic, a brief comparison of his views to those of Feyerabend may prove helpful.

At the very heart of Feyerabend's position seem to be the following claims. First, the methods of scientific technology are not static, but evolve through time. The methods utilized by the technoscientific disciplines today are, for example, quite different from those used in the seventeenth century. Second, the processes of scientific discovery are not generalizable, but rather, in his famous phrase, "anything goes." There has been considerable confusion regarding this claim.

Probably the best way to read Feyerabend on this point is not that anything goes in the testing phase of inquiry, but that anything in fact goes in the phase of inquiry that involves the formation of hypotheses, that is, the getting of ideas for further development. Third, science is not universal but perspectival, that is, culture-bound. Different assumptions and worldviews promote different approaches and even different solutions to similar problems. Medical practice, for example, developed in Asia differently than it did in Europe. Fourth, science operates in its own domain and does not have hegemony over other types of experience. To expect that the methods of the technoscientific disciplines should be applicable to the visual arts or to law would be to claim too much for those methods. Fifth, in true democracies, science should be "de-established" just as religion has been. This has been and continues to be a controversial point. Recent debates concerning the relation of "big" science to "small" science illustrate what this claim might mean in practical social terms. The failure of the struggle to secure funding for the Texas Superconducting Super Collider constitutes an excellent case study for this point.

Dewey's positions on these matters are the general subject of this essay, so I will not reiterate them in detail here. Nevertheless, two points are in order. First, except for Feyerabend's final point, each of these views (which many of Feyerabend's readers have generally regarded as radical) was present also in Dewey's treatment of science in his 1938 *Logic: The Theory of Inquiry.* Second, if Feyerabend's final point, that science should be "de-established," means that members of scientific institutions should be among many voices that play a role in the determination of public policy in a democratic society, then Dewey was clearly in agreement on that point as well.

A full comparison of Dewey's philosophy of science to that of Feyerabend is well beyond the scope of this chapter. I nevertheless present the preceding brief outline of an argument in support of my claim that Dewey's view of scientific technology was hardly an example of scientism. It was not a "mainstream" view during his lifetime (a time during which several varieties of scientism did in fact flourish), nor is it now.

V. *Agape:* Reinhold Niebuhr

Looking back on Dewey's work from the perspective of the 1990s, it is not difficult to find points at which he stumbled, and even blundered, as he sought to apply his productive pragmatism to the concrete problems of his own times and places.

Nevertheless, I believe that his central insights remain applicable to the social difficulties of our own time. The point to be emphasized is that the failure of an *experiment* is not the same as the failure of *experimentalism*.

To demand, for example, as Dewey did, that the claims and methods of religious communities and their leaders should be open to the same experimental tests that are applied to all others who seek to influence public opinion and policy is as appropriate now as it was in 1934, the year that Dewey published *A Common Faith*. To hold fast to this point is not to attempt to establish a hegemony of science over religion, as some religionists have claimed, and it is not to deny the important role of religious insight and motivation as materials for intelligent inquiry. Rather, it is a challenge to the proponents of various religions to abandon their own pretense to privilege, to join in public debates on equal terms with those whose primary activities take place in other areas of inquiry, and to accept the general criteria of experimental testing that characterize the successful application of the general pattern of inquiry to meaningful public discourse.

As I just indicated, these matters were the focus of Dewey's attention in *A Common Faith*, which he published in 1934. One of his central concerns in that work was to frame a reply to liberal theologian Reinhold Niebuhr, whose own book *Moral Man and Immoral Society* had appeared just two years earlier. Niebuhr had accused Dewey of mis-locating the source of social ills in "the failure of the social sciences to keep pace with the physical sciences which have created our technological civilisation."[19]

In this matter he thought that Dewey had gotten cart before horse: social justice would be improved not through the application of technoscientific methods in education, but through a type of social conflict whose primary motivation would be the "absolutizing moral principle" he termed Christian love, and whose primary tools would be "the right dogmas, symbols and emotionally potent oversimplifications."

"They [the industrial workers] may," Niebuhr claimed, "be very scientific in projecting their social goal and in choosing the most effective instruments for its attainment, but a motive force will be required to nerve them for their task which is not easily derived from the cool objectivity of science."[20]

Niebuhr's position on the political spectrum was certainly far removed from that of the Christian fundamentalists of his and our own time who have seen Dewey's pedagogy as a major threat to their own agenda. Nevertheless, the arguments Niebuhr used to support his position are remarkably similar to those advanced by the fundamentalists. In each case there is an appeal to the method of straight-line instrumentalism. In each case there is an inflexible social agenda, an inflexible principle, and a conviction that desired goals can be achieved only by utilizing irrational and oversimplified dogmas.

In his reply to Niebuhr, Dewey recognized the important place of ideals and emotions as motives for change, especially within the kind of problem-solving that leads to the control of matters that are not as we wish them to be. But he also denied that there is any "religious" experience *simpliciter,* and argued instead that those "elements and outlooks that may be called religious" (LW.9.8) should be emancipated from their servitude to the ideologies of sectarian religious institutions, including, by implication, even the one espoused by Niebuhr. He sought to reconstruct the noun "religion" as "religious," an adjectival term that would refer to the qualities of energy and enthusiasm that infuse and motivate all those experiences that produce enhanced adjustment within life's situations.

Dewey thus argued that undesirable social situations could be improved by education in the methods of experimental inquiry, or technology, that is, by improving citizen competence in the methods utilized by the general pattern of intelligence. He further argued that such methods were among the primary tools of democracy. But whereas he admitted that religious ideals and emotions may prove an aid in the struggle to achieve worthwhile ends, and he added that they frequently serve as important stimuli to the application of the methods of intelligence, he also argued that such ideals and emotions are themselves in continuing need of refinement by just those types of experimental methods that have proven successful in the technoscientific disciplines and elsewhere.

Niebuhr and Dewey were thus advancing remarkably different notions of democracy. For his part, Niebuhr claimed that the Christian religion had at its disposal a uniquely powerful tool, one that was much more effective than those utilized by the technoscientific disciplines. Whereas the instruments and conclusions of the latter were tentative, he argued, Christian love constitutes an "absolutizing moral principle" that is capable of "imparting transcendent worth to the life of others."[21] He held that democracy would result, if at all, when social conflict was coupled with Christian love and applied to solve immediate social ills.

Implicit in Niebuhr's argument was the claim that the Christian religion offered the greatest hope for the resolution of human problems because it was the most evolved of the world's religions. Dewey countered by suggesting that if religious thought had evolved (and he thought it had), then there was certainly no reason for its progress to stop with Christianity as it was understood and practiced in the 1930s. Its next stage might be a common faith, that is, one that would transcend sectarian differences and allow for common efforts to solve common problems.

A primary tool of advancing and refining such a common faith, Dewey argued, would be the method of intelligence. Just as the methods of technosciences transcend national borders and sectarian religious divisions, and just as the methods and products of the arts constitute an international "language," so could the experimental methods of the general pattern of inquiry be applied across boundaries previously thought impermeable, and this with an aim to the solution of social ills.

Dewey's approach was thus the inverse of Niebuhr's. He argued that the methods of democracy and scientific technology, motivated by a common faith in the desirability of an improved future and expressed in terms of experimental action undertaken to determine what courses of action are worthy of being desired, constituted the best hope for humankind. History has shown that no "absolutizing moral principle" is available within any particular religion, since each has claimed its own as absolute and since religious institutions have frequently resorted to open conflict with one another regarding whose principle is "more absolute."

Fortunately, however, no "absolutizing moral principle" is required for intelligent inquiry. On this question Dewey aligned himself against Niebuhr and on the side of Aristotle, who had argued that in matters of morals and social justice, intelligence works not from, but toward, first principles.

Dewey's notion of the motivating factors in the use of intelligent inquiry was thus much more sophisticated than that of Niebuhr, and it reflects his commitment to continuing reconstruction of the methods of the technoscientific disciplines and the arts in their ongoing transactions with the general method of intelligence.

For his part, Niebuhr seemed to prefer a utilitarian version of the arts that would render them subservient to political aims. To use a now famous phrase of Walter Benjamin, Niebuhr seemed to want to "aestheticize politics." Dewey's reply was that wherever the arts are utilized as little more than ancillary to the political, then inquiry in the arts is stifled and their larger contribution to desirable social ends is cut short. But where the arts flourish, that is, where artistic materials are expressed in ways that are intelligent, then several felicitous consequences ensue. First, experience is enriched because its aesthetic dimension is augmented and refined. Second, advances in inquiry within the arts feed into and enrich our understanding of the general pattern of intelligence. Third, improvements in the general pattern of intelligence serve to inform and ameliorate methods in the technosciences, in law, and elsewhere, with corresponding social gains. The same argument, of course, may be employed against the capture of the technoscientific disciplines, law, or historiography by political expediency.

Dewey's program for the enhancement of the role of the arts in social and political inquiry, and the corresponding enrichment of social life that would result from the refinement of the arts, revealed a much deeper grasp of the possibilities of the arts than was evident in Niebuhr's work. In fact, Dewey's position was in certain ways similar to that of Benjamin, who claimed that it would be much more productive to politicize art than to aestheticize politics, as the Nazis had done. By this I take Benjamin to have meant that aesthetics must play a role in a total program of social and political amelioration, and not be limited to a kind of veneer designed to mask and make palatable preconceived and therefore unreconstructed and un-reconstructable social ends. Put another way, both Dewey and Benjamin were saying that "the right dogmas, symbols and emotionally potent oversimplifications" that Niebuhr thought essential to political progress in fact tend to restrict social and political amelioration because they promote the "cult" values of art over their critical and expressive possibilities.

VI. A Note on Recent Critical Theory

Essential elements of Horkheimer's and Niebuhr's criticisms of Dewey's instrumentalism have resurfaced during the final decade of the twentieth century in connection with assaults on his philosophy of education. W. A. Paringer's *John Dewey and the Paradox of Liberal Reform* resuscitated many of their arguments. Drawing from arguments advanced earlier by members of the first generation of the Frankfurt School, as well as from the work of other radical philosophers of education, Paringer argued that Dewey was guilty of a naive optimism that ignored the realities of the American power structure, a structure that he thought legitimates itself through the use of brute power and oppression rather than through democratic institutions. Like Niebuhr before him, Paringer contended that "democracy begins only after reasonably egalitarian conditions and structures have been prioritized."[22] "In identifying 'scientific' with 'democratic,'" he wrote, "Dewey made a similar mistake to the one Plato had made. . . . Both presumed an epistemological basis (idealism) for their social theory."[23]

Paringer called on a passage from Herbert Marcuse to buttress his point: "Today, domination perpetuates and extends itself not only through technology but *as* technology . . . and provides the great . . . rationalization of the unfreedom of man and demonstrates the 'technical' impossibility of being autonomous, of determining one's own life."[24]

In other words Marcuse, and Paringer in his wake, held that it is the very methods of the technoscientific disciplines as they are practiced that have entrenched the patterns of inequality and oppression that are apparent in American society. Far from being a part of the answer to social problems, as Dewey thought they were, the methods of the technoscientific disciplines were in Paringer's view a part of the problem.

What did Paringer offer as an alternative to the methods of technoscience? His own approach, he wrote, "begins with a critical stance towards one's reality and engages in the contradictions which the option-makers have hidden. *While not abandoning the empirical means of science,* critical theory takes aim at hidden coercions, at the concrete contradictions consequent to any world picture, at an entirely different sort of emancipation" (emphasis added).[25]

There is a serious flaw in this line of argumentation, which betrays a misunderstanding of Dewey's program. Dewey's general pattern of inquiry, which stands in a relation of transaction to the methods of technoscience, is capable of absorbing the agenda of the critical theorists such as Marcuse and Paringer, insofar as they desire to engage in a critique of underlying ideologies and assumptions. Every account that Dewey provided of his general method of inquiry includes as one of its components just such a moment of analysis in which an inquirer or a community of inquirers delves as deeply into previously held assumptions as is possible within that situated process of inquiry. It was Dewey's contention that this pattern works in the arts no less than in the technoscientific disciplines.

What Dewey's general method of intelligence is *not* able to do, however, is to accept the notions of absolute truth and absolutizing moral positions that seem to be essential ingredients within the program advanced by Paringer.

When compared to other critics of technological culture who have found inspiration in the work of Marcuse, Paringer's criticism of Dewey seems thin and even a bit out-of-date. Andrew Feenberg, for example, who was a student of Marcuse, has adopted planks from the platform of productive pragmatism. I shall discuss Feenberg's program in chapter 9.

It is now time to draw together the arguments within this chapter. My suggestion has been that the methods of the technoscientific disciplines, together with the methods of other disciplines that have proven successful, such as the arts, law, and historiography, nourish and are refined by an overarching pattern of intelligence. This pattern, in general, involves the *invention, development, and cognitive deployment of tools and other artifacts, brought to bear on raw materials and intermediate stock parts, with a view to the resolution of perceived problems.* Philosophy, in its role as critic of this pattern of inquiry, can function as a kind of "liaison officer" for applying methods developed by the several disciplines to problems that are characterized as social.

Dewey argued strenuously that the methods of the technoscientific disciplines, though they in no sense exercise hegemony or even deserve to do so, have, in fact, set the pace for some other areas of human inquiry because their subject material is less complex than that of the social sciences, because of their refinement over time of the methods of hypothesis construction and testing, and because of their ability to develop and relate abstract meanings in ways that may be referred back to and that alter matters that are concretely existential.

Dewey at times called his general method "instrumentalism," and at other times he used the term "technology." Since the terms "technical" and "technological" are also utilized to refer to methods that are ancillary to the general method of inquiry, his equivocal use of these terms has been a source of considerable confusion. Why would Dewey insist on calling his general method of inquiry "technology"?

I believe that the answer to this question lies in Dewey's contention that every successful inquiry involves the *invention, development, and cognitive deployment of tools and other artifacts, brought to bear on raw materials and intermediate stock parts, with a view to the resolution of perceived problems.* This process may involve the concrete, tangible tools and artifacts normally associated with hardware technology such as that involved in the plastic arts and engineering, but it may also involve the conceptual tools and artifacts that do their work at more abstract levels of operation, such as in the musical arts and mathematics. Dewey's definition of inquiry is thus more or less his definition of technology in its broadest sense.

From the standpoint of Dewey's productive pragmatism, then, it makes little sense to condemn technology as the source of human ills, as Horkheimer, Paringer, and Marcuse have done. If the resources of a society have become concentrated in the hands of too few individuals, and if social ills result, then it is not technology that is at fault, and it is certainly not the method of intelligence that has failed. The fault rather lies with a failure to employ technology to solve human problems.

There are, therefore, good grounds for applying the methods that have proven successful in the technoscientific disciplines to social problems. The technoscientific disciplines, like the arts, law, and historiography, are themselves socially situated and cannot be divorced from social concerns. Conversely, no social problems exist outside the context of the physical conditions that the technoscientific disciplines have been developed to address. It is for these and other reasons enumerated above that Dewey thought that

> social phenomena cannot be understood except as there is prior understanding of physical conditions and the laws of their interactions. Social phenomena cannot be attacked, *qua* social, directly. Inquiry into them, with respect both to data that are significant and to their relations or proper ordering, is conditioned upon extensive prior knowledge of physical phenomena and their laws. This fact

accounts in part for the retarded and immature state of social subjects. . . . Without physical knowledge there are no means of analytic resolution of complex and grossly macroscopic social phenomena into simpler forms. (LW.12.486)

Just as Dewey continually argued that wherever democratic institutions fail to work properly there is a need for more, not less, democracy, he also argued that wherever technological institutions fail to enhance desirable human goals there needs to be more, not less, technology (taking the term in the broad sense in which he utilized it).

❖ 4 ❖

ART, TECHNOSCIENCE, AND SOCIAL ACTION

> Science states meanings; art expresses them.
> —John Dewey, *Art as Experience* (LW.10.90)

> Art thus represents the culminating event of nature as well as the climax of experience. In this connection the usual sharp separation made between art and science is criticized; it is argued that science as method is more basic than science as subject-matter, and that scientific inquiry is an art, at once instrumental in control and final as a pure enjoyment of mind.
> —John Dewey, *Experience and Nature* (LW.1.8–9)

> [N]ot only is scientific inquiry as it is conducted a highly skilled technology, but the consummatory fulfillments that are characteristic of the esthetic phase of life-experience play a highly important part in attaining the conclusions reached in science.
> —John Dewey, "A Comment on the Foregoing Criticisms" (LW.15.98)

I. Dewey's View of the Role of the Philosopher in Social Reform

It is not necessary to subscribe to any of the various formerly or currently popular cyclical views of history to recognize extraordinary similarities between our own time and an earlier one, some one hundred years ago, that was conterminous with the formative years of Dewey's public career.

Both are periods marred by racial strife, deterioration of the living standards of working men and women, and neglect and exploitation of children. Both are periods characterized by unchecked personal and corporate greed, capitulation on the part of federal and state governments to social Darwinist economic principles, the activities of powerful groups of religious fundamentalists[1] that seek to impose their supernaturalist agenda on a wider public, and by extensive (and controversial) waves of immigration. Perhaps even more significant, both are periods that exhibit widespread and unpenalized corruption within government and a stead-fast flight from reality by much of the voting-age public.

Dewey's response to the deplorable social conditions of the last decades of the nineteenth century is as appropriate today as when it was first written. It was to call for social reform—a cultural reconstruction in which philosophy would play several important roles. First, philosophy would serve as a reminder to the other disciplines (as would the other disciplines to it) of the importance of an ongoing reconsideration and reconstruction of its own ontological commitments. In this regard Dewey argued that philosophers must abandon their usual and too-intimate attachment to doctrines and prescriptions worn threadbare by habitual and uncritical use. He thought it essential, for example, that philosophers recognize the futility of attempting to describe reality in a general sense; that they abandon their hoary quest for certainty; and that they abjure supernaturalist and extranaturalist metaphysics in favor of a radical, experimental empiricism.

Should philosophers persist in clothing themselves in these comfortable but worn-out garments, he suggested, they would no longer be welcome in the company of those conscientious men and women in business, in the arts, and in tech-noscientific fields who take it as their task to identify, to resolve, and to reconstruct genuinely problematic situations. Their conversations would consequently lack the solid ring of relevance and would degenerate into jargon tossed to and fro among themselves.

A second role prescribed by Dewey for philosophy went beyond these admonitions. As I have already indicated, he thought that philosophers have at their disposal both a unique subject matter and a distinctive set of tools. Their unique subject matter is the method of inquiry by means of which distinctions are drawn and adjudications made with respect to values that are immediate and those that are ulterior, that is, between what is apparent and what is eventual. This method works in ethics, in aesthetics, and even in logic itself, that is, in the very theory of such inquiry. It also works in all the other arts and technosciences that consider particular cases of the relation of already-possessed tools and goals to their better, but not-yet-attained, alternatives.

The philosopher's distinctive set of tools includes both those instruments that are appropriate for use in philosophical inquiry in general, and the specific instruments that are unique to the various areas of his or her concern, such as aesthetics, ethics, or logic. An example of a general philosophical instrument is the recognition and avoidance of what Dewey called "the philosopher's fallacy." This mistake is committed when an inquirer analyzes a complex situation into its constituent parts for the sake of resolving some perceived difficulty, but then insists that the parts secured by means of inquiry were present all the while—*prior* to inquiry and in some absolute sense, in a way that is unrelated to the goals or ends-in-view that initially prompted their isolation from the total situation. Dewey's work offers an extensive account of general methods, such as the avoidance of the philosopher's fallacy, by means of which inquiry itself is illuminated, tested, refined, and suggested for use in the other arts and technosciences.

An example of the more specific instruments available to the philosopher are those tools developed specifically for use in aesthetics, in ethics, and in logic. These include theories of representation and expression in aesthetics, various deontological and consequentialist theories in ethics, and notions of class inclusion and of warranted assertibility in logic.

It is, Dewey argued, of great functional importance to differentiate these three things: the unique subject matter of philosophy, the set of general tools that it brings to bear on philosophical questions *qua* philosophical, and the specific tools that have been found to be of use in each of the specific areas of philosophical inquiry. And it is also important to recall that for Dewey's productive pragmatism, what functions as the unique subject matter of philosophy—the general method of intelligence that he thinks is present wherever and whenever genuine problem-solving occurs—also functions as a technology for tuning up other disciplines including the several technosciences, the arts, and the humanities. The difference is one of reflection: philosophy undertakes a self-conscious and systematic study of the general method of intelligence that is merely used, albeit often improved upon in use, by the other disciplines.

Were one to confuse the general method of intelligence *qua* subject matter of philosophy with the general method of intelligence *qua* tool of the arts and the technosciences, one might be tempted to think that philosophy has no unique subject matter, or that philosophers have no particular role—beyond their roles as good citizens—in the pursuit of social reform.

These are conclusions that have in fact been drawn by a sizeable contingent of contemporary philosophers. Richard Rorty, for example, has written approvingly of what he takes (erroneously, I will argue) to be Dewey's desire to "rub out" the distinctions among art, science, and philosophy, and to substitute for those distinct methods a "vague and uncontroversial notion of intelligence."[2] I believe that Rorty's confusion in this matter has led to substantial problems for his "liberal ironist." I shall return to Rorty's interpretation of Dewey presently.

That Dewey thought the general method of intelligence to be the subject matter of philosophy is apparent from his remarks in the final pages of his 1925 *Experience and Nature*. Philosophers, in Dewey's view, are capable of occupying a unique niche in the broad and ongoing enterprise called social reform, or the reconstruction of technological culture, because one of the functions of their discipline involves a "criticism of criticisms." "Philosophy," he wrote, "is inherently criticism, having its distinctive position among various modes of criticism in its generality; [it is] a criticism of criticisms" (LW.1.298).

On at least one occasion, Dewey put this point in terms that exhibit covert reference to the threefold distinction among categories that had earlier been elaborated by Charles Sanders Peirce. First, the philosopher, as well as the practitioner of the arts and the technosciences, has the task of going beyond the immediacy of "conscience in morals, taste in fine arts and conviction in beliefs" (LW.1.300) that characterizes inherited, habitual, naive, and other stances that are utilized daily and in an uncritical fashion.

In our own time such uncritical immediacy of response has included the emotional fever pitch generated by the use of patriotic symbols, such as the flag, especially during political campaigns. In the arts it has taken the form of preference for violence or kitsch in place of thoughtful and engaging studies of complex human situations. In the realm of religious taste it has meant literalist reinterpretations of what were formerly regarded as allegorical supernaturalist myths and consequent attempts to censor well-crafted and insightful literary and performance works on the grounds that they are immoral or even "satanic." In the area of mass media it has taken the form of an insidious sensationalism that conflates information with entertainment.

It may be objected that this list contains only negative instances, and that "conscience in morals, taste in fine arts and conviction in beliefs" (LW.1.300) may also include instances that have led to positive results. Dewey's answer to this point was the same as that of Peirce. Where unrefined experience leads to a good consequence, no more than luck can be claimed. It is, on the other hand, the function of intelligence to go beyond luck and to make sure that what is found to be valuable is secured.

The philosopher, then, shares with the political scientist, the historian or critic of art, the sociologist, and the media theorist the task of criticizing and refining uninformed impulses such as those just mentioned. Because it utilizes the general method of intelligence, however, in addition to the specific tools of each of the disciplines, this work can hardly be said to be uniquely philosophical.

But it is also the task of the philosopher (and Dewey thought it uniquely so) to operate in a venue that lies beyond those critical judgments of fact—Peirce's seconds—that are a part of the task of the individual arts and technosciences, from anthropology to nuclear physics and from mathematics to video art. One of the crucial functions of philosophy, in short, is to ensure that criticism operates at a level of generality not unlike Peirce's thirdness, a level at which it is "aware of itself and its implications, pursued deliberately and systematically" (LW.1.302). It is at this level that both general philosophical tools, such as the philosopher's fallacy, and tools that are unique to the more specific areas of philosophical concern, such as theories of "truth" as warranted assertibility, come into play. Taken together, these are the tools that have arisen from the activity Dewey called "criticism of criticisms." This is the stance from which philosophy can pursue its function of tuning up technology.

Dewey detailed some of the consequences of undertaking such a criticism of criticisms: they include the regulation of "the further appreciation of goods and bads," the engendering of "greater freedom and security in those acts of direct selection, appropriation, [and] identification," and the "rejection, elimination, destruction which enstate and which exclude objects of belief, conduct and contemplation" (LW.1.302). If Dewey's language regarding this matter fails to be elegant, it at least has the clarity and directness required to dispel any doubt concerning what, in his view, needs to be done.

Above all, the work of the philosopher is for Dewey situated in a cultural matrix from which it takes its problems and to which it must return for the checks and cues that afford its results a power that is both solvent and constructive. This is tantamount to saying that the role of philosophy in social reform has two moments. The first is an *excursus* from experience that is immediate and unrefined, as well as from the data and working hypotheses of the individual arts and technosciences. The second, once such material has been secured, worked over, and designated for use in the philosophical task of reformulation and transformation, is a *recursus* to the contents and the methods of the arts and technosciences and to quotidian experience in ways that ensure that "freer, richer and more secure objects of belief are instituted as goods of immediate acceptance" (LW.1.320).

These two moments, one solvent and the other reconstructive, constitute the drumbeats to which Deweyan social reform marches: the first is the resolution of problematic situations into meaningful elements by means of the application of instruments invented or chosen for that specific task; the second is the eventual and eventful *re*construction of such situations on the basis of the new meanings and the new possibilities that follow upon the intelligent application of appropriate tools to problematic situations.

A key word in the Deweyan lexicon of cultural reconstruction is "refinement." Dewey's arguments in *Art as Experience* reveal that he had few illusions regarding the tendency of most human individuals to take any available pleasure impulsively and without admixture. But he also understood that calls for censorship or for suppression of what is common, crude, or (short of violent) even patently disgusting to a majority is most often counterproductive. This is so because expression that is naive, intuitive, and unreflective often carries with it an energy that is fueled by cultural disturbance—distress that simmers outside of officially sanctioned channels of expression.

Dewey resolutely opposed those who would counter such expressions with instruments of suppression. His tactic of choice was instead the transformation of the raw materials of cultural disharmony by working to refine them, by focusing their energies, and by turning them toward ends that were better and more appropriate.

Dewey's views on the subject of the role of philosophy in cultural reconstruction are by no means uncontroversial, even among some neo-pragmatists who claim to be his adherents in general terms.

II. Neo-Pragmatism and Social Reform

As I have already indicated, Richard Rorty, whose variety of neo-pragmatism currently enjoys considerable popularity,[3] has written approvingly of what he takes to be Dewey's desire to "rub out" the distinctions between art, technoscience, and philosophy, and to substitute a "vague and uncontroversial notion of intelligence."[4] It is therefore surprising that even as he fuzzes these boundaries, putatively on Dewey's authority, Rorty establishes an implicit hierarchical privilege for the literary arts. As did Foucault and Heidegger before him, Rorty holds that science is now quietly receding into the background, and that it is being replaced by poetizing. A poet, in his broad definition of the term, is "one who makes things new."[5] But when he comes to specifics, it is usually spoken or written language that is the poet's subject material.

The effect of Rorty's hierarchy is that technoscience is not merely de-emphasized, but eclipsed as a tool of social reform. Rorty thinks this an important part of his task of laying bare the faults and failures of the Enlightenment project, which had, in his view, instituted a kind of cultural hegemony for technoscience. His "liberal ironist" responds to this alleged eclipse of technoscience with a shrug of her shoulders; she thinks that liberalism centers around novels, plays, and poems, and not around technoscience. She recognizes no particular vocabulary as more important than any other, just so long as there is enough overlap to allow one speaker to enter into another's "fantasies." In her view, the setting of the technosciences and the dawning of irony is just a case of one form of conversation being replaced by another. Her deconstructionist redescription may, Rorty suggests, serve quite as well to expand "our chances of being kind" as did the old scientific liberalism. It may even do better; it does not hold out the ungrounded hope of being "progressive" and "dynamic."

What, then, is Rorty's own view of the social function of philosophy? Unlike Dewey, he thinks that it has none. It would be better, he suggests, "to avoid thinking of philosophy as a 'discipline' with 'core problems' or with a social function."[6] To be sure, Rorty holds and presents certain ideas concerning what a good society would be like. It would be one in which free discussion was the norm rather than the exception, in which everyone had equal access to the means for self-creation, and in which, given that level playing field, people were then left alone to "work out their private salvations."[7] More recently Rorty has advised the political left to "kick its philosophy habit."[8]

Rorty singles out for special criticism what he takes to be the view of Habermas, that cooperative political action requires a common vision of what is universally human. Such a position, he argues, is unsatisfactory because it fails to come to terms with the failure of the Enlightenment idea of a foundational human nature on the basis of which its programs of absolute rationality and perfectibility were constructed. He recommends instead a view that what binds political groups are shared vocabularies and common hopes.

It would be redundant to present here an extended case that Rorty's work exhibits nothing that could be called a coherent social program. Richard Bernstein, Cornel West, and John R. Wallach have expended considerable ink establishing precisely this point.[9] My purpose is rather to illuminate the ways in which Dewey's notion of cultural *reconstruction* works by contrasting it with the liberal ironist's program of *deconstruction*.

What is remarkable in Rorty's neo-pragmatist/deconstructionist account of what philosophy does is that some of the most important philosophical underpinnings of Dewey's program for social reform drop out. It is as if Rorty has taken one half of Dewey's prescription for cultural reconstruction—its analytical or solvent moment—but ignored the other half: the moment in which it undertakes active reconstruction. Perhaps that is why the social dimension in Rorty's work, unlike that of Dewey's, turns out to be a liberalism without social action.

Dewey strenuously and consistently argued that the technosciences and the arts constitute different phases of inquiry in that they have different subject matters and different sets of tools. From a Deweyan perspective, Rorty's liberal ironist is correct on one important matter: there is no ultimate *ontological* distinction between the arts and the technosciences. The liberal ironist is also correct that the arts, the technosciences, and philosophy utilize the same general method of intelligence. But from Dewey's perspective she is mistaken in her conclusion that neither is there a *functional* distinction on which the differences between the arts, the technosciences, and philosophy rest.

III. The Distinctive Roles of the Arts and the Technosciences

It is precisely against the view that there is no distinction between the arts and the sciences—a view that is now a major plank in the liberal ironist's platform—that Dewey's argument was mounted. "Different types of problems," he wrote, "demand different modes of inquiry for their solution" (LW.12.82). He maintained that it is the function of the arts to comment upon the life and institutions of a particular culture and to express and intensify the meanings they find there—to render situations more perspicuous than they would otherwise be, to free experienced values from contexts that tend to militate against their use and development, and to enlarge the response of the imagination to perceived impasses: in short, to "perpetuate, enhance and vivify in imagination the natural goods" (LW.1.305).

Implicit in this characterization of the arts as a tool of cultural reconstruction is an argument against governmental interference in the arts, including restriction of government support to one type of artistic expression on the grounds that it is "safer" or less controversial than another sort. Dewey's position with respect to this matter is as relevant in our own time as it was when he first advanced it. From the 1980s to the present, the news has contained regular accounts of attempts to politicize the National Endowment for the Arts, that is, to create a political test for funding and to restrict support to those works of art that are considered "safe."

But what makes art art is not whether or not it is "transgressive," that is, characterized by some as containing subject matter that is obscene because it examines themes that are sexual or violent. What makes art art is its success in the performance of the functions just enumerated—freeing, enhancing, and expressing meanings. In the most general of terms, art must be expressive in ways that are not so much uplifting as clarifying, and not so much inspirational as insightful.

On this view, the difference between pornography and art, when art contains sexual material that some or even many may find offensive, is that pornography only serves to excite and exploit erotic fantasy, whereas art expresses such fantasy in ways that lead to its examination and refinement. On this definition, many of the images of women on MTV are pornographic, even though they are deemed socially acceptable and are viewed in millions of American homes; whereas the performances of Karen Finley, which were judged pornographic by a former director of the National Endowment for the Arts under admitted pressure from Senator Jesse Helms and others, constitute legitimate artistic expressions.

The function of the technosciences, in Dewey's book, differs markedly from that of the arts. The distinctions he draws between these disciplines is not prescriptive, however, but descriptive. They take into account what artists and scientists *do*, not some fixed ideal by which their activities are measured. The technosciences disclose relationships in ways that can be generalized to ever broader instrumental use, taking the term "instrumental" in this context to mean quantifiable and productive of new methods of quantification. In the arts, relationships are expressed. In the technosciences, relationships are stated and then stabilized by means of quantification, that is, by developing ever more complex languages that allow for ever greater precision and sophistication with respect to the substitution of variables. Technoscience develops cognitive tools and instruments that allow the comparison and contrast of things that were not theretofore understood as or taken to be relative, except perhaps by luck (LW.4.101).

Dewey provided an excellent example of this point in 1925, in the last chapter of *Experience and Nature.* Writing of the contributions of Jeremy Bentham and John Stuart Mill to the reform of the social ills of their time, Dewey suggested that their work had lacked the precision available when scientific instrumentation is utilized. Their work, he argued, was more like that of the literary artist Charles Dickens, whose expressed insights into the malaise of his time stirred individuals of good will to undertake meaningful reform. Their work operated, as he put it, as "literary rather than as scientific apparatus" (LW.1.323), though it would certainly be wrong, he was quick to add, to demean the work of any of these men. It is, after all, a function of art to refine and express brute experiences and to inspire action.

Mill's essay on *The Subjection of Women* provides an excellent example of Dewey's point.[10] As a polemical tract, one that involves a narrative account of perceived injustices and whose reasoning is predominantly analogical, Mill's story cannot have failed to touch and to sensitize a careful reader. Even today it functions as does good art. But it lacks a dimension that can now be furnished by careful empirical studies that go beyond the anecdotal in order to assert and defend detailed quantitative analyses of pay-scale differentials, the increasing feminization of poverty, and the consequences of continuing attempts by religious fundamentalists to effect legislation that restricts access to means of reproductive control, to mention only three of many areas of current technoscientific focus in this broadly problematic area.

This difference between the respective roles of the technosciences and the arts in social inquiry can perhaps be made more clearly by eliciting examples that are more current. The first involves successful works undertaken by artists and technoscientists that function in different but complementary ways to express, analyze, and reconstruct a particular social difficulty. Dewey's view regarding the unique function of philosophy is also manifest in this case. Because philosophy involves the study of the general method of intelligence, it is uniquely positioned to criticize the methods of the distinct disciplines that employ it. And because it functions as a criticism of criticisms, philosophy is also uniquely capable of arbitrating the differences and highlighting the similarities involved in alternative approaches to the same material.

Photographer Stephen Shames has done for the public of the 1990s what Jacob Riis did for his own public a century ago.[11] Shames's *Outside the Dream* expresses the meanings of the poverty and homelessness of many of America's children in ways that are unique to the work of the skilled artist.[12] As an artist, Shames's task has been to refine and detail those meanings; he has sensitized his public in a manner that constitutes a call to action, but does not define the means and methods involved in such action.

Shames's work, and its consequences, are thus of a radically different sort than the quantitative efforts of the behavioral scientists who have interpreted and published the data associated with the growing gap between rich and poor. Their charts, graphs, and tables do not so much "express" meanings as they serve to "state" them in ways that render them stable and manageable.

If Shames, as heir to Jacob Riis, has raised our consciousness and *expressed* the meanings of poverty and homelessness, then the more quantitative treatments advanced by Kevin Phillips's *The Politics of Rich and Poor,*[13] the editors of *Scientific American,*[14] and the Center on Budget and Policy Priorities, to take only three of many possible examples,[15] have *stated* those meanings in ways that constitute a call for specific action and set out the means by which it is to be undertaken. The difference between the inquirential functions of the arts and the technosciences in this case is clear in terms both of method and result. It is a difference that Dewey emphasized throughout his written work as one that must be understood in order for deliberate social action to be successful.

But this is precisely a difference that Rorty's liberal ironist tends to fuzz. The very different efforts of Shames and Phillips go well beyond the Rortian prescription of "entering into one another's fantasies." Their example involves distinct methods and tools that function in ways that are complementary. There is no vague and "undifferentiated" method of intelligence at work here. Instead, the works of technoscientist and artist are successful only as their different methods contribute to defining and sharpening an overarching method of intelligence, and then finding ways for that continually reconstructed method to feed back into their disciplines.

Productive pragmatism is a liberalism that involves social action. It therefore involves a variety of methods and techniques that go beyond a simple attempt to "work out our own salvation." Further, although both the arts and the technosciences utilize the general method of intelligence, neither discipline has that method as its subject matter. The analysis of that method, and of the ways in which it operates in a feedback relation with respect to the various disciplines, is one of the most important functions left to philosophy. Philosophy, as Dewey put it, is a kind of "liaison officer" between and among various disciplines.

At times the methods of the arts and the technosciences come into direct conflict. It is in such cases that philosophy can fulfill an important social function, engaging the "criticism of criticisms" that Dewey characterized as one of its unique functions. News reportage on television offers an excellent case for such analysis.

IV. The News as Bad Art

Some media critics have argued with great cogency that the very format of television militates against careful and detailed analysis of public issues. Because it is a mass medium and because it also constitutes a covert form of advertising (CNN, for example, is at the time I write owned by America Online–Time Warner), television news tends to reduce complex matters to their superficial aesthetic-affective dimensions and to reinforce common prejudices. In its quest to mimic the short bursts of simplistic, high-energy information developed and utilized so effectively by advertisers to condition their audiences, television news coverage has largely abandoned the critical debates that are an essential ingredient in the objectivity and fallibilism of the sciences. It has settled instead for highly stylized and aestheticized renderings of information, all the while claiming for itself a special ability to represent the facts of a case in a rigorous, definitive fashion (as "eyewitness" news, for example). To its critics, however, it functions at best as defective or bad art—defective in the important sense that unlike the successful arts it consistently fails to treat its materials with honesty.

Nowhere has this criticism been more warranted than in the televised coverage of the war in the Persian Gulf. The story Americans saw was one dominated by visual material furnished by the Department of Defense and its contractors, and by analysis and commentary furnished by the same sources.

Detailed, quantitative, scientific studies of the reportage of the Gulf War of 1991 have highlighted the inadequacies of the medium and its practitioners. Janet Steele and others, for example, have examined the backgrounds of the many consultants who were invited to appear on network news programs, including "Nightline," during coverage of the war.[16] Steele found that representatives of think tanks with Pentagon funding were rarely identified as such, and in some cases were actually misidentified in ways that contributed to the impression that they were objective analysts. One guest, for example, who appeared fifty-six times during the period from August 1990 to March 1991, and who was identified as a "university professor" and "national security analyst," was actually employed on the staff of a conservative Republican senator.[17] For its part, the editors of the journal *Extra!* surveyed the sources on NBC, CBS, and ABC nightly news during roughly the same period and found that "of 878 on-air sources, only one was a representative of a national peace organization. . . . By contrast, seven players from the Super Bowl were brought on to comment on the war."[18]

It is little wonder, then, that one public opinion poll found that only 13 percent of those sampled knew "that the U.S. responded to Iraq's threat to use force against Kuwait [in July of 1990] by saying it would take no action . . . [whereas] 81 percent of the [same] sample could identify the missile used to shoot down the Iraqi Scuds as the Patriot."[19] The televised news coverage of the Gulf War may have functioned well enough as a work of art designed to create and maintain public support for American involvement in the hostilities, but it was precisely to that extent that it failed to deal adequately with its putative materials. This sad situation was reenacted at CBS television in the late 1990s when the tobacco industry was allowed to kill a story on a whistle-blower who had revealed its misdeeds.

In Dewey's view, the methods of the arts and the technosciences at their best are also the methods of democracy. Where a work of art functions in an antidemocratic fashion, it compromises its own methods and loses its claim to artistic integrity. Under such conditions, "news" becomes little more than sensationalism or propaganda—in short, bad art.

V. The Pragmatist versus the Ironist

This matter of the distinctive functions of the arts and the sciences was the subject of Dewey's attention in 1934, in chapter 4 of *Art as Experience*. Once again, Dewey clearly articulated his view that it is the function of the technosciences to *state* meanings, whereas it is the function of the arts to *express* them. Dewey thought that technoscience functions as does a map or a directory: it sets out some of the conditions that must obtain if a particular experience is to be undergone and appropriated. But it is not that experience itself. An important difference between faulty technoscience and good technoscience corresponds to the degree of adequacy with which the supplied directions serve to lead to the desired experience. A formula for the combination of two chemical elements to form a third is adequate insofar as what has been predicted actually occurs under the specified conditions.

There is, however, a major difficulty in the way that some have interpreted the role of the technosciences. Philosophers and technoscientists of the seventeenth century—and they were in many cases the same individuals—often attempted to assimilate the new technoscience to an outmoded art form: they expected science to be an expression of the inner meanings of things. But when technoscience is thus asked to perform the function of art, when something is expected of it that it has not promised and that it cannot deliver, the resulting confusion is inevitable.

It was Dewey's view that this confusion of technoscientists and philosophers of the seventeenth century, their attempt to assimilate novel instrumental techniques to an outdated art form—a contemplative metaphysics of fixed and finished categories—was a great impediment to what might have been even greater progress during their time. What they in fact accomplished was highly productive: their de facto treatment of technoscience was as a matrix of indicators and as a directory of expectations. But what they *thought* they were doing, and the way they described their activities, turns out in retrospect to have functioned as a brake on their actual accomplishments: they persisted in their description of technoscience as expressive of the final and inner nature of things.

Thus a great gap existed between what seventeenth-century technoscientists thought they were doing and what they actually accomplished. They thought that they were getting ever closer to a final picture of reality, but, as Rorty's liberal ironist correctly points out, this path turned out to be a dead end. Their great accomplishment lay in what they did in fact, that is, in opening up new horizons through the development and refinement of new tools, techniques, and artifacts.

The move of the liberal ironist, then, is to reject that unfortunate assimilation by seventeenth-century technoscience and philosophy of the experimental method to an art form that claimed to be expressive of "reality." And she is certainly correct to do so. Where she goes wrong, at least from the standpoint of Dewey's productive pragmatism, is in failing to grasp the full extent of the error of seventeenth-century technoscience. She has consequently repeated it in another form. Whereas the seventeenth century assimilated technoscience to an old and now for the most part disused art form, namely the attempt to express the nature of ultimate reality, she assimilates technoscience to a newer and currently popular art form, namely the expression of experience through literary forms. Viewed from this perspective, her argument ultimately begs the question: since technoscience can no longer be assimilated to the old art form, it must therefore be assimilable to some new one. Her unspoken premise, as well as her conclusion, is the hierarchical privilege of the literary arts over the technosciences.

What the liberal ironist ignores, however, is the fact that technoscience had its own voice during the seventeenth century, and that its voice spoke loudly and clearly above the claims that were being made for it. Moreover, technoscience continues to have its own voice even today. The accomplishments of technoscience in medicine, in the exploration of space, in the manufacture and delivery of consumer goods, and in innumerable other areas constitute more than simply "another vocabulary." They constitute real indications of how real problems may be articulated, resolved, and reconstructed.

As I have indicated, an important consequence of the liberal ironist's assimilation of technoscience to the literary arts is that technoscience becomes only one "vocabulary" among others with no particular privilege. Even though the liberal ironist sometimes speaks of "desires" rather than "vocabularies," the point is the same.[20]

Regardless of the terms employed, the point that she misses is precisely the point of Dewey's productive pragmatist—Dewey's social reformer—namely, that both the arts and the technosciences continue to be privileged, but not hierarchically so. Each is privileged within its own peculiar domain, but each is a phase of inquiry in the broader sense and utilizes the other in its own investigations. A sculptor, for example, may use data generated by the technosciences regarding the strength and stress loads of various materials; and a technoscientist may utilize instrumentation whose design expresses the aesthetic qualities of glass, metal, plastics, wood, and other materials. In the contemporary examples just enumerated, the artist may utilize scientific data on poverty to target areas for aesthetic investigation, and the technoscientist may utilize the work of the artist to motivate his own interests and to engage his reader in the human dimension of abstracted data. In the same vein, the work of social scientists could be of great service to the artists who construct televised news, were they to avail themselves of it. Televised news might then open itself up to a wider spectrum of opinion, and work more diligently to construct balanced and defensible presentations of events that inform, as well as entertain. What is important in each of these cases is that neither the technoscientist nor the artist, *qua* technoscientist or artist, performs the unique function of the other, and that the philosopher has a unique social role as critic with respect to both.

In the view of the productive pragmatist, if it is the function of the technosciences to *lead* to an experience, it is the function of the arts to *constitute* one. The technoscientific or prosaic is set forth in propositions that indicate what is required for an experience. The artistic or poetic is "super-propositional": it involves what Dewey calls "an immediate realization of intent" (LW. 10.91).

A significant point of difference between Dewey's productive pragmatist and Rorty's liberal ironist, then, is that whereas the productive pragmatist argues that the technosciences and the arts constitute different phases of inquiry, each with its peculiar subject matter and set of tools, the liberal ironist wants to blur that distinction. Further, the productive pragmatist not only differentiates between the arts and the technosciences, but is ready to indicate some of the ways in which they are related.

Dewey's productive pragmatist, for example, reconstructs the popular notion, prevalent since the seventeenth century, that technology is "applied science." He thinks that the fault of this popular definition is that it is too "scientistic": it tends to make science the measure of all other areas of human experience. So the productive pragmatist views technoscience as functionally embedded within technology. He treats it as a special type of technological activity. But the productive pragmatist does not stop there. For him, technoscience could not operate in the absence of the "consummatory" moments of aesthetic experience. As Dewey wrote in 1948, in a reply to Benedetto Croce, "[N]ot only is scientific inquiry as it is conducted a highly skilled technology, but the consummatory fulfillments that are characteristic of the esthetic phase of life-experience play a highly important part in attaining the conclusions reached in science" (LW.15.98).

The productive pragmatist thus easily avoids the charge of scientism that is a central feature of the liberal ironist's frontal attack on the Enlightenment project and its manifestation in seventeenth-century science, as well as a feature of her attack on the productive pragmatist himself. Technoscience is privileged, according to the productive pragmatist, but only in its own domain. Far from being a paradigm for all of human activity, technoscience is at most instrumental to "the enrichment of immediate experience through the control over action that it exercises" (LW.10.294).

According to the productive pragmatist, progress is not only possible, but a frequent feature of our actual experience. It occurs whenever the possibility for amelioration is recognized, when technoscientific and other types of instruments are utilized to actualize and fructify what was theretofore only desired or hoped for as an "end-in-view," and when the resultant superadded value is enjoyed both for its own sake and as a platform for further progress, that is, as a means to enlarging meanings and securing further benefits. For Dewey, an important part of human life is a process of technological production, among whose tools is technoscientific inquiry.

The productive pragmatist's view of progress is therefore not bound up with practice, as some Marxists have suggested, or with the *vita activa*, as Hannah Arendt has argued, or even with enjoyment, as some aesthetes have thought. Progress is rather a cycle of production: this includes the production of new significances, the production of new feelings, the production of new means of enjoying, and the production of new techniques of production. For the productive pragmatist, to be human is to be involved in technological production, to generate an increase over what nature has given, to reconstruct our very selves on a continuing basis. This is one of the most important meanings of technology.

VI. The Liberal Ironist as Secular Calvinist

In the second volume of their admirable two-volume *A History of Philosophy in America*, Elizabeth Flower and Murray G. Murphey call to our attention a distinction that sheds considerable light on these matters. Characterizing the views of the mid-nineteenth-century German-American Hegelian Peter Kaufmann, they describe his socialism as one that "shares the Hegelian view of history as a process in which good emerges from evil through alterations and reform of the social institutions which transmit and mold values." They contrast this view with the prevalent "New England view that social reform depends upon the individual's change of heart."[21]

This distinction may provide a key to understanding the difference between Dewey's productive pragmatist and Rorty's liberal ironist. One finds Dewey's productive pragmatist active in education, in politics, in the arts, in the technosciences, and in every area where there are problems to be solved. Institutions are viewed as there to be improved. Social movements are viewed as opportunities for amelioration. Sleeves are rolled up, instruments are invented and applied, and matters are altered for the better. The project of amelioration undertaken by the productive pragmatist includes a continuing analysis and reconstruction of *both* the manifestations of our selves and the social institutions in which our selves are embedded.

But Rorty's liberal ironist is timid by comparison. The focus of her attention lies not in social institutions but in a change of heart—a conversion experience on the part of each individual. As Rorty put it, her hope is that individuals will be able "to work out their private salvations, create their private self images, re-weave their webs of belief and desire in the light of whatever new people and books they happen to encounter."[22]

What Flower and Murphey have called to our attention is that the position of the liberal ironist is a kind of secular Calvinism. Calvin had argued that there is a kind of pride associated with the use of natural and acquired tools, and that philosophy is of little use in the larger program of finding our place in the world. His emphasis, like that of the liberal ironist, was upon conscience and upon indi-vidual regeneration. As with Rorty's liberal ironist, so with the Calvinist; liberal-ism is possible, but it is a *liberalism without social action*. And a liberalism without social action, to use Rorty's infelicitous but revealing phrase, offers only "un-grounded" social hope.

Ralph Sleeper articulated this distinction between Dewey's social reformer and Rorty's liberal ironist with great precision:

> The trouble comes, not with Rorty's recognition of Dewey's pervasive "antifoun-dationalism," but with his construal of its consequences. We are left, he tells us, with "ungrounded social hope" and a philosophy that can provide us with noth-ing more than occasional illumination to dispel the gathering gloom. Philosophy, according to Rorty, is to give "edification," and there doesn't seem to be any-thing very edifying in Rorty's attenuation of philosophy's function to the point where it becomes indistinguishable from that of literary criticism. What rankles is Rorty's insouciant reductionism. Pragmatism—at least Dewey's sort—had seemed to offer us more than that. It had seemed to be teaching us how to trans-form the culture that is decaying around us, rather than just how to "cope" with its collapse."[23]

Following William James, Dewey thought that the question was not so much whether social hope was "grounded" in some final way as whether ways could be found to bring into existence what was hoped for. That novels, plays, and drama can and do set social agendas, motivate enthusiasm for social action, and promote common vocabularies is both undeniable and a source of great good. But to assert, as does the liberal ironist, that amelioration depends solely, or even principally, upon the "awareness of the power of [literary] redescription,"[24] that the methods that have been so effective in the technosciences have no special place in social inquiry, is to amputate one half of the method that has been tested and urged upon us by the productive pragmatist. In giving up the reconstructive moment for the sake of the solvent or analytical one, the deconstructionist liberal ironist abandons all hope for social action.

TECHNOSCIENCE EDUCATION FOR A LIFELONG CURRICULUM

> Why is it, then, that after a period of great technical success, the position of science is so subordinate and so precarious over so much of the world?
> —John Dewey, "Religion, Science, and Philosophy" (LW.11.456)

> "Science" in other words is still something that a group of persons, called scientists, do; something they do in laboratories, observatories, and places of special research. It is far from being the temper of mind with which human beings individually and collectively approach the problems that confront them.
> —John Dewey, "Religion, Science, and Philosophy" (LW.11.458)

I. Disparaging Technoscience

As Dewey frequently noted, one of the more interesting paradoxes of our technological milieu is the conspicuous fact that the defining methods and outlooks of the technosciences, despite their remarkable successes and widespread use, have been the subject of popular misunderstanding and even disparagement. This complex situation has been manifested both by negative appraisals of technoscience as a body of knowledge and by flights from technoscientific methods of thinking.

It is an undeniable fact that technoscience as an institution has been, and remains, a locus of controversy. Among the factors contributing to its present turbulence are cases of alleged scientific fraud such as those concerning research into the treatment of breast cancer, controversial practices such as the patenting of life forms, and the massive cost overruns incurred in the construction of publicly funded projects such as the Texas Superconducting Super Collider.

At a more abstract level, it is also undeniable that philosophers, among them Thomas Kuhn and Paul Feyerabend, have called into question what many had regarded as the most basic assumptions of technoscientific method, including the notion that it exhibits linear progress and the idea that there exists a clearly defined set of methods for hypothesis formation. Other philosophers, such as Jean-François Lyotard, have put the matter somewhat differently, announcing the end of technoscience as "grand narrative," that is, a privileged account that unifies all knowledge.[1]

As troubling as some of these factors may be, however, they can hardly be identified *simpliciter* as the sources of the low esteem in which many people now hold technoscience. Where technoscience is under attack, it is normally not the technoscience in which paradigm shifts are debated; nor is it the radical technoscience in which "anything goes" within the stage at which scientific problems are defined and articulated. These are more properly described as areas of legitimate exchange among technoscientists and philosophers, that is, among individuals who are presumably committed to an experimental attitude in the broadest sense of that term. Moreover, these debates are of a sufficiently abstract nature that they have not engaged the attention of the wider public to any significant extent.

The other difficulties just mentioned present a situation that is more ambiguous. Viewed from the standpoint of current institutional science, cases of technoscientific fraud are normally thought to be corrigible by the further application of technoscientific inquiry; technoscientific practices that are regarded as ethically questionable tend to become the subject of investigation by ethicists; and in the minds of most technoscientists, business people, and politicians, cost overruns and contractor fraud are more often laid at the door of shoddy or venal professional practice than taken as an indication of the failure of technoscientific methods.

As viewed by the wider public, however, these cases contain a common element that often leads to a different conclusion. In each case there appears to be a subordination by professional people of public good to private gain. Instead of the public's placing blame where it is deserved, however, the result has often been public confusion with respect to the general methods of technoscience and a consequent loss of faith in the applicability of those methods to areas of public concern.

II. Which Version of Technoscience?

Further complicating this situation is the fact that several overlapping technosciences are at work within the public sphere. This is a fact that is often neglected both in classroom science teaching and in science reporting for the general public.

One of these sciences is "Enlightenment" technoscience, or the technoscience that was developed during the late sixteenth and early seventeenth centuries. Dewey was highly laudatory of the gains made during this historical period. He thought that one of its chief inventions, the use of instrumentation as a part of controlled experimentation, had been the source of great advances over earlier methods, such as authority and empirical observation. But he also thought that many of its methods and outlooks have since been rendered obsolete.

Briefly put, Enlightenment technoscience held that the universe of objects of possible knowledge was finite, and that every problem solved was consequently indicative of one fewer to be solved. It was preoccupied with an epistemological skepticism, and consequently with a search for indubitable foundations for knowledge modeled in large measure on techniques of quantification. From these assumptions followed its faith in linear and inevitable progress through the exploitation of a machine-like nature that could be repaired and modified so as to conform to human needs and desires.

Dewey's own instrumentalist, or pragmatic view of technoscience was, however, quite different. His radical empiricism, inherited from William James, held that non-cognitive experience is much richer than modern technoscience had imagined, and that it offers access to relations within the focal areas of experience as well as to the vague areas at its fringes. He therefore recognized that non-cognitive experience offers the possibility of an expanding horizon of data for cognitive inquiry, including inquiry within the technosciences, and that the domain of potentially important technoscientific problems is enlarged as a result of inquiry.[2]

As a consequence of his fallibilism, inherited from Charles Sanders Peirce, Dewey held that certainty, even in the technosciences, is illusory. Whereas successful experimentation can furnish platforms for further inquiry, it does not furnish foundations of absolute knowledge. This is true of both technoscience as body of knowledge and technoscience as set of methods. In other words, both technoscientific knowledge and technoscientific methods evolve. Moreover, progress in these areas is neither linear nor inevitable; it must be secured piece-by-piece and step-by-step.

Finally, Dewey's evolutionary naturalism, largely the bequest of Darwin, held that human beings are within and a part of nature, that they transact business with other parts of nature, and consequently that there are grounds neither for rigid compartmentalization of the various areas where cognitive work is done, such as the technosciences, the arts, the law, and engineering, nor for a severing of facts from values within any of these areas of inquiry.

Dewey recognized that situations in which men and women ignore or reject the application of technoscientific methods to perceived difficulties often have origins that are murky and complex. He also recognized that it is frequently the case that technoscientific inquiry is thwarted by reliance on beliefs and methods that are emotionally comfortable but that have been historically outgrown or otherwise discredited. In some cases this involves the acceptance of non-scientific approaches to technoscientific questions. In other cases, however, it involves a misplaced loyalty to methods that served previous generations of scientists but that no longer represent the best technoscientific thinking. It was Dewey's recognition of this situation that led him to advance his well-known argument that it is the task of educators to tread a fine line between transmitting the received traditions of a society, on one side, and ensuring that the schools are places of social reform, on the other.

III. Transparency (or Self-Interest?)

I will draw attention to three instances of this flight from technoscientific thinking, although many other cases might also have been discussed. The first involves a decision to discontinue the application of proven experimental methods in the sphere of the public good, based on the very successes of the technosciences in that area. It is profoundly ironic that technoscience *as body of knowledge* frequently tends to prove sufficiently successful that it becomes virtually transparent within public life and consequently that technoscience *as a method of inquiry* suffers. As transparent, it is mistakenly taken for granted as a secure foundation on which other and sometimes competing values and goals are allowed to supervene.

One tragic example of this is the recurrence within the U.S. population of communicable diseases, such as rubella, that had once been virtually eliminated. On some accounts, at least, this unfortunate situation has been due to decreases in funding during the 1980s for the very public health programs that had all but eliminated these and other communicable diseases. Funding cuts were in their turn a consequence of a revised tax policy that shifted resources from the poor to the rich and from public to private spheres.[3]

At one level of analysis, this situation constitutes an excellent example of the normal application of the methods of Enlightenment technoscience. This view of technoscience, as I have already indicated, is characterized by a search for foundations, a sense of inevitable progress, a compartmentalization of technoscientific disciplines, and a diremption of facts and values. The control of rubella was regarded as complete, since this was an area where nature had been forced to submit once and for all. The explicit assumption was that once technoscience fixes something it remains fixed, and that there is therefore no need for continuing reappraisal of the facts of the case. And since the technosciences involved with public health were regarded as isolated from the technosciences involved with economic development, attention could then be turned to the latter without continued consideration of the former. Finally, the fact of the existence of a subclass of medically indigent citizens was viewed as unrelated to the values of an emerging investor class.

At another level of analysis, however, this situation may be viewed as resulting from a deficient application of the methods of post-Enlightenment or pragmatist technoscience as Dewey articulated them. From the standpoint of Dewey's productive pragmatism, it involved a failure to attend to the consequences of public policy, which in turn demonstrated a lack of understanding of the interconnectedness of the objects of experience and an ignorance of the principle of fallibilism. Nature was treated as adversary to be dominated and not as environment within which transactions are to be undertaken with a view to greater adjustment of the whole.

At a less charitable level of analysis, of course, this situation could be viewed as indicative of the readiness of public officials to place the private gain of themselves and their constituents above the demands of public good. The technoscientific literature of the 1980s contained numerous warnings about the consequences of cutting back inoculation programs; it would therefore be difficult to make the case that public officials were not cognizant of the dangers associated with their actions. On this analysis, it was not so much that Enlightenment technoscience was applied and failed, but that, despite the scientific facts of the case, private economic interests were allowed to take precedence.

At the level of public perception, however, the message associated with this event has been clear enough: technoscience appeared to suffer a setback and its status and influence were diminished.

As Dewey noted more than a half-century ago, however, failures such as the one just cited are ultimately not due to the failure of technoscience so much as they are to the failure to apply its finest and most appropriate methods in a consistent manner. As he pointed out in essays written during the depression era of the 1930s, economic and class interests, as well as tradition-bound thinking, stand ever at the ready to supervene upon and redirect public effort (as well as public funds) once hard-won scientific results are regarded as secure. The problem, of course, is that what appears stable today may well become perilous tomorrow.

IV. Fundamentalisms

A second and apparently more active anti-technoscientific movement is evident in the agenda of several types of religious fundamentalism. As the excellent studies edited by Martin E. Marty and R. Scott Appleby have demonstrated, there are many types of religious fundamentalism.[4] Their various aims and methods are colored by cultural contexts that include the technological factors at work in their respective cultures.

Islamic fundamentalists, for example, often see themselves in a proprietary relationship to science. Citing the contributions of the Arab world to medieval science, they describe a situation that in their view exhibits a harmony of science with revealed religion and that it is their mission to preserve.

Seyyed Hossein Nasr, for example, the noted historian of Islamic science, has written that "*scientia*—human knowledge, is to be regarded as legitimate and noble only so long as it is subordinated to *sapientia*—Divine wisdom. Muslim sages would agree with Saint Bonaventure's 'Believe, in order to understand.' Like him, they insist that *scientia* can truly exist only in conjunction with *sapientia*, and that reason is a noble faculty only insofar as it leads to intellection, rather than when it seeks to establish its independence of its own principle, or tries to encompass the Infinite within some finite system."[5]

As Everett Mendelsohn points out, however, the demands of exercising and retaining power in Islamic republics such as Iran often temper the more severe attitudes toward technoscience harbored by hard-line revolutionary fundamentalists who have not yet come to power.[6] Once in control of the government and faced with the responsibility for pumping oil, deploying missiles, and providing telephone service, for example, even hard-liners tend to compromise this vision of wholeness.

It is a point of considerable interest, especially for observers in non-Islamic countries, that a part of the success of moderate fundamentalist groups, such as the Muslim Brotherhood, is attributable to their focus on small technoscience, such as the delivery of health care to their constituents, at the same time they ignore or reject the big technoscientific projects that have been undertaken by the official governments of their countries. Their implicit argument is that the projects of big technoscience are largely irrelevant to the needs of the general population, and too susceptible to the corruption that tends to siphon off the foreign aid that would otherwise improve general living standards. There may be a lesson here for rapidly developing countries such as Turkey, and even for information-based countries such as the United States.

The case of Christian fundamentalism in the United States presents a similarly complex picture. The apparently oxymoronic "creation science" ardently advanced by Christian fundamentalists appears to be an attempt to replace a curriculum of technoscientific studies with one based on religious doctrine. As I write, the balance of power in Kansas seems to have shifted to religious fundamentalists on this issue.

In other curricular matters, such as sex education, and especially discussions of homosexuality, Christian fundamentalists appear to want to develop quasi-disciplines that parallel or even challenge normally accepted psychological and medical technosciences. The *Village Voice* reported in 1993 that fully 25 percent of U.S. school districts were teaching the fundamentalists' sex education curriculum, including the views that the only safe sex is no sex and that abortion is equivalent to killing a baby.[7] Even on a charitable reading, the first of these claims is false and the second relies on a controversial semantic assumption.

Paradoxically, it seems, Christian fundamentalists tend to couple these programs with an extensive commitment to the use of the tools and media of advanced technoscience. From one vantage point, this might be taken as a case of non-technoscientific and anti-technoscientific messages being conveyed by scientific media such as their satellite networks and the massive computer banks they use in their direct mail campaigns.

Viewed from another angle, however, this apparent paradox takes on a different aspect. As James Moore has argued, much of what the fundamentalists are espousing is not so much anti-technoscience as it is an attempt to revive the values and even some of the hypotheses of the Enlightenment, replete with many of the metaphysical commitments of that earlier stage in the history of technoscience.[8]

For one thing, many contemporary fundamentalists advance a view of the origin of life on the earth that is remarkably similar to the "normal" technoscience of Darwin's lifetime, and which some of the best of Darwin's technoscientist contemporaries stoutly defended. Two of the most ardent of Darwin's creationist opponents were Lord Kelvin and Louis Agassiz, the first a highly regarded physicist, the second a leading geologist and glaciologist.[9]

Further, as Northrop Frye has noted, the fundamentalist reading of the Bible as an example of what he has called "third-phase" or "literal-demotic" writing would be a study in anachronism if viewed as an attempt to return to a golden age of faith prior to the rise of Enlightenment technoscience. Third-phase writing was, in his view, "signaled by the ideology of humanism, with its cult of plain sense [thus demotic] and the use of ordinary language [thus literal]."[10] Frye has convincingly argued that the main idiom of the Bible is "kerygma," or rhetorical proclamation, and therefore that any attempt to present it as literal history or technoscience has its roots not in an archaic tradition, but in the Enlightenment.

If one probes beneath the surface phenomena, then, the implicit agenda of the Christian fundamentalists may be viewed as similar to that of their Islamic fundamentalist cousins. In both cases there is an attempt to regress to a time when technoscience—or perhaps the observational science that preceded technoscience—and religion were in putative harmony. In both cases there is an attempt to argue that some recent technoscientific developments should be rejected because of the consequences to the respective theologies. And in both cases these attempts are dampened by a reluctance to jettison the entire history of technoscience in one deft move.

Taken together, these factors might shed light on the fact that some of the staunchest defenders of "creation science" hold faculty positions within the engineering departments of otherwise respectable universities. (Civil and mechanical engineering appear to be the preferred fields.) It is not so much that these professionals are anti-technoscience, but that in this area of their thinking, at least (i.e., where peer assessment of their bridges, hydraulic systems, and other professional work is not at stake), their technoscience and its attendant metaphysics are some 150 years out of date.

Dewey did not directly address Islamic fundamentalism, but he was well aware of the agenda of Christian fundamentalism, and even called attention to its affinity with Enlightenment thought. "The craving of human beings for something solid and unshakable upon which to rest is ultimate and unappeasable. . . . Fundamentals are the answer to man's cry for security, living as he does a life of uncertainty in a world that is always on the move" (MW.15.3). Nevertheless, he thought the name a misnomer, since a true fundamentalist would inquire into fundamentals, and not just dogmatically advance a favorite candidate (MW.15.5).

It might be objected that the fundamentalists' search for foundations has its roots not in the Enlightenment, but in a Platonized Christianity that antedates the Enlightenment by some fifteen or sixteen centuries. There is a sense in which this is true. But this is only one side of a metaphysical split that, as Dewey repeatedly pointed out, rends fundamentalist thinking to its very core. And as Frye pointed out, revealed religion prior to the Enlightenment was mythic and metaphoric in nature, and not literal-demotic. What renders the current fundamentalist position untenable, at least from the perspective of the type of productive pragmatist or post-Enlightenment technoscience advanced by Dewey, is its very abandonment of the mythic and the metaphoric in favor of the literal. The current attempt of "creation scientists" to justify revealed religion in technoscientific terms has its roots in Enlightenment technoscience, and not in first-century C.E. Christianity.

From the standpoint of the tradition of its own sacred texts and history, then, the agenda of "creation science" amounts to little more than bad faith. From the viewpoint of instrumentalist or post-Enlightenment technoscience, it represents little more than bad technoscience. And finally, from the viewpoint of the sociology of technoscience, its increasing popularity represents a failure of technoscience education.

Published surveys underscore this last point. A study published in 1986 indicated that more than half of undergraduates surveyed in three states said that they were creationists.[11] Another survey indicated that "less than 2 percent of [730 Ohio] school board presidents were able to correctly select the statement that best described the theory of evolution from a list of five choices."[12]

This analysis was implicit in Dewey's pragmatic criticism of fundamentalism. Although he understood the fundamentalists' need for security, he had little sympathy with their chosen method of attaining it. "Until they have been reborn into the life of intelligence," he wrote, "they will not be aware that there are a steadily increasing number of persons who find security in *methods* of inquiry, of observation, experiment, of forming and following working hypotheses. Such persons are not unsettled by the upsetting of any special belief, because they retain security of procedure" (MW.15.7). To read the Biblical account of creation literally, he suggested, is not simply to reject the cardinal procedures of post-Enlightenment technoscience in favor of its Enlightenment precursor. At this stage of the history of technoscience it amounts to a "crude, illiterate Philistinism" (MW.15.5).

V. Isolation and Misinformation

A third instance of technoscience disparagement is based neither on economic and class interests nor on religious commitments, but on a general lack of information about technoscientific projects. In this case it is not so much that technoscience is rejected as just that it is misunderstood or ignored. Public opinion polls taken in the United States in 1994, for example, indicated that a large percentage of the population feels increasingly isolated from the work of technoscientists. A survey of 1,255 adults from across the United States by the American Museum of Natural History in New York indicated that 87 percent of those polled could not "identify the cause of the hole in the ozone layer." Another survey found that 92 percent of the respondents could not correctly identify the causes of acid rain.[13]

Exacerbating this situation is what might be called a "splintering" phenomenon within scientific disciplines. Increasing specialization within the more abstract technoscientific disciplines and the increasing bulk of technoscientific output have reached the point at which experts in one field no longer possess either the vocabulary or the time to follow developments in contiguous fields. This situation tends to be even worse within fields such as engineering and agriculture, where concrete application often proceeds in the absence of an understanding of theoretical context. The case already mentioned, of mechanical engineers who go about their professional work even while advancing a version of pre-Darwinian technoscience at the theoretical level, provides one example of this phenomenon.

Dewey was particularly interested in the relation of theory to practice. Against the Enlightenment notion that technology is applied science, he argued that what are generally termed "the technosciences" are types of technology. A cardinal feature of his productive pragmatism was his view that theory and practice must function as partners in the construction of novel products, and that these new products must be tested against previous products and against the requirements of the wider situation. (This is a matter to which I will return in some detail in chapter 9.)

The current "splintering" effect would, in Dewey's view, be the result of the failure of professional people to address the wider social implications of their work, that is, to explore the moral dimensions of their projects by a conscious and systematic treatment of the interactive relations between what they are doing and what others in the scientific community are doing.

Put another way, this deteriorating situation involves a failure of scientists to engage the imagination of the public, a failure of technoscience reporting to indicate the consequences of scientific discoveries for enriched experience, and an absence of political initiatives designed to nourish community involvement in technoscientific undertakings. The methods that have proven successful in the technosciences will not find application in the moral sphere until working technoscientists and technoscience educators begin to see it as their task (and devote the time, even if it involves pro bono activities) to explore the consequences of their work and to communicate their insights to the wider public.

VI. Dewey's Three-Point Program

Dewey advanced a three-point program for improving the status of technoscientific thinking within the schools and, for the public, within a lifelong curriculum. First, he argued that mainstream or "liberal" religious communities need to examine their own interests and goals with an eye to distancing themselves from the outmoded technoscience of the fundamentalists. This will not be achieved, he argued, until they have become clear in their own minds on two points: "What is the relation of a specially organized community and institution like the church, whatever be the church, to religious experience? What is the place of belief in religion and by what methods is true belief achieved and tested?" (MW.15.7).

Dewey's relation to liberal religious institutions was highly complex, and he seems to have been torn between several alternative courses of action. His own view of liberal religion, which was probably a result of what he called the "permanent deposit" of Hegelianism in his thinking, was that it constituted a stage in the development of religious experience that represented an advance over the more primitive literalism of the fundamentalists. But he thought most institutional religions also somewhat out of date and wondered why the next evolutionary step could not be taken.

This would be a step toward an evolutionary naturalism according to which the adjective "religious" would be used in place of the noun "religion," that is, used to characterize any experience, whether scientific, aesthetic, moral, or political, that led to a "better adjustment in life and its conditions" (LW.9.11). This would be a view of "religious" experience sufficiently ecumenical to be taught in schools without fear of undermining the wall of separation between church and state. This would also be a correlative of his view of the proper place of "values" in the curriculum, namely, that the teaching of "values" requires no special place since, properly understood, such instruction permeates the entire curriculum and infuses it with meaning.

Dewey's productive pragmatism is at work in these suggestions. William James had argued that in matters where evidence is lacking but options are live, forced, and momentous, we have the right to choose our beliefs. Dewey added that the public consequences of such beliefs, provided there were any, should be subject to public tests. Where the consequences of liberal religious belief enhance the adjustment that Dewey thought necessary for individual and social progress, there is no apparent reason to disparage such belief.

This was perhaps in the forefront of Dewey's thinking during the mid-1930s as he entered into dialogue and sought alliances with liberal religious thinkers against the fundamentalists. But he thought his religious interlocutors had not devoted sufficient attention to the consequences of their own beliefs, and that this would be necessary before a firm alliance between their institutions and the institutions of post-Enlightenment technoscience would be possible (MW.15.7).

Second, as I have already indicated, Dewey argued that professionals in the technoscientific disciplines must take the lead in demonstrating to the public the ways in which the application of the methods of the technosciences can effect social amelioration. This would amount to a kind of life-curriculum for the public that would present the methods, successes, and aims of technoscience in ways that render them more perspicuous and more relevant to daily life by engaging the imagination of the public. It would require that public figures be public educators, that is, that they put themselves forward as public practitioners of technoscientific methods.

A part of the problem, he suggested, is that all too often influential persons "make use of appeal to authority, prejudice, emotion and ignorance to serve their purposes in political and economic affairs. Having done whatever they can do to debauch the habit of the public mind in these respects, they then sit back in amazed sorrow when this same habit of mind displays itself violently with regard, say, to the use of established methods of historic and literary interpretations of the scriptures or with regard to the animal origin of man" (MW.15.50).

This point is particularly important given the characteristic features of democracy in the United States. In this country as nowhere else, the public registers its views through opinion polls, call-in radio, newsletters, and even computerized news lists and chat rooms. These phenomena are the result of advances in the sphere of the technosciences, and it is obvious that they can, at least in principle, serve to enrich democratic practices. The problem, however, as Dewey saw it, is not so much participation as it is discrimination. "The conditions which have enabled the public actively to intervene have failed in providing an education which would enable the public to discriminate, with respect to the matters upon which it is most given to vehement expression, between opinions untouched by scientific method and attitude and the weight of evidence" (MW.15.48–49).

What Dewey called "a loose, scrappy and talkative education" (MW.15.50) (a type of education that, he lamented, its proponents have sometimes termed "progressive") tends to reinforce the worst elements of this situation. Where such practices prevail, there has been little success in "converting prejudiced and emotional habits of mind into scientific interest and capacity" (MW.15.50). In short, democracy in America tends to be long on personal opinion and short on devotion to the type of thinking that characterizes the technoscientific attitude.

But if Dewey was against what is "loose, scrappy and talkative" in education, he was equally opposed to rigid hierarchical educational structures. He regarded such structures as both anti-technoscientific and anti-democratic. As he wrote in *The Quest for Certainty*, "The scientific attitude may almost be defined as that which is capable of enjoying the doubtful; scientific method is, on one aspect, a technique for making a productive use of doubt by converting it to operations of definite inquiry. No one gets far intellectually who does not 'love to think,' and no one loves to think who does not have an interest in problems as such. Being on the alert for problems signifies that mere organic curiosity, the restless disposition to meddle and reach out, has become a truly intellectual curiosity, one that protects a person from hurrying to a conclusion and that induces him to undertake active search for new facts and ideas" (LW.4.182).

Dewey's view of what he termed the "scientific attitude" has important implications for both administrator-teacher relations and teacher-student relations at every level of education. Where administrative decisions leave teachers without adequate space for intellectual curiosity, initiative, and an active search for new facts and ideas, education is bound to fail. Similarly, where teaching methods do not encourage these traits in students, time spent in school has little value. In Dewey's view, the nurturing of technoscientific attitudes requires ongoing transaction between inquiring individuals and the materials of their chosen inquiry, and it also requires continuing transaction among members of a community of inquiry. In far too many cases, however, "inculcation of fixed conclusions rather than development of intelligence as a method of action still dominates [educational] practice" (LW.4.201).

This brings us to Dewey's third suggestion. "The fundamental defect in the present state of democracy," he wrote, "is the assumption that political and economic freedom can be achieved without first freeing the mind" (MW.15.51). But this is not something that happens on its own and without, as he puts it, "the unremitting nurture of right habits of observation and reflection" (MW.15.51).

How is this to be done? Dewey's approach is holistic without being either totalizing or utopian. First, the material conditions necessary for learning must be present, both for the schools and for a lifelong curriculum. It is only common sense that when illness, hunger, fear of bodily harm, or other forms of debilitation intervene, learning is rendered more difficult. Dewey argued for the application of the tools of the scientific disciplines to the elimination of these problems, which he regarded as moral in character.

But the material means to pursue universal and lifelong learning constitute only the first stage in democratic education. Dewey also argued that both schools and workplaces would have to be redefined and reorganized so that the means and ends of both education and industrial production could be better integrated, and hence that the experience of children and workers alike could be aesthetically richer and intellectually more satisfying. A key element in this conversion would be a greater appreciation and application of the attitude of the best of current technoscience (LW.13.169).

In short, Dewey argued that the interests and aptitudes of child and worker alike must be engaged, coordinated, and liberated through education that continues throughout a lifetime. Where this fails to occur, both study and work become dull, rote, and "mindless." Splits open up within society. On the other hand, minds become "free" as they are engaged and enlarged, and more precisely as they are enabled to appropriate the meanings of experience through an enhanced command of the methods of technoscientific thinking.

The danger of the propagation of "creation science" in the classroom and among the wider public is not, then, that evolution as fact and as theory will cease to be a part of the body of technoscientific knowledge. As Dewey suggested, for such a challenge to "affect seriously the course of scientific inquiries, a number of persons should have been strangled in their cradles some three hundred years ago" (MW.15.48). The danger is rather to the capacities of affected individuals to appropriate the technoscientific attitude in ways that allow them to adjust to changing circumstances by means of the clarification and enlargement of their own experiences.

The reconstruction of technoscience for a life curriculum must involve the rejection of the putative gulf between moral and non-moral knowledge. "At any moment," Dewey wrote in 1932, "conceptions which once seemed to belong exclusively to the biological or physical realm may assume moral import. This will happen whenever they are discovered to have a bearing on the common good. When knowledge of bacteria and germs and their relation to the spread of disease was achieved, sanitation, public and private, took on a moral significance it did not have before" (LW.7.282).

Dewey thought that the attitude that technoscience is somehow set apart from moral matters was a relic of an earlier period of its development, and one that has long since been rendered inappropriate. It is a moral responsibility of technoscience to mount what Dewey called a "contagious diffusion of the scientific attitude" (LW.13.171) that would have widespread and profound public consequences.

Technoscience is a moral enterprise because it is capable of influencing the goals and ideals by which people live. If technoscientists and educators shrink from the performance of this task, then men and women will have their ideals and goals nevertheless; but they will be those of an earlier stage of technoscience, or worse, ones nurtured by anti-scientific forces.[14]

On the eve of World War II, Dewey argued that there is no reasonable alternative to the plan of action just discussed. "Science," he wrote, "through its physical technological consequences is now determining the relations which human beings, severally and in groups, sustain to one another. If it is incapable of developing moral techniques which will also determine these relations, the split in modern culture goes so deep that not only democracy but all civilized values are doomed. . . . A culture which permits science to destroy traditional values but which distrusts its power to create new ones is a culture which is destroying itself" (LW.13.172).

One further point needs to be made about Dewey's conception of technoscience education for a lifelong curriculum. He did not think technoscience a "master narrative," in the sense in which Jean-François Lyotard uses the term.[15] This is to say that he thought technoscience neither universal in its applicability nor the measure by which all other cognitive activities should be judged. Dewey's view of technoscience was not "scientistic."

It was Dewey's view, however, that there is a general method of intelligence that is both fed by, and feeds back into, the scientific disciplines, the arts, historiography, and law, as well as other cognitive undertakings. This is the method he outlined in *How We Think* and elsewhere. That the physical technosciences have been the most successful among these various enterprises is undeniable: but this has been in part due to the fact that their materials are inherently more manageable.

Dewey consistently argued that it is one of the tasks of technoscience education to demonstrate the connections between the methods of the physical technosciences and those of other forms of cognitive activity, especially the arts, with a view to amelioration of public problems. It is only by this means that technoscience can become a part of a life curriculum, and thereby achieve its full potential as a moral enterprise.

LITERACY, MEDIACY, AND TECHNOLOGICAL DETERMINISM

[T]he only meaning of essence is teleological, and . . . classification and concep-
tion are purely teleological weapons of the mind. The essence of a thing is that
one of its properties which is *so important for my interests* that in comparison
with it I may neglect the rest.
                                        —William James, *Principles of Psychology*[1]

Essence, as has been intimated, is but a pronounced instance of meaning; to
be partial, and to assign a meaning to a thing as the meaning is but to evince
human subjection to bias.
                                        —John Dewey, *Experience and Nature* (LW.1.144)

I. Traditional Texts versus Technological Texts

Among those who make it their business to think about the nature and function
of texts, there is a remarkable lack of consensus regarding just what should be
counted as one. There is also deep disagreement about how to sort texts by type.
Discussions about the identification of text-tokens within text-types don't seem
to fare any better. A part of the problem, as Joseph Margolis has reminded us, is
that talk about how texts refer often gives way to talk about "textuality" and "ref-
erentiality."[2]

For some, a text is a literary text. Period. Others have invited us to share their
view that there is an essential difference between paper-based texts and those that
are produced or reproduced on other media. During the mid-1980s, for example,
Albert Borgmann began to construct just such a textiary.[3] The text-type he termed
"traditional" includes literary texts, printed musical scores, and architectural drawings. The text-type he termed "technological" includes information on tapes,
disks, silicon chips, and celluloid.

To some of his readers at that time, Borgmann's choice of terms seemed a bit curious. It seemed fairly obvious that the printing press in its many varieties is the product of technology and therefore that the printed page must also be counted as technological. For that matter, parchment, quill pens, and ink are technologically produced artifacts, so handwritten manuscripts must also be technological texts. The same could be said of stories told in languages that have no written form and even of cave paintings: aren't they also technological texts, since they are artifacts whose production involves the deliberate cognitive deployment of tools and other artifacts, including language, which Dewey called "the tool of tools"? (LW.1.134).[4]

More recently, in his 1999 book, *Holding on to Reality,* Borgmann has sought to clarify this confusion.[5] Expanding his thesis somewhat, he now focuses on the three ways that he thinks information engages what he calls "reality."

First, there is natural information. Natural information is information *about* reality. It was, he says, the "big bang of divine information" available to Abraham in the book of Genesis. It was the natural signs that the Native Americans of Montana encountered in their ancestral home. This reality, Borgmann tells us, is characterized by "gratuitous beauty and sacred magnificence," and it is disclosed by natural signs such as clouds, smoke, and tracks.[6]

Second, there is cultural information. Cultural information is information *for* reality, that is, for the shaping of reality. Architectural drawings, musical scores, and the printed page are examples of such information. They do not convey the eloquence of reality so much as they reveal its structure, or, like the printed word or the grid system of the American West, impose structure upon it. Because there is so much contingency in reality, however, cultural information can never completely convey reality. It is always an abstraction. Even in the most adequate cultural information there is always a remainder—and a reminder—of contingency. In his view, this is good. It keeps us on our toes.

Third, there is technological information. Technological information is information *as* reality. It is the virtual reality of technologies such as the Internet and CDs. Seeking to avoid the ambiguity of the term "technological" in his earlier work, he now indicates that he is using the term in a special and restricted sense. "I use the word 'technological,'" he writes, "to refer to modern and in fact to the most recent technology of information."[7] Its identifying marks are "digital rigor, the massive logic and data structures, and the rapid processing of technological information."[8]

Borgmann dislikes "technological" information for several reasons. First, unlike cultural information, it is not legible without the aid of complex machines. Written languages and architectural drawings will be accessible to future generations regardless of the state of their machinery. Strings of 1's and 0's will not. Second, technological information disburdens us from having to think about contingency and therefore makes us lazy. It releases us from the rhythm of structure and contingency by getting rid of contingency altogether. Third, technological information is totally ambiguous; it provides information only about itself. The "gratuitous beauty and sacred magnificence" of reality are completely stripped out.

What does Borgmann think we can do to stop what he views as the headlong flight from reality that is inherent in technological information such as the Internet? We must get back in touch with the aura of reality by means of live performance and celebrations of life, "erecting enduring things and seeing to truthful signs." We must forsake CDs and the Internet and once again become readers of books and tellers of stories, hikers of trails, and skiers of slopes.

Leaving natural signs aside, and considering only those that are abstract, Borgmann thus wants to separate the world of texts into the two hemispheres that he terms the traditional and the technological. He also wants to claim that one hemisphere is superior to the other. He tells us that traditional texts are superior because they are permanent, self-contained objects that are closed off and distanced from reality, that their rigor is guaranteed by their immutable identity and their pure form, and that they enforce certain community experiences and practices that are salutary.

On the other side, technological texts are inferior because they tend to make us lazy. They give us so much information that they require little reconstructive participation. Their realization and appropriation does not demand of us the effort required by literary texts such as books, musical scores, and architectural drawings. They divorce us from reality and create in us responses that prevent our participation in a community. Books, in his view, as traditional texts, provide a richer and more enduring wellspring of conversation than would "technological" texts such as films.[9] In his view, the communal virtues of literacy are mortally threatened by the electronic media.

Since it seems reasonable to assume that many of the readers of this chapter spend time developing their own literacy (and in the case of some of its readers, urging their students to do likewise), perhaps Borgmann's manner of demarcating texts and the order of superiority and inferiority he assigns to them will find ready acceptance. Is it not after all true that a great obstacle to the careful reading of philosophical texts by university students is the time they spend with "the media"—meaning the *other*, non-print media? Aren't those media the sources of their confusion of psychological and biographical factors with good, sound logical reasons? Isn't it, after all, from those media that they get their subjectivism, their idea that one opinion is as good as another, that they are right just in case they think they are?

Borgmann's dark warnings during the 1980s were echoed by Allan Bloom, the author of a 1987 bestseller, *The Closing of the American Mind.* Bloom, whose title thesis appeared to some observers ironically to have been supported by his sales, assured his readers that it is impossible for students to know how to view films unless they have first read Dostoevsky and Dickens. "As films have emancipated themselves from the literary tyranny under which they suffered and which gave them a bad conscience," he wrote, "the ones with serious pretensions have become intolerably ignorant and manipulative. The distance from the contemporary and its high seriousness that students most need in order not to indulge their petty desires and to discover what is most serious about themselves cannot be found in the cinema, which now only knows the present."[10] Perhaps these somber warnings are correct. Perhaps non-print "mediacy," or the reading (never mind whether critical or not) of "technological," non-print texts, crowds out literacy, or the reading of "traditional" ones.

Confident rejection of new text-types was of course not invented by Borgmann and Bloom. In the *Phaedrus,* Plato has the Egyptian king Thamus (whom the Greeks called Ammon) warn Theuth, the inventor of writing, that his newfangled papyrus-based information retrieval system will prove a disaster. If the young and inexperienced begin to occupy their spare hours with reading and writing, they will no longer avail themselves of the rich tutelage of those who are older and wiser. (They might, for example, go so far as to write to and for one another.) Learning will be more accessible—more democratic—but thinner and less personal. The realities comprehended by the oral texts will be lost, and the dissolution of the community will follow as surely as the night the day. The world will then consist of people filled not with wisdom, but with the conceit of wisdom. Literacy will crowd out memory, and democracy will crowd out the authority of the cultural elite. Civilization as Theuth knows it will be at an end.

Borgmann shares Thamus's concerns but, given his commitment to traditional texts, does not seem to see the irony in doing so. "In the natural economy of information," he writes, "signs and things keep a fine balance. Natural signs emerge, refer, and disappear. They do not get in the way of things. Writing, to the contrary, allows for an endless accumulation of information, and unchecked accumulation leads from perspicuity—the signal benefit of natural information—to confusion."[11] Nevertheless, he admits that writing is here to stay and that it can be liberating. If we can no longer have "natural information," or information *about* reality, then let us at least have what is second best: cultural information, or information *for* reality. Beyond that, disaster lies in the next step—in capitulation to technological information, or information *as* reality.

II. Text-Type Determinism versus Productive Pragmatism

One of the principal difficulties with the contemporary version of Thamus's view, the version held by both Bloom and Borgmann, is that it constitutes a species of technological determinism that, like others of its genus, ignores certain facts.[12] I shall call the Bloom-Borgmann thesis "text-type determinism." It claims that once a type of text is utilized it shapes us in ways that are beyond our control; that on balance, what our texts *are,* and consequently what they do *to* us, is of greater significance than what we do *with* our texts. Texts of the print type, including musical scores and architectural drawings, are said to have the essential feature that when they are utilized they make of us critical and intelligent people. Technological texts, which include those of the cinematic, photographic, audio, and computer types are said to have essential features that are different: their use is said to make us less intelligent and less critical people than we would be if we did not use them.

The claim of text-type determinists is thus much stronger than the productive pragmatist claim of John Dewey, for example, that the kinds of instruments we utilize (in this case our choice of texts) constitute a form of life, a platform, a fabric of habits and working hypotheses, by means of which we enter forearmed into novel and often problematic situations. This productive pragmatist view differs from text-type determinism in its assertion that it is the task of intelligence, regardless of the type of text to which it gives rise or to which it is applied, to generate and improve hypotheses with a view to the reform of habits.

The text-type determinist also appears to reject the pragmatic claim that we grasp and utilize different types of tools, including texts, in different ways. That hammers are designed to be handled and used in different ways than saws or drills would seem clear enough. Moreover, to use a hammer is not to condemn the use of drills and saws. As tools, they do not compete. They complement one another. In much the same way, the increasing variety of complementary tools and implements available for use in technological societies undercuts technological determinism and its commitment to essentialism. It attests to the prodigious adaptability and inventiveness exhibited by human beings.

The claim of the text-type determinists is thus much stronger and less defensible than that of the pragmatist: it holds that once chosen, mechanical and electronic production and reproduction of images and sounds (as opposed to mechanical and electronic reproduction of marks on paper) de-civilizes and renders passive and inert those individuals who involve themselves with such texts. The claim of the text-type determinists is that non-print mediacy, the use of non-print texts, casts out literacy because if we are mediate we cannot also be literate. They tell us that non-print mediacy involves the loss of critical skills, including the ability to interact constructively with literary texts. Their claim holds that text-types are uniquely linked to certain forms of life, and that this is true because each type of text has a unique essence and because the acceptance and use of one text-type in lieu of another closes out certain parts of our future.

It might be objected that I have been unfair. Perhaps the view I am opposing asserts no more than that people spend too much time going to the movies, watching television, listening to recorded music, and playing video games—and not enough time reading books, writing essays, and making their own music. But the relative amount of time spent doing these things is not the central concern of the text-type determinists.[13] What alarms them is that people go to films or watch television or listen to recorded music *at all.* It is not just that such activities take the time that would otherwise be spent reading, but rather that they diminish us as we use them. They make us poorer in spirit than we would otherwise have been.

In lieu of the view of the text-type determinists, then, I offer the following alternative. Following the lead of Dewey's productive pragmatism, I suggest that texts, whether printed, on celluloid, on mylar, on photographic paper, on silicon chips, on CD-ROM, or for that matter carved in stone, are nothing more or less than tools for enjoyment and use. I further suggest that energy spent attempting to find ways of solving perceived problems by experimenting with existing and proposed tools—finding out what we can do with them—is far more productive of augmented critical skills than attempting to discover their essences, their pure forms, their inherent qualities. To put this suggestion another way, what our tools do to and for us is dependent upon choices we make and continue to make, dependent upon our relations to our tools, and not upon their "essence" or "pure form." If my analysis is correct, then text-type determinism is a variety of Platonism.

Text-type determinists contend that our tools have fixed essences and that we are what we are because of what they, our chosen tools, are. To this I would answer that ontological inquiries into the essence of our tools may possess certain aesthetic charms, but that such inquiries have notoriously failed to provide guides for action. One of the dangers of this ontologizing of texts, as well as other types of tools, is that it prevents meaningful inquiry into what they *can be.*

It was not clear, for example, during the first hundred years of printing what could be done with literary texts. The invention of the novel, to take an obvious example, was yet to come. And those readers in the years that immediately preceded the publication of *Ulysses* and *Finnegan's Wake* who thought that they had ascertained the "pure form" or "immutable identity" of literary texts must have been greatly surprised at what James Joyce wrought. Given the history of literary texts, it would be arrogant indeed to say that the essence of that particular text-type has now been, or ever will be, completely revealed. The "novel" is still being invented.

Even if today it were known with certainty that we have once and for all time run out of genres, types, and approaches to literary texts, that the fountain of invention would henceforth and forever be dry, the argument of the text-type determinists that the essences of literary texts are secure would still be far from convincing. The texts of Shakespeare, Dickens, and Woolf still provide new insights even (perhaps especially) for their most accomplished readers. Discoveries of new uses of printed texts and the choices we can and do make about their use run backward into the past and reconstruct it just as surely as they look forward to and influence the future.

To say of a whole group of texts, then—to say of electronically and mechanically produced and reproduced images and sounds—that their essence has been grasped and that they can be nothing more than what they now are, or that their use denotes and promotes lack of critical intelligence, seems to me to fly in the face of well-established fact. Text-type determinism is a thesis that competes for lack of sophistication with Marx's claim in *The Poverty of Philosophy* that the hand mill begets a feudal society, and the steam mill begets capitalism.

The view advanced by these determinists ignores the work of video artists such as Peter Campus and William Wegman, who have richly informed our vision. It neglects the work of film makers such as François Truffaut and Stanley Kubrick, who have expanded the boundaries of what it means to construct a moving image. It demeans the work of photographers such as August Sander and Irving Penn, who have provided us with the means to look at the world in new ways. And most fundamentally it belittles the audiences that these artists have created, those individuals who work *with* and alongside these artists in libraries, in their homes, in museums, and in darkened theaters, to reconstruct those texts for their own needs and purposes.

III. Objectivism without Essentialism

As Dewey and the other pragmatists of the classical period attempted to tell us, rejection of text-type determinism need not involve a commitment to any type of subjectivism or relativism. The bald, indisputable fact is that most human beings are in constant communication with others of their species. We communicate intentionally and unintentionally. Even some who are long dead still communicate with us. Nor is great spatial distance any longer a barrier to communication. It is only by means of tools, including printed texts, photographs, films, videotapes, and compact disks, and the Internet, that we are able to do this. The photographer Russell Lee still speaks to us eloquently of the life of the dust-bowl farmers of the Great Depression, just as do the recording artist Woody Guthrie, the filmmaker John Ford, and the novelist John Steinbeck.

The sources and types of significant texts are many and varied. Like other types of tools, some texts, perhaps most, are inherited. Some are found lying about, and some are available from stocks that are common. Some are available only from sources that cater to the specialist. Some are borrowed, some are modified for personal use from stock items, and some are invented. We discard some texts as no longer useful, and we use some texts only once and then replace them with another of their type. Some texts never leave the planning stages, remaining forever in barest outline.

In all of this talk of texts as tools I have made no reference to inner and outer, subjective and objective, real and ideal. Like other types of tools, a text is an artifact that is produced for use and enjoyment. It may be a simple text designed for a specific task, such as a list of the current prices of mutual funds or a snapshot or videotape of a family outing. It may be a complex text capable of multiform usage and such as to give great delight, as do certain novels by Dickens and certain films by Truffaut. Good texts, texts that serve us well, are constructed so as to take into account the environing conditions that occasion their construction, use, and enjoyment. Poor texts are not well constructed; so their use and enjoyment is flawed.

That there is much that is dreary on television and on film and on audio recordings is beyond dispute. There is also much that is dreary in print. That commercial television is used by some as a refuge from thought, only a fool would wish to deny. But it is also beyond denial that there are books—even some written by philosophers—that function in the same way.

What I urge, then, is that we put an end to speaking of tools, and therefore of texts, as having complete essences that predetermine and provide the measure of our ways of involvement with them. I suggest that we instead speak of the ways in which texts can and do serve to enhance delight and to resolve problems, that is, to enlarge the meanings of our experiences.

A corollary of this view is the thesis that critical intelligence is not split into higher and lower realms along lines of division between involvement with texts that are "traditional" and texts that are "technological." What the text-type determinists argue is that films, photographs, videotapes, and compact disks are incapable of being viewed critically, that there is something in their essence that prohibits critical involvement with them. It seems to me rather the case that if contemporary college and university students do not know how to view a film, or how to look at a photograph, then it is because they have not been taught how to do so. If they are manipulated by images used for the purposes of commercial or political propaganda, then it is because they have not been trained to view images with care and insight. And if they do not demand high standards for the images and sounds that are produced by our culture, then it is not because they spend too much time with non-print media but because they are not sufficiently "mediate." To be mediate, as I use the term, is to have a critical understanding of the ways in which texts do and can work—both within and across text-types.

IV. Scarcity, Significance, and Creativity

This is precisely the debate that Walter Benjamin joined in his 1936 essay "The Work of Art in the Age of Mechanical Reproduction."[14] A part of Benjamin's purpose in that essay was an assault on the cult of high culture, the equation of scarcity with significance. Though this cult still exhibits vital signs, I believe that Benjamin was substantially correct when he argued that it was a symptom of an unfortunate and anachronistic social arrangement. But Benjamin also argued that there is an act of reconstruction, of complicity, in the way we deal with mechanically reproduced images. In looking at a film, he says, we identify not with the actor, but with the camera. Viewing a film is montage in reverse.

In his novel *Three Farmers on Their Way to a Dance*, Richard Powers has provided a felicitous paraphrase of Benjamin's point. He denies that when we look at a film or photo we look at its subject matter. Instead, we look "over" it. We remake the scene, looking for something else. In the case of a still photo, "the lens slices a cross-section through time, presenting an unchanging porthole on a changed event. The frame invites us to feel a synchroneity with the photographer the way museum-case glass, slicing through a beehive, invites us to live in the colony. . . . If the path between sense and significance opens, it will open in those moments when, momentarily delighted by some overlooked detail or construed resemblance, we become aware of what lies in front of the plane of the photo."[15]

What Benjamin and Powers have attempted to tell us is that there is work that is constitutive, work that is productive, going on not only behind the lens but also in front of the surfaces of the photograph, the film screen, and the cathode ray tube. There is no simple act of looking; the eye is a prehensile organ that handles and feels and grasps its subject, turning it over and manipulating it to get a clearer view not only of the image itself, but of possible contexts from which it has been abstracted.

Powers's metaphor of the photographic image as cross section is itself a productive one, for it reconnects two kinds of activities between which the text-type determinists have attempted to drive a wedge. The activities that give rise to the creation and appreciation of images are reunited with those of the type we call "knowing" in a broader sense than is usually admitted by epistemologists.

Powers treats the cross section as a kind of hypothesis. It is a grasp put forth within a field of experience, a freezing of action, an arrest of movement. It is a location of sharpened focus. Productive knowing utilizes such specimens in order to get a firmer grasp on the broader field from which they are abstracted. Cross sections/hypotheses allow experimentation with experienced fields; they help to indicate the possibilities of what experienced situations can become as a result of productive intervention into them. To look for the pure form or essence of the cross section is to miss the point of its function. A cross section, whether a printed essay, an idea, or a photographic image, is a proposal for something to be done.

Put another way, both creation and appreciation, whether of ideas or of photographic, cinematic, or video images, involve the bringing of a creative activity to a provisional close. Stopping the action is to some purpose: this, rather than that, is selected from a busy field. But the stop is provisional because it is the occasion for evaluation, for the positioning of the image or idea in ways that allow it to be utilized in the future with respect to things we can and should do, as well as with respect to cross sections that are not yet had. With images, as with ideas, creation and appreciation broaden the field of actual and possible connections. They heighten critical awareness.

The text-type determinism advanced by both Borgmann and Bloom is a part of a long and still powerful tradition that stands opposed to this view of the unity of intelligence and the critical activity of vision. Descartes spoke for the tradition of which Borgmann and Bloom are a part when in Rule Twelve of the *Rules for the Direction of the Mind* he treated vision as a passive conduit that is sensate only when being *acted upon*. His metaphor was still a passive one when he turned in the third of his *Meditations* to the visual metaphors clarity and distinctness as criteria of truth. For this tradition, sight operates in a fashion that may be called "linear" insofar as it establishes a point-to-point conductance of information from the pure form of a complete and finished object to the visual orifice and thence to the common sense of the mind.

Against this view Benjamin argued that vision is "non-linear," that it is not passive and inert but active and exploratory. This alternative account of vision constitutes a radical departure from Descartes's metaphor of rays entering the eye from a complete and finished object. In this alternative account the eye is a probing tool that moves and checks and interacts. Sidney Hook drew attention to this constructive activity of vision in 1927 in *The Metaphysics of Pragmatism*. "We use our eyes," he wrote, "as we do our hands—to grope, to pry, to scan, to escape danger, to signal a friend. Sense activity, like all behavior generally, is not inertly receptive in the presence of stimuli or explosively active in their absence. It is *interactive*."[16]

V. Two Fallacies of Technological Determinism

There are two significant fallacies involved in technological determinism, hence in the species of that position that I have called text-type determinism. The first is a reductive fallacy that says "artifacts of the type A have effect *x*, therefore no other type of artifact can have effect *x*." Bloom's comment on Dickens offers a clear example of this fallacy: "students today have nothing like the Dickens who gave so many of us the unforgettable Pecksniffs, Micawbers, Pips, with which we sharpened our vision, allowing us some subtlety in our distinction of human types. It is a complex set of experiences that enables one to say so simply, 'He is a Scrooge.' Without literature, no such observations are possible and the fine art of comparison is lost."[17]

Bloom tells us in this passage that literary texts and no other kind of texts allow us to sharpen our vision with respect to human foibles and character flaws. It is his view that such insights are not attainable as a result of interaction with any other type of text. We cannot expand our understanding of human behavior by viewing films critically.

It is doubtless true that there are some novels that should never be translated into film. E. M. Forster said that his *Passage to India* was one of those novels, and I for one think it unfortunate that director David Lean did not take him at his word. Further, I take it as obvious that there is a *prima facie* richness about a novel—among other considerations simply owing to the time required to read it—that is difficult to approach in the two or fewer hours it takes to view a film. But the same may be said of the text-type we call the short story. To say this is just to admit the obvious, that we use the tools we call texts in different ways, and that there is no perfect translation from one medium to another. Films based on books must overcome enormous problems of translation; but the same could be said about books (and essays) about films.

To say, however, as do the text-type determinists, that we get a more detailed impression of the poisoned political prisoner in Manuel Puig's novel *Kiss of the Spider Woman* than we do in Hector Babenko's excellent film version of that novel is nothing short of nonsense. Words on a page cannot convey the convulsions of a poison victim with the same intensity that is managed by a moving image in the hands of accomplished film actors and directors. To take a case of political documentary, no assemblage of print texts was able to galvanize a nation against the indignities of racial segregation as did the film footage of Bull Connors turning his dogs loose on demonstrators in Selma, Alabama. If Borgmann wishes to speak of media in terms of their abilities to provide wellsprings for conversation, then I submit that particular bit of film footage as an example of a text of enormous and lasting consequence.

There are those who will object that images, because they can carry heavy emotional charges, are capable of political abuse. In the hands of the wrong people, images can become instruments of repression and destruction. Another form of this objection is the claim that filmmakers sometimes serve purposes that are evil even though their own motivations are more innocently aesthetic, as the motivations of the director of *The Triumph of the Will* arguably were. Thus put, what has been said is unquestionably true. But the text-type determinist wishes to go further to say that cinematic and video and photographic texts are capable of manipulation in ways that print texts are not because they, unlike print texts, are not amenable to critical interpretation. This is precisely the type of reductionism advanced by Bloom.

Unfortunately, however, his view ignores several important facts. It ignores the fact that print texts have also functioned as means of manipulation, as did Harriet Beecher Stowe's *Uncle Tom's Cabin,* Tom Paine's *Common Sense,* and Adolf Hitler's *Mein Kampf.* It ignores the fact that print texts can and do function as instruments for critical assessment of non-print texts, as has Eisenstein's *Film Form.* And it ignores the fact that communities of inquiry into non-print texts, such as film societies, have grown up around their respective texts in the same way that other communities of inquiry have focused upon print texts.

Even more significantly, however, this type of reductionism abandons the field to those who create commercial and political propaganda. It denies that intelligent estimation of image texts or music texts is possible; it denies that education in this field can be effective.

The remarks of Sergei Eisenstein, who was also interested in the works of Dickens, provide a kind of vaccine against the reductionist fallacy of Bloom and Borgmann. Eisenstein argued that cinema and literature have features that they share, as well as certain features that are unique to each. His remarks should not be taken in an ontological sense, however, but in terms of the ways in which cinema and literature can be utilized. In a passage that constitutes a sharp contrast to Bloom's, he writes:

> Perhaps the secret lies in Dickens's (as well as cinema's) creation of an extraordinary plasticity. The observation in [Dickens's] novels is extraordinary—as is their optical quality. The characters of Dickens are rounded with means as plastic and slightly exaggerated as are the screen heroes of today. . . . It is absolutely thus that Dickens draws his characters—this is the faultlessly plastically grasped and pitilessly sharply sketched gallery of immortal Pickwicks, Dombeys, Fagins, Tackletons, and others.[18]

Later in the same essay, Eisenstein chides as "thoughtless and presumptuous" those who think that they "can erect laws and an esthetic for cinema."[19]

Eisenstein's point is that literary texts share many structures with the texts of other media, and that some of the same critical tools by means of which we operate in one arena quite often serve us well in another. He invites us to read Dickens from the standpoint of cinema mediacy, as well as to read cinema texts from the standpoint of the literary structure of Dickens's novels.

The second significant fallacy of the text-type determinists is what Dewey called "the philosophic fallacy." This is the mistake of taking some result of inquiry, reifying or hypostatizing it, and then positing it as something that was already fixed and finished prior to inquiry, that is, treating it as if it had been there all along. The text-type determinists conclude that non-print texts are for the most part treated uncritically in our culture. No impartial observer would deny them that conclusion. But then they turn their conclusion into something that is said to be an essential feature of non-print texts. They hypostatize what they have found in inquiry into something that existed previous to their inquiry and then they say that it has existence in its own right.

The text-type determinists call attention to the widespread use in American culture of image texts and music texts. They also point to an equally evident fact, that ours is a society that has not come to terms with its educational needs, a society that has not developed meaningful patterns of leisure-time use. They conclude that the use of non-print texts constitutes a determining factor for de-education and laziness. In the view of Borgmann and Bloom, that is the essence of non-print or technological texts.

But they have put the cart before the horse. It is not that we have text-types with essential structures at work determining human behavior, but rather that poor decisions have so limited our perspective that full inquiry into the possibilities of non-print or technological texts has been lacking. One can admit that television texts and cinema texts are sometimes silly and sometimes even downright dangerous—and at the same time reject the determinist thesis that those text-types are essentially flawed and beyond redemption.

The view I have presented has no quarrel with those who say that there is much work to be done to improve the quality of most of the non-print texts utilized in our culture. There is also much that could be done to improve the use and enjoyment of print texts. What I have argued instead, along the lines advanced in Dewey's productive pragmatism more than a half-century ago, is that the development and use of critical intelligence is not uniquely linked to the use of one text-type; that we must intelligently engage texts of all types, even if some of the text-tokens within those types are silly, dreary, or even dangerous. To be mediate is to be literate, but it is to be more than literate.

Borgmann's brand of reductionism holds that the essence of television is that it is silly and destructive of intelligence and that it should therefore be avoided. It is true that television is often silly and often destructive of intelligence. But it is more. It can also be educational, or entertaining, or soporific, or even an aphrodisiac. His reductionist view also recommends that we forsake CDs and the Internet and once again become readers of books and tellers of stories, hikers of trails and skiers of slopes. If we do not, he warns, we will miss the contingencies of reality that keep us on our toes. To this I suggest that there is no apparent reason why a Saturday surfer of the Internet cannot also be a Sunday skier of the slopes. And there is also no apparent reason why printed books, the Internet, and CDs cannot be used as complementary tools for research and enjoyment. Borgmann's observation that there is much that is cheap and inauthentic on the Internet is hardly debatable. But is this fact not just one of the contingencies of reality that keep us on our toes?

POPULISM AND THE CULT OF THE EXPERT

> [D]emocracy is belief in the ability of human experience to generate the aims and methods by which further experience will grow in ordered richness. Every other form of moral and social faith rests upon the idea that experience must be subjected at some point or other to some form of external control; to some "authority" alleged to exist outside the processes of experience. Democracy is the faith that the process of experience is more important than any special result attained, so that special results achieved are of ultimate value only as they are used to enrich and order the ongoing process. Since the process of experience is capable of being educative, faith in democracy is all one with faith in experience and education. All ends and values that are cut off from the ongoing process become arrests, fixations. They strive to fixate what has been gained instead of using it to open the road and point the way to new and better experiences.
>
> —John Dewey, "Creative Democracy—The Task before Us" (LW.14.229)

I. The Issues

One of the most persistent problems of our milieu may be put quite succinctly: "What should be the role of the expert in technologically based democracies?" This matter was the subject of especially intense debate during the late 1960s and early 1970s, the crisis years of American involvement in Southeast Asia. Some, including philosopher Emmanuel Mesthene, responded to this situation with a call for increased central planning in which cadres of experts would formulate and implement public policies, largely bypassing public opinion. Others, including political analyst John McDermott, offered solutions that would merge populism with a mild form of Luddism, eschew large-scale planning, and sharply limit the influence of experts within the domain of public policy.

Complicating this issue, experts in some societies such as the United States have convinced policy makers to apply techniques of centralized planning that have included subsidizing large industries such as General Electric through enormous tax incentives and cushioning the losses of financial institutions such as the savings and loan industry even while claiming to march under the banner of laissez faire capitalism. This is a situation that John Kenneth Galbraith, with his customary precision, once termed "the approved contradiction."

In this chapter I shall examine three important—and competing—contributions to this debate. The first two were published during the Vietnam War era of the late 1960s and the third in 1927, a year in which a crisis of another sort—the great Mississippi flood—brought the issue of expertise to the forefront of American political life.

Although not widely available until 1970, Mesthene's technocratic view was developed as a part of a 1968 report prepared by the Harvard Program on Technology and Society. McDermott's populist view, advanced in his now classic essay "Technology: The Opiate of the Intellectuals," was published in 1969 by the *New York Review of Books.* The third position, and the one that I contend offers the most promising approach to the problem, is the productive pragmatism articulated by Dewey in *The Public and Its Problems* in 1927. As a part of my presentation and defense of Dewey's position, I shall review recent studies by Bruce Bimber of the history of the Congressional Office of Technology Assessment and by Michael Eldridge of the work of San Francisco political activist Randy Shaw.

II. From the Cowboy to the Engineer

The last decade of the nineteenth century saw the beginning of an enormous public fascination with the most visible of all experts: the engineer. When Dewey began to write about technology in the 1880s, the cowboy—the symbol of lonely self-reliant individualism—was still the dominant national cultural symbol in the United States. The Eiffel Tower—the great monument to the expert—had not yet been built. By the time Dewey published *The Public and Its Problems,* however, the cowboy had long since been replaced, as Cecilia Tichi reminds us, by the engineer—the expert solver of great public problems.

During the first two decades of the twentieth century the engineer was the hero of hundreds of silent films and best-selling novels. "In the imaginative literature of industrialized America," wrote Tichi, "[the engineer] figures as a new hero who enacts the values of civilization. He is at once visionary and pragmatic."[1] His role was to signify "stability in a changing world. He was technology's human face, providing reassurance that the world of gears and girders combined rationality with humanity. And he represented the power of civilization in the contemporary moment. Popular texts present the engineer as the descendant of once-powerful ministers and statesmen; his is ethical *and* utilitarian power. In an industrial era, in a gear-and-girder world, the engineer wears the mantle of civilizing power and ethical judgment."[2]

From 1880 to 1920 the number of engineers in the United States increased from 7,000 to 136,000. A decade later, their number had swelled to 226,000.[3] Efficiency expert Frederick Winslow Taylor, who invented the term "scientific management," designed more efficient factories and then turned his attention to the design of more efficient societies. He was not the only engineer interested in social problems. Another expert intent on riding the crest of the wave was Herbert Hoover.

Hoover, who would become president of the United States less than a year after the publication of *The Public and Its Problems*, had a career as just such an engineer. He remains to this day the only one of his profession elected to the White House. At the time of the great flood of 1927, which inundated 1.5 million acres and displaced almost a million people, Hoover was secretary of commerce. By means of a brilliant public relations campaign, however, he was able to parlay his assignment to bring relief to the flood victims into major political capital, and ultimately to occupancy of the White House.[4]

Although Dewey was not exactly infected by the disposition within American popular culture to apotheosize the engineer, his writings nevertheless reflected and even contributed to this rise of interest in the possibilities of technoscientific planning. As early as the 1890s, long before he articulated the technologically based version of pragmatism that he called "instrumentalism" (and that I have termed "productive pragmatism") in *Studies in Logical Theory* (1903), Dewey was already using the language of engineering and social planning. In "Moral Theory and Practice" (1891), for example, problems of ethics are presented as analogous to problems of engineering (EW.3.94–95). He was even more specific in an essay published a year later, in which he compared the solution of ethical problems to the engineering feat of building a tunnel under the St. Clair River (EW.3.157).[5]

Some four decades later, during the difficult period that followed the stock market crash of 1929, Dewey extended his engineering metaphor to social planning of all types. "The first lesson of scientific method," he wrote in 1931,

> is that its fruit is control within the region where the scientific technique operates. Our almost total lack of control in every sphere of social life, international and domestic, is, therefore, sufficient proof that we have not begun to operate scientifically in these fields. . . . For the ultimate issue is not between individualism and socialism, capitalism and communism, but between undisciplined thinking and confused action, and scientific planning and action. (LW.6.50–51)

Quite simply put, Dewey saw the social disaster generated by the Great Depression as a consequence of the failure to apply the very techniques that had worked well enough in the technosciences and industry to other public areas in which they might be expected to work quite as successfully. He regarded social problems as little more than complex problems of technology. This remarkable thesis has to this day not been adequately appreciated. One of its consequences is that technoscience is not value neutral. I shall return to this matter later in this chapter.

Dewey's interest extended beyond the engineer proper to a consideration of how all those who are regarded as experts differ from those who are not so regarded. One of his favorite means of explicating his view on this matter was in terms of habits. Taking his cue from William James, Dewey argued that habit was both mainspring and flywheel, both inner tension and live inertial weight, of human action. Habits bind us to old ways of doing things and make us reluctant to initiate novel courses of action. But they, and especially the shared habits that we call "institutions," also provide the springboard from which new discoveries can be made and new paths of action can be entered upon.

Habit and thinking are thus for Dewey not polar opposites, but phases within human experience. Habit determines the channels within which thought operates, and thinking takes place within the fabric of habits. As I argued in chapter 1, *technique* is the expression of existing habits and *technology* is the inquiry that forms new ones. They indicate different types of occupations, but they also operate as correlative within sequences of inquiry.

> The sailor, miner, fisherman and farmer think, but their thoughts fall within the framework of accustomed occupations and relationships. . . . Scientific men, philosophers, literary persons, are not men and women who have so broken the bonds of habits that pure reason and emotion undefiled by use and wont speak through them. They are persons of a specialized infrequent habit. (LW.2.335)

Dewey's "experts," those who engage their specialized situations intelligently, have learned the methods of managing their habits in ways that allow greater control of indeterminate and problematic situations than are generally available to other members of the public. In contrast to these experts, the majority is caught up in the apparatus of tools and appliances: cell phones, computers, automobiles, microwave ovens. These technoscientific fruits sometimes tend to function as surrogates for the critical thought that solves problems. This majority, then, to whom technoscientific quotidiana have become transparent in use, stands in stark contrast to the experts—those who have gone beyond satisfaction with the embodiments of technoscience "in practical affairs, in mechanical devices and in techniques which touch life as it is lived" (LW.2.338), that is, beyond preoccupation with the fruits of technology to the manipulation and control of tools and other artifacts in ways that resolve problematic situations. The expert is one for whom a portion of the technoscientific life-world has ceased to be transparent and is instead an object of a special type of focus that allows deliberate and considered intervention.

Dewey argued that active engagement of existing habits is effected by means of experimentation, and experimentation is the necessary condition for an understanding of *how* things may be made to work more efficiently. This is no more or less than what Dewey meant by "intelligence." Where intelligence is lacking, he suggested, individuals are at the mercy of circumstances. Sometimes luck or good fortune intervenes and they are able to turn matters to their own personal benefit, but there is still a lack of systematic management (LW.2.338).

But is there not a danger in all this? Do not the activities of experts, especially when they are directed toward the formulation of public policy, tend to create a new oligarchy, a technocracy that is by its very nature antipathetic to democracy? Dewey's response to these questions takes on additional relevance when placed beside the positions of Mesthene and McDermott. They present positions that he regarded as extreme and that he had already rejected some forty years earlier.

III. Government by Experts

In *Technological Change: Its Impact on Man and Society,* Emmanuel Mesthene (who had received three degrees from Dewey's Columbia University between 1948 and 1964), writing for his colleagues at the Harvard Program on Technology and Society, presented his case in terms that could at first sight have been a paraphrase of Dewey's productive pragmatism.[6] Technology, he wrote, is more than just hardware. It is "tools in a general sense, including machines, but also including such intellectual tools as computer languages and contemporary analytic and mathematical techniques. That is, we define technology as the organization of knowledge for the achievement of practical purposes."[7] And in language that even more specifically recalls Dewey's, Mesthene summarized what he termed his book's central argument.

> The argument in brief is that new tools—it takes some of the awe and mystery out of "technology" to think of it as tools—create opportunities to achieve new goals or to do things in new ways. This means that people and groups of people generally must organize themselves differently from before in order to take advantage of the opportunities offered by new tools. (It takes some of the awe and

mystery out of the concept of "social institutions" to think of them as groups of people organized in certain ways to accomplish certain purposes.)[8]

Mesthene thus painted a picture of available tools and methods that lie at the ready, but at the same time in tragic disuse, while vested economic interests and intransigent bureaucracies hold a brake on the application of those tools to persisting social problems. Among the many things that he thought could be done to improve this situation were (a) "the proliferation of what might be called scientific or knowledge agencies in government itself,"[9] (b) "introduction of the professional scientist into the policy-making process," and (c) the expansion of "computerized information-handling procedures."[10] As I write, some thirty years later, each of these proposals has been implemented in concrete terms and has become a prominent feature of the American sociopolitical landscape.

How will this increased utilization of "professional cadres of technicians and experts" affect traditional democratic forms of social organization? How will people organize themselves in this new world? What kind of new publics will be created? It is on these points that Mesthene's program departs in subtle but important ways from that of Dewey. His language—which includes talk of tools and publics—echoes that of Dewey's productive pragmatism. But his prescription for the role of the voting public in a technological society could not be further from the one that Dewey developed during more than a half-century of public life.

Mesthene argued that the imperatives of decision-making processes in a modern technological society would probably create the need to rethink traditional forms of democracy. It would still be important that citizens register their preferences, but such free expression would increasingly be irrelevant to the task of the experts, who would in any case be occupied with the prediction of consequences. More specifically, the electorate would probably have no particular role to play in the "technical process of government itself." The job of the expert would increasingly be to lay out alternative scenarios and then attempt to determine their likely outcomes. Although they would remain accountable to the public in the long term, "consultation and accountability remain distinct from the technical decision making process, and no amount or combination of them—that is, no amount of 'participation' in the populist sense of the term—can substitute for the expertise and decision making technologies that modern government must use."[11]

The role of the public is thus in Mesthene's account reduced to approval or disapproval of policies worked out from afar. Democracy is redefined as the ability to recall policy makers, but not necessarily to redirect their policies, which in any event remain the best courses of action because they have been sanctioned by the experts.

IV. The Populist Response

John McDermott's essay "Technology: The Opiate of the Intellectuals," which appeared in the *New York Review of Books* in 1969, constituted a major assault on Mesthene's position.[12] McDermott argued that the Harvard report was little more than a call for greater numbers of technocrats who were even further divorced from and impervious to the wishes of the public than those currently in charge. He cited as evidence Mesthene's analysis of what he had called "the negative externalities" of technology, among which were pollution, overpopulation, and occupational hazards. Mesthene had suggested that such problems are merely the result of confused signals among the leaders of industry regarding whose business it should be to attend to such matters. McDermott, on the other hand, suggested that the "negative externalities" had not so much fallen through the cracks as been the result of conscious choices made by the captains of industry to put profits above public responsibility. He criticized what he took to be a central claim made by Mesthene and others, among whom he included Zbigniew Brzezinski (who was later to become President Jimmy Carter's national security advisor), that the answer to technology is just more technology. He objected to their view that technology was a self-correcting system that would eventually take care of such "negative externalities" in the event that the free play of technological factors was allowed to run its course.[13]

McDermott accused Mesthene and his Harvard group of embracing a modern version of the old laissez faire doctrines of the British empiricists and utilitarians. "Just as the market of the free play of competition provided in theory the optimum long-run solution for virtually every aspect of virtually every social and economic problem, so too does the free play of technology, according to its writers. Only if technology or innovation (or some other synonym) is allowed the freest possible reign, they believe, will the maximum social good be realized."[14]

Contrary to what he perceived to be Mesthene's "combination of guileless optimism with scientific tough-mindedness," McDermott thought that he saw ample evidence that decisions made by technocrats during the 1960s were in fact de-democratizing American society. He argued that the decline of popular literacy, by which he meant the increasing inability of the man or woman on the street to understand the language used by technocrats, was one such indication. Another was said to be the growth of a two-tier society: increasing regimentation of low-level employees into mind-numbing tasks at the same time that those in the upper echelons were allowed to pursue fulfilling agendas. Finally, he pointed to what he saw as the truncation of the lives of "men and women in the lower and . . . middle levels of American society . . . cut off from those experiences in which near social means and distant social ends are balanced and rebalanced, adjusted, and readjusted." [15]

Much of McDermott's evidence and many of his central metaphors came from the tragic American experience in Vietnam, which he viewed as a case study of what goes wrong when technical information is withheld from those who need it in order to do their jobs. (He mentioned technical scenarios developed by computers at base camps, for example, that were then applied to situations in the field without input from the units on the ground there. He complained that the individual soldiers were often badly informed about the factors that were utilized to determine the missions.) McDermott thus encountered incontrovertible evidence of his thesis that the rarified decisions of technocrats inevitably fail when they ignore the experiments of those who are concretely involved in specific problematic situations. He argued with considerable irony (I suspect that Dewey would have agreed with him on this point) that the concretely experimental low-tech North Vietnamese and Vietcong had proven themselves more proficient in technological terms than had their high-tech Yankee opponents. As Dewey might well have put it, the North Vietnamese and the Vietcong had understood the situation in terms of a delicate interplay between means and ends that took into account subtle existential distinctions. The Americans had not.

In retrospect it is difficult to disagree with this last point. The architects of America's involvement in Southeast Asia seemed never to have had a clear goal or end-in-view. But because they were convinced that they had superior tools, or means, their unstated hypothesis seemed to be that the employment of those superior means would bring about a superior end. The problem was not that their goals were flexible, since flexible goals are generally preferable to those that are inflexible. The problem was that their goals were vague. The means they employed, on the other hand, were single minded and inflexible. They bordered on a technophilic obsession with the use of tools for their own sake.

Although Mesthene and McDermott were both ostensibly writing about "technology," they were in fact writing about different issues under the same rubric. Worse, each writer used the term "technology" in ways that were inconsistent with other uses of the term within his own essay. Mesthene used the term in at least two important senses. The first was his stated instrumental one: "the organization of knowledge for the achievement of practical purposes." But the second was quite different: technology is whatever is formulated and implemented by experts. Mesthene's unquestioned assumption was that at the level of large social and political organizations, these are the same. As I shall suggest, one of Dewey's central arguments in *The Public and Its Problems* was that what was to be Mesthene's second sense of "technology" is not technology at all but something else: it purposely cuts itself off from whole areas of potentially important information and so fails to be inquiry in an honorific sense, a component that Dewey thought essential to technology in *its* honorific sense.

McDermott, too, used the term "technology" in several incompatible senses. Throughout most of his essay he wrote of technology as equivalent to what President Dwight Eisenhower had called "the military-industrial complex" (a phrase that a character on the television series "The X-Files" has since enlarged to include "the military-industrial-*entertainment* complex"). If technology in this sense is said to be self-correcting, then the situation is even worse. Since its growth entrenches existing power structures, its self-correction will lead to even further entrenchment. It is only buried within a footnote on John Kenneth Galbraith that we finally get a glimpse of McDermott's "alternate" vision of technology: "My own feeling," he wrote, "is that the fundamental point to take account of in constructing an alternate vision is the fact that technology itself and its need for a skilled and knowledgeable population has created within the population ample resources for self-management even of the most complicated activities."[16]

V. Productive Pragmatism's Alternative

Each of these opposing arguments gives token acknowledgment to a view of technology that is consistent with Dewey's productive pragmatism, but each chooses to focus on an alternative view of technology that has drawbacks that Dewey had already demonstrated. It is ironic that Mesthene, trained at Dewey's Columbia, found a technocratic view of technology appealing, or at the very least that he saw no inconsistency between a technocratic view and a democratic one. McDermott confronts Mesthene with the defects of the technocratic view and gingerly approaches the subject of a more acceptable alternative, but because of his failure to develop his treatment of technology in its more democratic sense, his critics cast him in the role of moderate Luddite.

In brief, Mesthene's essay may be read as a paean to the cult of the expert, and McDermott's as an attempt to tar all forms of expertise with the same unsavory elitist brush. Neither writer attempts to spell out the ways in which constructive interaction between expert and public may be effected.

What were Dewey's suggestions regarding this issue? In *The Public and Its Problems,* he suggested that dynastic and aristocratic forms of oligarchy had yielded to a new form based on economic considerations. "At all events, it is a shifting, unstable oligarchy, rapidly changing its constituents, who are more or less at the mercy of accidents they cannot control and of technological inventions" (LW.2.362). What is to be the check on the new oligarchy? Some have argued that ordinary men and women, since they are too distracted to form effective publics, are incapable of filling such an oversight role. It has therefore been suggested that only an "intellectual" aristocracy—a cadre of experts of a different sort than those interested solely in economic matters—would be capable of providing an adequate balance. The trick is thus to pit one group of experts against another for the benefit of the broader public. Those who hold this view, Dewey continued, also contend that democratic movements have been just transitional,[17] at one time a necessary antidote to the powers of landed aristocracy and ecclesiastical authority but no longer appropriate to the making of policy in a complex technological society. In short, this view holds that contemporary problems are addressable only by "expert intellectuals," even though those experts may in fact form different groups, have different allegiances, and operate from different stances.

Allowing for the anachronism, this is a remarkably accurate paraphrase of the conclusion advanced by Mesthene, who wrote almost exactly four decades later. Against it Dewey mounted a frontal attack. He first argued that if the "common" people are as "irredeemable" as the argument indicates, then "they at all events have both too many desires and too much power to permit rule by experts" (LW.2.363). The very factors that allegedly render the common people unfit for rule also render them incapable of submission to the rule of a class of experts.

The target of Dewey's criticism is a view that is only slightly less extreme than the situation depicted by George Orwell in *1984* of a proletariat that is perpetually prevented from forming an effective public because of its preoccupation with sex and drugs.[18] In Orwell's novel, the experts found it unnecessary to take steps to "control" the proletariat, since the proletariat had proved uncontrollable in any case. At the same time, however, the experts had realized that the proletariat had set its own boundaries, constructed its own prison, so to speak, and so constituted no real threat to the continued rule of the experts. The attitude of the experts toward the proletariat was, to use a phrase made famous by Daniel Patrick Moynihan, "benign neglect."

Second, Dewey argued that any attempt by the experts to rule would ultimately be the consequence of their alliance either with the members of the economic oligarchy or with the non-expert voting classes. In the former case the experts would tend to be subservient to the economically privileged, just as engineers and other technoscientists often become the servants of big business. In the latter case, ordinary men and women would once again have a share in government.

But Dewey thought that there is an even more serious objection to the thesis that would later be advanced by Mesthene. Experts could never achieve monopoly control over the knowledge required for adequate social planning because "in the degree in which they become a specialized class, they are shut off from knowledge of the needs which they are supposed to serve" (LW.2.364). In other words, experts can be experts only if they are in close contact with the problematic situations concerning which they are the putative experts. There is no such thing as an expert in the abstract.[19] This argument is as effective against Plato's vision of an intellectual aristocracy as it is against Mesthene's vision of a technocratic one. In a slightly different form it is also one of McDermott's arguments against Mesthene.

Finally, Dewey followed Tocqueville in claiming that a democratic form of government is not just *one* way of associating among many, but the *only* manner of association that is truly *educative,* both for its officials and for its voting citizens. The strength of democracy is that

> it forces a recognition that there are common interests, even though the recognition of *what* they are is confused; and the need it enforces of discussion and publicity brings about some clarification of what they are. The man who wears the shoe knows best that it pinches and where it pinches, even if the expert shoemaker is the best judge of how the trouble is to be remedied. Popular government has at least created public spirit even if its success in informing that spirit has not been great. (LW.2.364)

Dewey thus argued that the activation of social intelligence is an affair of knowing in the sense in which knowing is instrumental and experimental— which is to say dynamic, flexible, and in need of constant revision. It was in this context that Dewey rejected the idea that societies should be *planned* and argued instead that they should be *planning.*

But there are many reasons why the expert may fail or refuse to take into account changing public needs: he or she may have put private interests above public ones, or have opted for *a priori* formalism above active experimental knowing. When the members of a class of experts become divorced from the public needs they are called upon to serve, then, says Dewey, their knowledge is private knowledge. This means that as far as the public is concerned, their expertise is not knowledge at all.

On the other side, rejecting what would become the McDermott thesis, Dewey recognized the fact that an uninformed electorate can create prodigious public problems as a result of its failure to vote intelligently, and that it must depend upon experts for the gathering of facts and the construction of scenarios. "Majority rule, just as majority rule, is as foolish as its critics charge it with being" (LW.2.365). Dewey refused his unconditioned blessing either to the decisions of experts, which sometimes tend to take the form of "apart" or *a priori* knowledge, or to the popular will *simpliciter,* which when implemented without adequate consideration can have disastrous consequences.

Dewey would, for example, probably have been quite opposed to the proposals now being put forward in some quarters that public referenda should be expedited by instant voting on the Internet or cable television. What would be missing in such situations would be the debates and deliberations that make citizenship educative and meaningful. At the same time, I think that he would have been critical of the manner in which information is presented by news programs on commercial as well as public television, since the "experts" who are invited to provide background information and comment on current events usually represent no more than a narrow cross section of public life. I leave aside what would have doubtless been his reaction to the concentration of ownership of media outlets and the control of news by corporations who are the subject of their reports.

What is important about balloting, Dewey argued, is not the expression of popular will, but the process of antecedent debates, the modification of views to provide adjustments to the opinions of minorities, the discussions, the consultations, and the attempts at persuasion, all of which should precede any public decision that is, to use the vocabulary of William James, based on options that are "live, forced and momentous."

Dewey thought that the problem of promoting and maintaining meaningful debate in which minority opinions are respected is "*the* problem of the public" (LW.2.365). Tools, methods, and artifacts must be measured in terms of the extent to which they promote such interchanges, enhance knowing, and thus facilitate the solution of public problems.

Inquiry, indeed, is a work which devolves upon experts. But their expertness is not shown in framing and executing policies, but in discovering and making known the facts upon which the former depend. They are technical experts in the sense that scientific investigators and artists manifest *expertise.* It is not necessary that the many should have the knowledge and skill to carry on the needed investigations; what is required is that they have the ability to judge of the bearing of the knowledge supplied by others upon common concerns. (LW.2.365)

The central problem of the public was thus for Dewey not that of making each of its members an expert, but in reforming and maintaining itself in such a way that enlightened debate concerning its vital interests can continue unimpeded. To those who would argue, as did Mesthene, that the public must in principle be barred from participation in the activities of policy making, and this because of lack of information or sophistication or intelligence, Dewey had two counter arguments.

First, such a judgment is based on existing conditions that include the unfortunate effects of secrecy, prejudice, and misrepresentation. There is in fact no way of knowing how capable the public might be if facts were openly available and undistorted by propaganda, and if inquiry were otherwise unimpeded. This was precisely the issue that Dewey faced in defending his view of education against its critics on both left and right. He had no sympathy, for example, with those who decided upon *a priori* grounds that Irish-Americans or Italian-Americans or African-Americans were "uneducable," as some during Dewey's time thought members of those ethnic groups to be.

Dewey advanced a second and related argument. Neither expertise nor the ability to render informed arguments regarding public policy is inborn: "*effective* intelligence is not an original, innate endowment, . . . the actuality of mind is dependent upon the education which social conditions effect" (LW.2.366). Intelligence in public affairs, like intelligence of all other types, is not a private and personal matter, but a function of a rich inheritance of tools and artifacts of all types, including meanings and significance, which has been bequeathed to each individual by his or her forebears. "The notion that intelligence is a personal endowment or personal attainment is the great conceit of the intellectual class, as that of the commercial class is that wealth is something which they personally have wrought and possess" (LW.2.367).

VI. The Office of Technology Assessment

An excellent example of the manner in which Dewey's arguments can be expanded and applied to the current political situation can be found in Bruce Bimber's book *The Politics of Expertise in Congress*.[20] Bimber has provided a carefully researched and tightly reasoned assessment of what the subtitle of his book terms "the rise and fall of the Office of Technology Assessment."

Created in 1972 by legislators concerned with the social implications of technological innovation, the OTA functioned successfully for more than two decades as a source of expert advice on technological matters for members of both parties in both houses of Congress. In 1995, however, following the Republican "revolution" led by Newt Gingrich and the subsequent shift of power in the House of Representatives from committee chairs to the Speaker, the OTA was abolished.

Bimber demonstrated that the success of the OTA was built on its adherence to a strategy of strict neutrality that precluded participation in the making of policy.[21] He reports that "nearly every committee of Congress occasionally relied on OTA for information, from the Budget and Appropriations Committees to Veterans Affairs."[22]

Bimber's central argument, however, is that "*[t]he degree of politicization of expertise may be more an institutional phenomenon than a product of the preferences or style of politicians, the moral or professional commitment of experts, or an inexorable trend away from neutrality.* . . . If the view here suggested is right, the way [toward neutral competence in government] lies in the design of political structures and the incentives to which experts respond, and there is no reason to believe it impossible for balanced, neutral-tending experts to exist inside some political institutions."[23]

The solution that Bimber envisioned avoids the extremes presented by Mesthene and McDermott in much the same manner that Dewey's did. It is not that legislators cast their votes based on instructions furnished by the experts at OTA, but that they utilized the information provided, the scenarios developed, and the outcomes projected by those experts as the basis for their political judgments. Moreover, legislators' political judgments, as well as the institutions that provide their context, are (at least ideally) continually open to oversight and revision by the various publics that they serve and to whom they must justify their actions. And the degree to which the various publics are capable of political technology, including intelligent oversight and revision of legislative decisions, is a function of the degree to which the values of critical thinking—educational values or what Dewey termed "technology"—permeate the wider society.

If Mesthene's vision involves top-down management by a cadre of experts, and if McDermott's involves a bottom-up populism, then Dewey's and Bimber's analysis is much more complex. They view interaction among the various levels of expertise, policy making, and popular opinion as exhibiting a dynamic give-and-take. And this, as Dewey constantly reminded his readers, just underscores the need for a stronger emphasis on public education. Only when democratic forms of government are secured by strong educational moorings will the various publics that make up the larger body politic have sufficient weight to counterbalance the effects of institutionally isolated and protected expertise.

In Dewey's view, it is not necessary that the members of those various publics become experts themselves. But it is necessary that they should have been taught the use and benefits of critical skills and commitment to public goods. And it is necessary that neither technical experts, nor policy makers, nor popular movements gain a measure of power and influence that upsets the delicate balance among its co-partners. The goal of each sector should be the growth of social intelligence through cooperation with each of the others.

VII. Political Technology: Randy Shaw and Ralph Reed

Consideration of the most advantageous balance between technical experts, policy makers, and popular movements within the context of the topic of this book leads to the inevitable question: Did Dewey have a "political technology"? Michael Eldridge takes up just this question in his admirable book *Transforming Experience*.[24] He concludes that Dewey was headed in the direction of a political technology, but that he didn't go quite far enough. He supports this conclusion by drawing our attention to the work of Randy Shaw, an activist at the Tenderloin Housing Clinic in San Francisco, whom Eldridge says utilizes Deweyan methods.

Eldridge defines political technology in Deweyan terms as "a specification of the means to the ends desired." Discussing Shaw's program, he expands this somewhat: political technology should be practical, ameliorative, deliberative, and consequentialist. Even more specifically, he says, it should be systematically situated; it should involve public discussion and concerted effort; it should call for strategic planning; it should hold elected officials responsible; it should build coalitions; and it should rely on direct action, including the use of lawsuits.

As Eldridge describes it, Shaw's work as an expert political organizer has incorporated each and every one of these elements. But surely this description cannot be sufficient. The same might be said of the work performed for the Christian Coalition by the conservative political activist Ralph Reed during his tenure as its director. Reed's service in that capacity appears to have incorporated each of the elements on Eldridge's list. If political technology is defined in terms of "a specification of the means to the ends desired," then Reed appears to have been right on target. If it is a matter of coalition-building, holding politicians' feet to the fire, the use of lawsuits, and so on, then it looks as if Reed's program fit Eldridge's bill perfectly—perhaps even better than Shaw's, since Reed was an actor on a much larger stage.

Given the political interests that motivate *Transforming Experience*, it is apparent that Eldridge does not have the same enthusiasm for Reed's work that he does for Shaw's. So unless his views are based on no more than tenacity or prejudice, there must be something more at work.

It might be asked, for example, whether either Shaw or Reed has a type of faith in his own ideals that the other lacks. But this doesn't seem to work very well. Shaw and Reed appear to be driven in similar ways by faith in their ideals. Shaw is apparently motivated by a faith in social justice, and more specifically by a desire to empower the poor to stand up to the pressures of large corporations. Reed also appears to be motivated by faith, but a faith in what?

Following Dewey, Eldridge makes a distinction between two types of inquirential strategies. On the one hand, he says, there are attempts to render intelligence practical. Political movements that use this strategy begin and end with ideals that are intractable. The situation at hand has to be constantly adjusted to the ideal, and it almost never happens the other way around. The second strategy starts with practice as we find it and then sets out to make it more intelligent. This strategy calls for continually testing our ideals with a view to adapting them to our experienced situations. Since one of the main planks in Dewey's instrumentalist platform was the claim that inquiry begins where we are and not where we are not, he rejected the first strategy and embraced the second one.

At first glance, neither Shaw nor Reed seems to have employed the first strategy. Both started with a perceived difficulty. Both defined a problem. Both formed a hypothesis. Both tested their hypothesis against the facts of the case. Both applied the test results with respect to the existential situation that occasioned the inquiry. And both have been highly successful at their chosen tasks.

Eldridge points out the flaw in this analysis, however, by arguing two theses. First, politics may be about power, but a democratic politics must be about the widespread distribution of power, not its concentration. This is not a matter of political left versus political right, but of political inclusion. Nor is it a matter of "big government" versus "local control," since both terms are relative. "Big government" sometimes reins in repressive local governmental entities, and sometimes local governments function as laboratories in which experiments are performed that ultimately help big government do its job better.

By this measure, Shaw's goal seems to have been to include a fragile segment of the citizenry in the political process, whereas Reed's goal seems to have been to form coalitions of people who wish to protect their own economic and social status against perceived threats such as racial minorities and homosexuals, among others, and to see their own religious values taught in the public schools to the exclusion of the religious values of others. So one difference between Shaw's political technology and Reed's is that the former is more democratic than the latter. It is not that Shaw is democratic and Reed is not, but that their commitment to democracy differs—perhaps even significantly—in degree.

Second, Eldridge argues that making practice intelligent involves experimentation and not just discussion. As I shall argue in chapter 9, this is the watershed that separates Dewey's political technology from that of Habermas. As Dewey reminded us, participation may be a necessary condition for democracy, but discrimination, and the formation of habits of discrimination, and action that grows out of habits of discrimination are even more important. If the current popularity of talk radio teaches us anything, it is that the venting of preconceived ideas is not the same as intelligent debate based on the results of experimentation. Moreover, experimentation must go beyond analysis of the best means to predetermined ends, or "straight-line instrumentalism." It must also involve the evaluation of cherished values.

Shaw, for example, encouraged his clients to experiment with their cherished value of maintaining the status quo, namely, preventing the hotel development that threatened their neighborhood. In other words, he encouraged his clients to treat their goals as ends-in-view instead of intractable ideals. As a result, their ideals were modified to accommodate the situation as it presented itself. Reed, on the other hand, sought to organize people who believe that it would harm our society if gays and lesbians were to have equal rights to employment, adoption, and so on. He and his clients have held this as an intractable value despite the fact that there is a large body of experimental evidence that they are wrong. To take only one of many examples, longitudinal studies of children raised in same-sex households indicate that their mental health tends to be no better or worse than that of children raised in heterosexual households.

Viewed from the standpoint of Dewey's political technology, this creates considerable difficulties for Reed's political technology. He and his clients could only defend their cherished value on the basis of an authority brought in from somewhere outside of experimentally warranted evidence. This means that Reed's political technology is not sufficiently experimental with respect to his cherished values. Reed is indisputably a genius in the area of experimentation with the *means* of forming coalitions of people who hold similar intractable values. He is very good at the techniques of straight-line instrumentalism. But he doesn't extend the same experimental techniques to an evaluation of the *ends*, the cherished values, that those means serve.

This is a crucial difference between his political technology and the political technology of productive pragmatism. As Dewey put the matter, "Only recognition in both theory and practice that ends to be attained (ends-in-view) are of the nature of hypotheses and that hypotheses have to be formed and tested in strict correlativity with existential conditions as means, can alter current habits of dealing with social issues" (LW.12.490–91).

In order to be responsible, political technologies, just like the technologies involved in building bridges and writing software code, must be both experimental and democratic. This is what makes them sustainable. By drawing our attention to the work of Randy Shaw, Eldridge has provided an excellent example of the ways in which Dewey's productive pragmatism can and does work. If Dewey did not go far enough in terms of the application of his own ideas, as Eldridge has claimed, he was going in the right direction and his insights are still applicable to our increasingly complex technological milieu.

To sum up, the role of the expert in Dewey's vision of a planning society is that of the researcher and clarifier of facts, hypotheses, and the means and methods of bringing about resolution of experienced difficulties. Experts get from members of various publics an increased awareness of what the public problems are and how those problems relate to existing public institutions. They bring to public discourse clarified scenarios and possible courses of action, as well as new insights into pertinent facts. They treat their hypotheses as ends-in-view and not as inflexible goals. When they fall short of this role or go beyond it, situations arise such as the one described by McDermott in his critique of the policies that led to the disastrous American presence in Vietnam. In such cases the "cadre of experts" described by Mesthene ceases to be a public resource and instead becomes a public problem.[25]

❖ 8 ❖

HOPE, SALVATION, AND RESPONSIBILITY

> But it is a lazy abdication of responsibility which assumes that a genuine culture can be achieved except first by an active and alert intellectual recognition of the realities of an industrial age, and then by planning to use them in behalf of a significantly human life. To charge that those who urge intellectual acknowledgment or acceptance as the first necessary step stop at this point, and thus end with an optimistic rationalization of the present as if it were final, is a misconstruction that indicates a desire to shirk responsibility for undertaking the task of reconstruction and direction. Or else it waits upon a miracle to beget the culture which is desired by all serious minds.
> —John Dewey, *Individualism, Old and New* (LW.5.110)

I. Myths

Some have suggested that what we call myths may have begun as religious stories —imaginative, prescientific accounts of the origins, nature, and eventual outcome of the world. Few today would deny that cosmogonies, cosmologies, and eschatologies, as we now call such stories, are myths in some sense of the term. And some have suggested that religious stories were derived from even more primitive accounts—tales about individuals, real and imagined, such as Prometheus, Hector, and Achilles, acting and suffering in modes that we call heroic, which is to say, on behalf of and within the context of social concerns.

Dewey held a very different view. He thought that myths had arisen from what he called the "industrial" activities of the early human, from concerns such as "the utensils, tools, instrumentalities that secured him a constantly improving life." He suggested that the early human's "nature-myths, his conception of natural forces as hostile and favorable, his interpretation of the events of his daily life, grew out of this industrial basis. His modes of associated life, family relations, political control, etc., were intimately dependent upon his industrial occupations" (MW.1.233–34).

Whatever else may be true of myths, it seems fair to say that once the point in the life cycle of a story is reached at which it is called a myth, the content of the story has already been reflectively transcended. The moving fan blades have slowed to the point that they have become visible.

For true believers, to characterize *their* story as a myth is tantamount to charging that it is suspect or even false. Religious fundamentalists and other literalists, for example, are inclined to choke on the term "myth"—except when it is applied to stories that are someone else's. For those who are more critical, such as philosophers or sociologists, to call a story a myth might simply indicate that it should be accepted as one account among many viable alternatives (even though perhaps as the best among them, it might still issue a call for action).

This chapter will employ the term "myth" in a sense that is quite broad. It will be used to designate any coherent blend of assumptions and beliefs that humans develop from their existential situations and concerns in order to fill up gaps in their experiences. Myths are in this sense ideal overlays to concrete data that are for some reason incomplete or unsatisfactory. Even though all myths involve the ideal, it does not follow that all myths are created equal.

That mythmaking in the sense in which I use the term is a uniquely human social activity is beyond doubt. We may now speak with confidence about languages that are learned and used by chimpanzees, for example, but not even the most sanguine proponent of interspecies communication has so far been able to produce evidence that chimps or dolphins tell the kind of stories that I have called myths.

Myths, then, are stories that human beings tell about their existential situations in order to fill gaps, to render soft spots hard, to sharpen poorly focused images, to get an overview of problematic situations, or to celebrate certain activities and outcomes above others. While these stories remain vital, they seize us. They entertain, they motivate, they provide a beat to which we can march. They can even help us find and recognize new facts.

II. Acquisition and Loss

The primary myths of advanced technology and quotidian technique alike have tended to involve instrumental control or management. The story of Prometheus's theft of fire from the gods; the Enlightenment myth of nature as a well-oiled machine; the myth of the human brain as a computer; the myths of augmented personal power through the instrumentality of Calvin Klein briefs, Arid Extra Dry, or BMW motorcars—these are all myths of control.

But the type of control conveyed by this type of myth can take radically different forms. Some celebrate the *acquisition* of control. Prometheus steals fire from the gods and gives it to humans. Humans become like the gods because they have this important tool. The myth of nature as a machine is also a myth of the acquisition of control. That myth, which seems so alien and alienating to us now, at one time had a liberating effect with respect to medical practice. After the human body began to be thought of as a machine within the larger machine of nature, the old myths of medical practice that were couched in the Galenist language of quiet observation began to recede. Machines can be repaired.[1]

Technical and technological myths sometimes compete for acceptance as accounts of acquisition of control. During the seventeenth and eighteenth centuries, for example, myths of control by mechanization competed with myths of control by mathematization. As Dava Sobel has reminded us, one of the great conflicts in the larger struggle to control the determination of longitude pitted the mathematization of lunar-position theories, favored by Isaac Newton and others, against methods of mechanization, in the form of John Harrison's shipboard clocks.[2]

Technological and technical myths have also included stories about *loss* of control. As David Edge has reminded us, nineteenth-century American folk songs depicted a delicate balance between the railway engineer, whose job was to keep the engine on its rails, and the fireman, whose job was to provide its enormous power. The engineer, the symbol of control, was inevitably portrayed as a sober family man. The fireman, the symbol of potential loss of control, was depicted as a lustful drunkard with a girl at every station. Edge has also reminded us that for emerging middle-class Americans of the nineteenth century the railway myth was one of endless possibilities, journeys of adventure, and personal enrichment. In the blues tradition of poor, southern African-Americans moving to the industrial north in search of jobs, however, the railway myth was one of separation from family and loved ones, of desolation and despair.[3]

In some stories about technology and technique human beings have ceased to be the users of instruments of effective control. They have themselves become the instruments of some outside force, perhaps benevolent, perhaps malevolent. Among the arts, Arthur C. Clark's book *Childhood's End* is an example of the former, and films such as Fritz Lang's *Metropolis* and Charlie Chaplin's *Modern Times* are examples of the latter. As for philosophy, two classic myths of loss of control have been advanced by Jacques Ellul and Martin Heidegger.

III. Hope

In *The Technological Society,* Ellul argued that what he termed "technique" has become autonomous, that it is outside of human control, and that it has totally usurped human freedom.[4] Technology, as he described it, is so pervasive that there appears to be no means of evaluating it from outside, much less any way to control it. It obeys only its own laws, its own logic, and it is self-augmenting. Human beings can no longer understand or regulate it. It is like a cancer growing within human society. Ellul saw no possible human or historical possibility of controlling technology. Like the Hollywood Frankenstein story, the human inventors in Ellul's story have created an inhuman force that has become greater than they. It threatens to destroy them.

Later, in *The Technological System* and in *Perspectives on Our Age*, Ellul tempered this harsh judgment.[5] In place of the desperate situation he had described in his earlier work, he advanced a different kind of myth. His new story was an appeal for an ungrounded religious hope.

It was not religion per se, however, that excited his interest. Institutionalized religious faith, as he described it, is based on human feelings of anxiety and it tends to rise toward God as a means of controlling such feelings. Ellul identified institutionalized religion with attempts to do business with God. Like Euthyphro in the Socratic dialogue of the same name, or like Pat Robertson on channel forty-two, religions attempt to use the divinities to effect certain existential changes, to assure an entrance ticket into heaven, and so on. Ellul characterized such religious practice as little more than ill-conceived and faulty technique. Its proponents bargain with the gods in much the same way that Faust bargained with the devil. A soul is offered in return for a cure from cancer or financial prosperity. Prayerful devotion is offered in return for steering a hurricane away from a favored city (or toward an offending one).

Ellul was particularly critical of mass-media Christians in this regard. He claimed that whenever it utilizes electronic media, popular Christianity models itself on the propaganda techniques of mass political movements. Religious faith of this type was in Ellul's estimation no better in its Christian manifestation than if it were directed toward technique itself as a kind of god. In fact, that is what institutionalized Christianity has more or less done.

As an antidote to this loss of control, Ellul offered what he called "hope." Hope offers a place to stand—a place he described as the *only* standpoint outside the technological system. If technology is all-pervasive in an empirical sense, then something transcendent is needed in order to escape it. In his book *Hope in Time of Abandonment*, Ellul defined this hope as "man's answer to God's silence."[6] As he put it, "Hope comes alive only in the dreary silence of God, in our loneliness before a closed heaven, in our abandonment." Further, hope is "this absurd act of confidence placed in those who declared that it was the Word of God which they had received (and which we are no longer receiving)."[7] He presented the biblical character Job as the hero of hope, and this because he "dares to declare God unjust because he fails to show himself as he said he was."[8]

For Ellul, it is hope that makes our history our responsibility. But this is true only in the sense that we believe that history has a beginning and an end, alpha and omega points. Ellul urged Christians not to reject technology, or to be indifferent to it, or even to engage it superficially, as they might, for example, engage in politics. Christians should instead address technology critically in order to "destroy the deified religious character of technology."[9] Ellul characterized the Christian as someone who works within the interstices of the technological machine with a view to increasing the amount of free space within the system. But his only concrete suggestion was a negative one: it is the task of the Christian to recognize technology as a false god—an idol—and to work for its destruction as an object of veneration.

Ellul's story of loss of control can be summarized as follows: technology is ubiquitous and insidious. It is a system with its own laws, and it is beyond the control of any human institution or combination of them. It allows no standpoint for criticism from the inside. Increased control by human beings is no longer possible. Institutionalized religions offer no hope against it because they too have accepted the false myth. Ironically, the more that institutionalized religions buy into the myth of technological control, the less effective they become. Only the hopeful Christian can ameliorate this situation because only he or she has the possibility of transcending the system, of judging and altering it.

Ellul's story thus presents myths of acquisition of control as examples of idolatry. His primary story is the technical myth of loss of control, and he tells it in order to set the stage for its replacement by a special kind of religious story. Despite his best efforts, however, his religious story is also a myth of control—of covert control. He urges the hopeful Christian to *do* something creative, to *work* diligently for control within the interstices of the technological society. His technological myth, his story of loss of control, turns out to be a foil for his religious myth. But his religious myth contains a second and subordinate technological myth: a covert story of control. This is a component that he cannot avoid if he is to propose any action at all.

IV. Salvation

Like Ellul, Martin Heidegger was profoundly troubled by the status of contemporary technology. Heidegger did not speak as unambiguously of the autonomy of technology as did Ellul, nor did he argue that it has completely crowded out human freedom. For Heidegger, it was not so much that technology has caused human beings to lose control, but that it has caused them to lose their way. Technology has become a mere gimmick or superstructure (*Gestell*) that gives a false rendition of what he called "Being" *(Sein)*. The "enframing" of contemporary technology, by treating objects, means, and even human beings as stock parts, as standing reserve, prevents Being from "coming to presence," or being revealed.

"Being" is a term that serves as the linchpin of Heidegger's philosophical work. No definition of "Being" is possible, since far from being an object or event it is the possibility of there being such things. Being is what occasioned the astonishment of the pre-Socratic philosophers, and Being is what the Western intellectual tradition since Plato has forgotten.

To some of his readers, including George Steiner, Heidegger's Being sounds remarkably like the God of Augustine, Pascal, or Kierkegaard.[10] Being is not, and it cannot be, the object of control. It can be called forth if approached lovingly by artistic means: by *poietike techne*—the poetic arts. Heidegger suggested that before Plato, the Greeks had a sense of making palpable and luminous that which is already inherent in physical nature. A proper attitude toward technology would involve a return to such a custodianship of Being. Instead, contemporary technology has provoked Being and has entered into an adversarial relationship with it. Contemporary technology has masked Being rather than allowing it to shine. It has divorced *poietike* and *techne*. *Teche* in its contemporary form, technology, has been undertaken in ways that are insensitive to the poetics of wonder and the "shepherding" of Being.

In the now famous interview with *Der Spiegel* published shortly after his death in 1976, Heidegger argued that as a consequence of its will to control, its will to power over nature, humanity has become uprooted from the earth. Neither philosophy nor human endeavor of any type can any longer effect a turn away from this bleak and deteriorating situation.

What then are the prospects for humankind? Heidegger sketched two scenarios, but endorsed neither of them. In the first, technology destroys itself, and perhaps humankind as well. Little imagination is required to envision how this scenario could be realized. Nuclear disaster, toxic pollution of the seas, global warming, and a depleted ozone layer are just a few of the more obvious candidates.

In the second scenario, an accidental opening to Being is discovered (or revealed) and then taken. In other words, a god comes to save humankind and humankind pays heed. In either case, a return to the concerns and activities of the poets will serve as preparation for what might come. Heidegger put this clearly and succinctly in the *Der Spiegel* interview. "Only a god can save us. The sole possibility that is left for us is to prepare a sort of readiness, through thinking and poetizing, for the appearance of the god or for the absence of the god in the time of foundering; for in the face of the god who is absent, we founder."[11] On being asked by the interviewer what the individual is capable of doing within the bleak situation he had sketched, Heidegger replied that the individual is capable only of "this preparation of the readiness, of keeping oneself open for the arrival of or the absence of the god."[12]

Heidegger's story, like that of Ellul, begins with a myth of failed control. But whereas for Ellul human beings have created a monster that they can no longer control, for Heidegger the control undertaken by technology has been misdirected. Being is provoked, and there is consequently the prospect of devastation. Since humankind has taken a wrong turn and has become lost, there is a need for salvation. But salvation can be effected only by means of an epiphany: a god who comes to show a path in the thicket.

Heidegger's primary myth is thus a religious myth. Like Ellul, however, he used the technological story as a foil for his religious story. In his account, the best that humankind can do is to prepare itself to be the instrument of divine intervention: the revelation of Being. Humankind is to prepare itself to be able to recognize the epiphany, should it come. As in Ellul's story, there is a recondite myth of control embedded in his religious myth. The poetic art that he urges upon us will, he believed, have the effect of self-control—of preparation for the epiphany.

What type of god is it whose salvific epiphany Heidegger awaits? We are not told. If Heidegger's flirtation with Nazi ideology and his emphasis on the superiority of a German-Greek cultural axis are any indication, however, it would hardly be a god whose appeal was universal.

V. Responsibility

Dewey employed technological and technical myths very differently. He did not wish to deny that technological decisions have at times failed to be of service to humanity, or that control has sometimes been lost and that the result has been alienation and suffering. But he argued that whenever this has been the case, it has not been the fault of technology per se, but rather of a failure of imagination or nerve, of stubborn adherence to inappropriate forms of social and political practice, of placing self-enrichment above the common good, or perhaps even of inability to resolve a situation that could not be resolved given the available tools and resources.

The story told by Dewey is thus quite different from the ones told by Heidegger and Ellul. The messages of Heidegger and Ellul are structured as a standard sermon, with three points. First, there is loss of control (a story of failed technology); second, there is either ungrounded hope or preparation for an epiphany (a religious-eschatological story); and third, building on the first two points, there is something that can be done to regain control in the short term (a covert myth of technological control).

Dewey's account is quite different. Instead of abandoning a myth of control for a religious myth that turns out to conceal yet another myth of control, his account is a myth of control in which loss of control is not massive, and not due to the hegemony of out-of-control technology. For Dewey, loss of control and securing it again is a part of the rhythm of organic life. For Dewey, technology is not the enemy. It is the means of putting things right that have gone sour or gotten off the track.

Dewey viewed the history of human problem-solving and knowledge-getting as the history of effective adaptation to specific environmental problems by means of the development of increasingly complex instrumentation. Those instruments have included organic structures, extensions of limbs and senses, and ideas. Problems and difficulties were thus for Dewey not an occasion to abandon technological instrumentation, including the projection of imaginative ideals and goals, but to enlarge their domain and to renew them in order to render them appropriate to whatever problem is at hand. Whereas Heidegger recommended that we prepare ourselves in the event that a clearing (*Holzweg*) appears in the forest, Dewey called for sharper tools with which to cut a way through the dense underbrush of conflicting events and relations. Writing of the use of rules such as the Golden Rule, for example, Dewey says: "About the specific act to be done it tells, I repeat, not a jot. But it is a most marvellous tool of analysis; it helps me hew straight and fine in clearing out this jungle of relations of practice" (EW.3.101).

In short, Dewey's message was that perceived difficulties call for active and direct experimentation, that experimentation must be related to the original difficulties and constantly tested against the existential situations from which they have arisen, and that solutions usually prove to be temporary. They become parts of situations that give rise to new problems and require new forms of experimentation. In other words, Dewey also told a story of the loss of control, but not one that was global or that called for supernatural intervention. In Dewey's story, loss of control is a continual, quotidian event, an ordinary part of a general pattern of problem-solving as well as the highly abstract problem-solving that goes on in the advanced technosciences. The world of human beings exhibits resistances, and those resistances are the occasion for the productive inquiry we call technology.

Whereas Ellul and Heidegger deserted faith in human intelligence for ungrounded hope and the prospect of salvation, respectively, Dewey argued that if human problems are to be solved then it will be human intelligence that will have to do the job. His story is not a myth of hope, or even of salvation, but of human responsibility.

This is not to say that there is no religious element in Dewey's critique of technology. In 1934, in *A Common Faith,* Dewey suggested that religion is a collective term, but that the collection for which it stands is not logically coherent (LW.9.1–58). He proposed the "emancipation of elements and outlooks that may be called religious" from religion (LW.9.8). He denied that there is any religious experience in itself, and suggested instead that there are religious qualities in many types of experiences.

What are these qualities? They include enthusiasm brought to bear in the pursuit of ideals, the qualities within experience that lead to better adjustment to life and its conditions, and whatever introduces genuine perspective into what is fragmented or incomplete.

What Dewey rejected, however, was any attempt to make religious faith *supervene,* rather than *intervene,* with respect to human affairs. He wrote of faith in human intelligence as having a religious dimension, and he thought that some proponents of supernatural religions properly feel such a faith a dangerous rival.

By 1903 Dewey had already rejected the claims of supernaturalists that there is a context or body of experience that is just given by a transempirical deity. The language he used to set out his views was the language of technology. The failure of idealisms of various sorts, he argued, especially those that espouse forms of supernaturalism, is their attempt to posit a system that is self-contained and that ignores the "control of the environment in behalf of human progress and well-being, the effort at control being stimulated by the needs, the defects, the troubles, which accrue when the environment coerces and suppresses man or when man endeavors in ignorance to override the environment" (MW.10.333).

Dewey's theory of human inquiry, which he called "instrumentalism" and later "technology," and which I have termed productive pragmatism, characterized knowledge as "the outcome of competent and controlled inquiry" (LW.12.15). He argued that one of the greatest of philosophical mistakes is the attempt to separate knowledge from the specific practice that gives rise to it in each particular situation. Human inquiry is technological in the sense that it signals a shift from acquiescence with respect to beginnings and endings, the contingencies of nature, to a search for the means of control of consequences. Immediate use and enjoyment give way to the production of what is determined to be desirable. When human beings were just content to enjoy fire, or to think of it as a gift of the gods, there was no inquiry, no technology, no effective control of it. But when they began to *make* fire, they began to institute a "method of procedure" (LW.1.181). They took a major step on the road to technology. When such a change occurs, mere enjoyment of fire and consideration of its essence or "whatness" is supplanted by a concern with the "how" of its production and use.

Both Ellul and Heidegger treated technology in a manner that can be viewed as a foil for their deeper stories, stories that involved hope or salvation. On this reading, both were at bottom idealistic religious thinkers who found in technological myths a convenient instrument. In contrast, Dewey was a thinker who was entirely at home with technological accounts. The story he told us is about human beings responsibly solving the problems that confront them by means of "sharpening their tools." Among those tools is the enthusiasm with respect to ideals that he terms "religious," but it is only one tool among others. Like other tools, it must be used responsibly and appropriately, that is, only in situations to which it is properly applicable.

Because he rejected myths of hope and salvation such as the ones told by Ellul and Heidegger, some of Dewey's critics have taken his call for responsible technology to be a myth of domination and control in the worst of senses—a species of vulgar, straight-line instrumentalism. In chapter 3 I argued that Max Horkheimer, for example, misread his work in this way. I shall revisit Horkheimer's assessment in more detail in the next chapter. What redeems Dewey from criticism of this sort is his account of the delicate balance that must be maintained between means and ends whenever problem-solving is undertaken.

I have suggested elsewhere that Dewey's relationship to nature was similar to that of field naturalist Aldo Leopold.[13] Both men eschewed the notion of control in the sense of *domination* and embraced it in the sense of *management*.

Unlike Ellul, Dewey viewed hope as effective only when directed toward ideals for whose realization we are prepared to work from the inside of our technological milieu, all the while maintaining a careful balance between means and ends. And unlike Heidegger, Dewey thought that if there is a way out of our current difficulties, whatever they may be at any particular time, then it will be through the responsible use of the tools and artifacts that men and women have made and utilize, not as a result of preparation to hear the voice of a god.

THE NEXT TECHNOLOGICAL REVOLUTION

> We must wrest our general culture from an industrialized civilization; and this fact signifies that industry must itself become a primary educative and cultural force for those engaged in it. The conception that natural science somehow sets a limit to freedom, subjecting men to fixed necessities, is not an intrinsic product of science. Just as with the popular notion that art is a luxury, whose proper abode is the museum and gallery, the notion of literary persons (including some philosophers) that science is an oppression due to the material structure of nature, is ultimately a reflex of the social conditions under which science is applied so as to reach only a pecuniary fruition.
> —John Dewey, *Individualism, Old and New* (LW.5.105)

I. Talk about Revolution Is Easy, but Revolution Is Hard

"Talk about revolutions is easy," Marx Wartofsky has reminded us, but "revolutions are hard."[1] Compared to the technological revolutions that replaced wood with steel and steel with synthetics, he predicted, the next one will be much more difficult. We will have to politicize technology.

But what does it mean to politicize technology? If that's how activists are going to mount the next technological revolution (or how determinists are going to recognize it when it gets here), then perhaps it's time to get clear about what the idea means. The problem, of course, is that the very idea of politicizing technology has invited a smorgasbord of interpretations.

It's worth remembering, for example, that some of the programs that have been billed as attempts to politicize technology have been less than felicitous. For the hardline "scientific" Marxists,[2] for Stalin and his grey clones who dominated the technological and technical programs of the Soviet Union and its satellite states during the half-century following the end of World War II, politicizing technology most often meant attempts at centralized control of just about everything by political hacks and a relentless pursuit of what Langdon Winner has called "straight-line instrumentalism."[3] Winner characterized this approach as beginning with certain preconceived ends, then deciding on the appropriate instruments to reach those ends, and finally using the instruments to achieve the results.

In the hands of the Soviets, straight-line instrumentalism (which holds that predetermined ends justify the means) led to absurdities such as the rejection of Mendelian genetics and attempts to reverse the course of major rivers, as well as tragedies such as the poisoned air, soil, and water in much of central and eastern Europe. Historians now argue that in cases where Soviet technoscience was successful, such as the brilliant work done as a part of its space program, exemptions from the official system of control had been the rule. If the Soviet space program had gone its way completely unhindered by the "scientific" Marxists, the first human on the Moon might well have spoken Russian instead of English.

The "scientific" Marxists had read that the hand mill gives you feudalism and the steam mill gives you industrial capitalism, so they determined to give technological determinism a jump start. Since tools and techniques tend to determine forms of political life, they selected and enforced the tools and techniques that would yield the forms of political life that they knew in advance were the best for everyone concerned.

Of course these weren't the only Marxists intent on politicizing technology. There were also the softer Marxists—including the critical theorists of the Frankfurt School—who preferred the younger, more flexible, more humanistic Marx to the older, tougher, intransigent one. They viewed matters quite differently. As one of their number, Max Horkheimer, put it, they "reject[ed] the kind of knowledge that one can bank on . . . [and] confront[ed] history with that possibility which is always concretely visible within it."[4] Beyond that vague rejection of historical determinism, however, there was a remarkable lack of consensus among first-generation critical theorists regarding what it means to politicize technology.

Horkheimer, for example, was profoundly pessimistic about the prospects. In the end, he suggested that revolutionary practice demands the ascendency of an "intransigent" theory. Herbert Marcuse called for a radically new technoscience that would be ushered in as scarcity was abolished by the current incarnation of technoscience and as "final causes" were taken off their pedestals and treated as technical problems. Unfortunately, he provided little in the way of specific directions regarding how to realize that goal. Walter Benjamin also pointed to the end of scarcity as the beginning of a new relationship to technoscience, and suggested concrete ways in which the means of "mechanical reproduction"—the printing press and the camera, for example—could facilitate this change. But for all its insights, his program remains narrowly applicable. I shall examine the programs of these early critical theorists in more detail in a subsequent section of this chapter.

Today, some of the heirs of early critical theory—especially those who take Benjamin seriously—devote considerable time and energy to the analysis and critique of various forms of communication, especially television and film. Some of them write books on film studies and even produce programs on television. Others struggle to get an increased understanding of the ways that political communication takes place within technological societies and how such communication can be improved.

There can be little doubt that the heirs of early critical theory have produced excellent critiques of the media. They have also made valiant attempts to teach their students to look and listen critically—to be "mediate" as well as literate. The problem, however, is that those of us who appreciate their work and use their textbooks in film and media courses don't seem to be making much headway toward technological revolution. Commercial and political advertisers spend billions of dollars each year to influence how college and university students think, whereas most of us who teach film and media courses tend to have annual budgets in the mid-to-high two digits.

Even public television is from time to time threatened with extinction in the American heartland because it is perceived by some legislators, including a recent Republican Speaker of the House of Representatives, as "leftist and elitist." Despite the best efforts of the heirs of critical theory and those of us who are sympathetic with their work, it is the new philistines—from Rush Limbaugh to Rupert Murdoch—who increasingly control the media of communication. Apparently, the next technological revolution will not be broadcast on television—either public or private.

Wartofsky's own view, which he presented with tantalizing brevity, was that to politicize technology means to democratize technology. To democratize technology, in turn, he told us, means first the sharing of power and second, the "education, in a major way, of the scientific and technical understanding of the public to the extent that some forms of democratic participation in scientific-technical policy-making becomes feasible and useful, and not simply an empty populist piety."[5]

There are probably few who would deny that these are worthy objectives, even though some might be tempted to question the sequence of Wartofsky's steps to revolution. Following the lead of Dewey, for example, I would suggest that education is *always* education for power-sharing. Failing that, what passes for education is little more than either indoctrination on the one hand, or haphazard self-expression on the other. It now seems more obvious than ever that in the absence of healthy public education we run the danger of getting a kind of talk-radio populism that is long on opinion and short on discrimination. To make matters worse, efforts to enlarge the sphere of home-schooling and vouchers for private religious schools often proceed from the assumption that public education is flawed beyond repair—that public education is one aspect of the great American experiment in democratic living that has already failed and needs to be abandoned.[6]

In the United States of the late 1990s, politicizing technology has often been confused with pursuing political goals by means of electronic media. The vast amounts of soft money raised by politicians and spent on mass-media advertising is but one example of this phenomenon. Another is the increased blurring of the traditionally sacrosanct lines between news information and commercials. A third is talk radio, a kind of village party-line gossip session writ large in which unconsidered opinion is accorded weight simply because it has been broadcast. A fourth is the type of Internet site made famous by Matt Drudge, where unsubstantiated rumor is purveyed as if it were hard currency.

The great techno-prophet Marshall McLuhan warned us as early as the 1960s that one of the first casualties of the electronic revolution would be civility. Electronic media, he argued, would create the new form of tribal interaction that he called the "global village." But unless educational reforms accompanied the rise of the new communications techniques and technologies, the new electronic village would have many of the same defects as the old pre-industrial ones. It would be a place where rumor and disinformation are rampant and where people are less interested in creative debate about matters of common interest than they are in the titillating effects of sticking their noses into everyone else's private affairs. Public officials would give up their right even to minimal privacy as one of the costs of their election. The new electronic village would turn out to exhibit the very features that led both Plato and Aristotle to treat democracy as a defective form of political association. Perhaps Plato and Aristotle were correct. If I may be allowed to shift from Greek to Hebrew, it now appears that even the Garden of Eden that we once thought the Internet to be now has its serpents and its original sinners in the form of hackers, spammers, and virus code writers.

Leaving aside the failed program of the "scientific" Marxists, which now seems to have been consigned to the dustbin of history except in places such as Belarus and Myanmar, let us assume that Wartofsky, Horkheimer, Marcuse, and Benjamin are in general correct. Let us suppose that we need a technological revolution, that such a revolution would be brought about by politicizing technology, and that politicizing technology means making our technological-technical infra-structure more user-friendly. What's the next step? Do the mainstream methods of philosophy offer us any help in getting our revolution under way?

II. Analytical Philosophies

It must now be more or less apparent, even to its practitioners, that the tradition of Anglo-American analytic philosophy has been either unwilling or unable to develop a robust philosophy of technology in the sense in which I characterized it. Apart from its historic interest in the basic concepts of science (which was in any event never understood or treated as a type of technology, as I have argued it should be), and apart from its emerging interest in artificial intelligence and cognitive science, analytic philosophy has had amazingly little to say about the cultural context of technology and, consequently, about technological revolution. This may be one of the reasons why Thomas S. Kuhn's now classic work *The Structure of Scientific Revolutions* created a sensation at the time it was published.[7] It insisted that the "laws" of technoscience cannot be understood independently of their historical—indeed, their instrumental—context.[8]

Several characteristics of analytic philosophy have contributed to this situation. First, the primary interest of analytic philosophy has been spoken, written, or "conceptual" language, whether in its ideal (so-called "artificial") or its ordinary (so-called "natural") manifestation. Even Wittgenstein, who during his later career adopted a view of language as instrumental, never seemed to get beyond his preoccupation with language to a full-fledged consideration of the role of other sorts of instruments within human life. Even in Wittgenstein's rich and suggestive discussion of human interaction with material objects such as slabs and bricks, for example, non-linguistic artifacts seem to function as little more than props for a discussion of language. It may well be, as Dewey once observed, that language is "the tool of tools."[9] But for a robust philosophy of technology, it is hardly the only tool. In the case of Wittgenstein, this situation is all the more remarkable given his interest in architectural design and even his occasional practice of that art.

Second, although the later Wittgenstein and his followers attempted to under-cut the assumptions of "substance-accident" metaphysics, much of the rest of analytic philosophy has remained solidly within its sway. This commitment is not always apparent, since some of the practitioners of this view express themselves indirectly by means of propositional analyses. But substance-accident metaphysics, because of its commitment to fixed substances that possess or fail to possess fixed properties, is entirely too rigid to respond to the dynamism of the contemporary technological milieu, and especially to the functional subtleties and multiple taxonomies spawned by electronic technologies.

Put another way, it is fair to say that substance-accident metaphysics is not inimical to a comprehensive philosophy of technology as long as it is not taken literally, but only as one functional metaphor among many. Unfortunately, however, because of their strong commitment to correspondence theories of truth, the tendency of most substance-accident philosophers seems to be to get at the literal truth of literal propositions that correspond to literal states of affairs. Of course commitment to substance-accident metaphysics and the scientific realism that usually accompanies it is not unique to analytic philosophy, nor is it held by all analytic philosophers. On one side, the followers of the late Wittgenstein have tended to reject such views. On the other side, they are a feature of philosophical critiques of technology mounted by some neo-Heideggerians, of which the work of Albert Borgmann provides one of the best examples.

Third, and perhaps most important, analytic philosophy has tended either to ignore or to deprecate the role of the body in intelligent behavior. Viewed from one perspective, there is high irony in the fact that current analytic philosophy, which is the heir of logical positivism, has become the most metaphysical of contemporary philosophical schools. Viewed from a slightly different angle, however, this makes perfect sense. The concern of analytic philosophy is analysis, which is to say, theory. In their preoccupation with "possible world" semantics, for example, some ideal language philosophers seem blissfully unconcerned with the techniques and technologies that influence the way we live in this one. In their preoccupation with speech acts, some ordinary language philosophers appear myopic with respect to the technical and technological matrix in which illocutionary acts are performed and by which they are colored. Even in cases where practitioners of "action theory" (as it is often understood within analytic circles) examine simple acts such as the raising of one's arm, the object of the examination sometimes tends for all practical purposes to be a disembodied or context-free arm.

Even some social and political philosophers who have been trained in the analytic mode continue to suffer from this narrowness of vision. It is possible, for example, to read hundreds of pages of discussion about the role of John Rawls's "veil of ignorance" as an instrument for enhancing social justice without ever once encountering a discussion of the many and varied ways in which the embodied situatedness of human beings affects their self-perception, and therefore the preconditions for their entering into the type of contract in which a "veil of ignorance" might prove a significant tool. Perhaps this is one of the reasons that Habermas has charged Rawls with doing political philosophy "on the drafting table."[10]

To be fair, it should be said that Rawls has softened his position to the point that in the response to Habermas he published in 1995, he could write of "background culture" that "contains comprehensive doctrines of all kinds that are taught, explained, debated one against another, and argued about—indefinitely without end as long as society has vitality and spirit."[11] Still, I can find no evidence even in Rawls's recent work, apart from vague references to "learned and scientific societies" and the like, that he has taken into account the technological dimensions of that "background culture."

It might be objected that the work of philosophers such as Stanley R. Carpenter, Kristin Shrader-Frechette, and Paul B. Thompson constitutes a counterexample to my general thesis concerning the relationship between technology and analytic philosophy. Carpenter, for example, has published meticulously detailed analyses of ecological sustainability. Shrader-Frechette has examined the application of Bayesian methods to policy-making and provided expert analyses of proposed sites for the deposit of nuclear waste. Thompson has published influential analyses of the ethical problems associated with the development and use of genetically modified agricultural products. Even though these philosophers are carefully "analytic" in terms of their approach to their research materials, however, none of them counts as an analytic philosopher in the sense that Russell, Wittgenstein, Ayer, and Ryle devoted themselves to the analysis of so-called ordinary language or in the sense that Carnap, Reichenbach, and others occupied themselves with the analysis of so-called ideal languages.

It is not the point of this exercise to discredit or demean any of the various schools of analytic philosophy. The works of the late Wittgenstein and J. L. Austin, to take two examples, continue to provide insights into the mazes of language use. My point instead is to distinguish the pure, abstract atmosphere in which most analytic philosophers have done their work from the concrete world in which they, and the rest of us, live our lives as embodied human beings.

Because he was a philosopher, and because analysis is a philosophical tool, Dewey was of course interested in analysis. He viewed it as a phase of inquiry and as a part of abstraction, and he thought the work of abstraction essential to the enlargement of knowledge. Nevertheless, he warned against what he called the "philosopher's fallacy," namely, conferring on the results of analysis or abstraction a reality independent and prior to the inquiry of which it was a consequence. "Artificial simplification or abstraction," he wrote, "is a necessary precondition of securing ability to deal with affairs which are complex, in which there are many more variables and where strict isolation destroys the special characteristics of the subject-matter" (LW.4.173). Nevertheless, he warned us that we err "when the results of an abstractive operation are given a standing which belongs only to the total situation from which they have been selected" (LW.4.173–74).

William James expressed much the same view, but with considerably more flair, when he compared the work of abstraction and analysis to the air above an aquarium. If the air were not there to oxygenate the water, the fish could not live. The air may be *what* the fish eventually breathe. But it is not *where* or *how* they live or breathe, and it must be transformed before they can breathe it. It is necessary to their existence in the sense that it is required, but it is only one of the factors that sustain them.[12]

III. Early Critical Theory: Horkheimer, Marcuse, and Benjamin

As I have already indicated, some non-analytic philosophies have taken a major step beyond the philosophies of analysis and toward the development of a comprehensive philosophy of technology. I have already mentioned the work of Max Horkheimer, Herbert Marcuse, and Walter Benjamin—representative members of the first generation of critical theorists—and I have briefly described their critique of what they termed "Enlightenment rationality" as well as their analysis of what they took to be the prospects of the reform of technological culture. Now I shall deal with their respective programs in greater detail.

As Thomas McCarthy crisply characterized it, critical theory does not concern itself only with "the construction of a theory of social evolution (the reconstruction of historical materialism); its primary aim remains a historically oriented analysis of contemporary society with practical intent (a reconstruction of the critique of capitalist society)."[13] In other words, critical theory is a philosophy of praxis.

Max Horkheimer, who witnessed the rise of National Socialism in Germany, was profoundly pessimistic about the reform of technological culture. He blamed the disasters of culture as he knew it on the type of rationality that had been spawned by the Enlightenment. "Enlightenment," he wrote, "behaves toward things as a dictator toward men. He knows them in so far as he can manipulate them. The man of science knows things in so far as he can make them. In this way their potentiality is turned to his own ends. In the metamorphosis the nature of things, as a substratum of domination, is revealed as always the same. This identity constitutes the unity of nature."[14]

In other words, the technosciences are essentially locked into a method—the straight-line instrumentalism and its attendant domination that now colors all of life, obscuring individuality as it goes. The early Enlightenment promise of a rationality that would displace superstition, as the sun evaporates the early morning fog, has been corrupted. "With the abandonment of thought, which in its reified form of mathematics, machine, and organization avenges itself on the men who have forgotten it, enlightenment has relinquished its own realization."[15]

What is the remedy for this appalling situation? Horkheimer does address the subject, even if somewhat vaguely: "true revolutionary practice depends on the intransigence of theory in the face of the insensibility with which society allows thought to ossify."[16] In short, revolutionary practice demands the ascendency of a stronger commitment to theorizing.

Herbert Marcuse, another representative of the early critical theorists, argued that the reform of technological culture could never be brought about by piecemeal reform. The problems were simply too big to be repaired in that fashion. Technology, by which he meant the prevailing technoscientific rationality of quantification and domination, would have to undergo a "catastrophic transformation." There would have to be "the emergence of a new idea of Reason, theoretical and practical . . . expressed in Whitehead's proposition: 'The function of Reason is to promote the art of life.'"[17]

Contrasting what he called "the real" (the domain of technoscience) and "the good" (the domain of philosophy), Marcuse argued that the technosciences had for the most part gone about their work in the absence of input from philosophy. The technosciences had done a credible job of mechanizing socially necessary labor, thus liberating men and women and providing them with the leisure to think philosophically, that is, about values or "the good." Further progress, however, would involve a radical break with the past—a reconstruction of the technosciences whose issue would be an entirely new reality. The historical relationship between technoscience and philosophy would then be reversed. This would not be merely a superimposition of values upon the current technosciences, as some have recommended. Rather, radically new technosciences would have to be developed whose task would be to quantify values. As a result, this development would confront science with "the unpleasant task of becoming *political*—of recognizing scientific consciousness as political consciousness, and the scientific enterprise as political enterprise."[18]

In short, technoscience would finally "arrive at essentially different concepts of nature and establish essentially different facts."[19] Recent work in feminist philosophy of technoscience, or perhaps better put, the recent inclusion of women within technoscientific fields that had traditionally been the exclusive province of males, has proven Marcuse correct, at least on this one point. Beyond that, however, how is the politicization of technology to be accomplished? How is the new technology to be brought about? We are told little more than that it will involve the end of scarcity as we know it.

Steven Vogel pointed to another problem in Marcuse's account that is perhaps even more important. He argued that Marcuse's take on technology ultimately suffers from his reluctance to accept the idea that nature is socially constructed. In other words, Marcuse reified an independent nature and he located it over against the technosciences, relegating it to playing the role of object to technoscience's subject.[20] At the same time, he located the technosciences over against the human sciences, as the bearer of an ideology that must be overcome and replaced before cultural reform can occur.

For Marcuse, then, one of the paths to a radical new technoscience is the abolition of scarcity. Another is the rejection of "final causes" as fixed and finished and their reconstitution as technical problems. As I shall suggest a few pages hence, this theme—presented as little more than a hint in Marcuse—is one of the key features of Dewey's program for the reform of technological culture. Marcuse's own program, however, despite its good intentions, ultimately remains utopian at best, debilitated by its vagueness.

Walter Benjamin, another of the first-generation critical theorists, had a radically different view of the technosciences. His criticism of the Nazis was that they wanted to aestheticize politics, whereas he wanted to politicize aesthetics. What Benjamin meant by this was that technical instruments such as the camera have the capacity to liberate much of what is limited and limiting within human life in two respects. First, they are able to democratize life by severing the bond between beauty and scarcity. (If Marcuse's discussion of scarcity is theoretical and vague, Benjamin's is beautifully practical and specific.) Mechanical reproduction of images by means of the printing press, for example, removes much of the "aura" of oil paintings, for example, in the sense that it makes it possible for even the poorest person to own excellent reproductions of works of art. And second, the camera has the capacity to democratize because it turns every man and every woman into an auteur, that is, into producer, director, and actor in the work of art that constitutes their own life. As Benjamin put it, "the distinction between author and public is about to lose its basic character. The difference becomes merely functional."[21]

Benjamin's insights are even more relevant now than when they were first published. That the now-ubiquitous video camera has been the agent of social change should be evident to anyone knowledgeable about the events that followed the taped beating of Rodney King in Los Angeles. Performance artists now push Benjamin's thesis to the limit as they make even the most intimate moments of their lives available to cyber-voyeurs twenty-four hours a day, 365 days a year, all for a modest fee. On a larger scale, traditional conceptions of democracy are under increasing scrutiny as a result of the growth of the Internet. How do you run a totalitarian state when your people have computers and satellite dishes? As I write, the governments of China and Iran are attempting to find out.

But is this enough? Despite Benjamin's brilliant analyses and his pertinent prescriptions for democratizing the aesthetic dimensions of life, his thesis remains thin, with little to say about the broader themes of reforming technological culture. Even though important, is the self-expression of the auteur a sufficient basis for democratic life? It would seem that more is required. Dewey argued that such is precisely the case.

IV. Later Critical Theory: Habermas, Winner, and Feenberg

Jürgen Habermas, whose work is representative of later critical theory, also exhibits a deeply ambivalent relationship to the technosciences. On the one hand, as Steven Vogel has convincingly argued, his need to maintain the idea that technology is ideologically conditioned has led him to reject the positivist notion that technoscience is value free.[22] On the other hand, his need to distance his own position from any charge of relativism has led him to insist that the technosciences just deliver "the facts" and that meanings are solely the province of the human sciences. Vogel has argued that this split in Habermas's thought, which opposes socially constructed nature to noumenal nature, ultimately disables his critique of technology.

Matters are even worse, however, since this is not the only rift in Habermas's philosophical edifice. On one side, for example, are the technosciences that Habermas considers nefarious because their methods involve what he calls "strategic action" or straight-line instrumentalism. On the other side is communicative action, which is the lubricant of democratic organization, in tandem with emancipatory action, which supplies the critical component that helps communicative action to keep strategic action in its place. In Habermas's view, the strategic action of the technosciences attempts to colonize the human life-world because it is essentially, and even more important irrevocably, committed to the use of straight-line instrumentalism as its primary method. This situation is not remediable because it is rooted in the very life of humanity: men and women must work in order to survive, and work involves strategic action. The split between the strategic action of the technosciences and the communicative and emancipatory action of the human sciences thus runs the length of Habermas's program.

Given this impasse, what then is to be done? Beyond the treatments in his early work, Habermas has had very little to say about the technosciences since the 1970s. Early on, he criticized Marcuse's idea that the technosciences could be reformed. But in the process he created a considerable problem for his own position. The recent inclusion of women in traditionally male-dominated technoscientific disciplines, for example, has precipitated palpable reform in some of them. In other words, his thesis has been undermined because "the facts" have changed as the interests of those who "collect" the facts have changed.

Since the 1970s, Habermas seems to have been interested in the technosciences tangentially and intermittently at most. His real interest is in communication, and more specifically in the manner in which free and unhindered communication within democratic societies can be grounded so that it operates between the "facts" of ordinary or technoscientific discourse and the "norms" of a constitutional system. If Habermas's position on the reform of technology avoids the difficulties of Horkheimer's pessimism, Marcuse's utopianism, and Benjamin's narrowness, it nevertheless exhibits its own problems. As I have indicated, one of those problems is his profoundly ambivalent treatment of nature. Another is that he seems to want to isolate the technosciences by creating a bulwark against their further incursion into the human life-world. Because of these unresolved splits in his thinking, it is difficult to know what Habermas's positive program for the reform of technological culture might be, unless it rests entirely on the building of consensus within formal public-sphere debates.

Langdon Winner is representative of the many contemporary critics of technology who have been influenced by the early critical theorists through the "New Left" of the 1960s. In "Technē and Politeia," published in the mid-1980s, Winner argued that the traditional relationship between technology and politics has been reversed. It was once thought that politics, or what Plato called "statecraft," was the loftiest form of human production. Plato borrowed the metaphors of the technical arts for his discussion of the leadership of his ideal republic. And modern political thinkers such as Rousseau, Locke, and Jefferson drew upon metaphors of the reigning technoscientific paradigm, namely that the universe is a machine and that societies and individuals are lesser machines inside the greater one. Even as late as the early years of the nineteenth century, Jefferson was still well within the Greek tradition when he asserted that civic virtue and material prosperity are antithetical, that technical innovation and expansion threaten the civic virtues.

By the middle of the nineteenth century, however, as Winner indicated, this model began to be eclipsed by a different one, one whose claim was that material abundance is equivalent to, or at least necessary for, political freedom. Put another way, the new claim was that technological development is the key to an enriched and enlarged democracy, and therefore that technology should drive politics. (As I shall argue, Dewey accepted the first half of this statement, but he would have been puzzled by the formulation of the second half, since he called for a political technology.) Almost imperceptibly, Winner suggested, old political constitutions were replaced by new, de facto sociotechnical ones.

Winner argued that a social order based on a sociotechnical "constitution" is at once larger, more centralized, and more hierarchical than one based on a political constitution. In addition, sociotechnical arrangements tend to crowd out forms of human activity that do not conform to its demands of efficiency. Such arrangements are also very good at managing the very social and political institutions that would have formerly effected control over technological growth. In short, or so Winner's argument went, technological institutions now dictate to political ones. He suggested that the new order even has its own "founding fathers." Unlike Jefferson, whose goal was the institutionalization of the liberties we now know as the Bill of Rights, the founding fathers of the sociotechnical order, the Fords and the Rockefellers (writing today, he would probably include Bill Gates), have been more interested in profits, organizational control, and the pleasures of innovation for its own sake.

In Winner's view, the current situation calls for two corrective steps. The first is that there must be more widespread recognition that "every political philosophy in a given time implies a technology . . . and . . . that every technology of significance to us implies a set of political commitments that can be identified if one looks carefully enough."[23] In other words, we must recognize that politics have artifacts, and artifacts have politics. Second, there must be a shift from the present preoccupation with the "impacts" of technological change to a consideration of the "material and social infrastructures specific technologies create for our life's activity. We should try to imagine and seek to build technical regimes compatible with freedom, social justice, and other key political ends."[24] In short, Winner urged a turn away from technology assessment as it has most often been done and argued that technologies should be driven by and serve political ends.

Winner's arguments were clearly and plausibly articulated, and the examples he offered in their support are certain to retain their relevance well into the twenty-first century. But the solutions he proposed also have a rich past. They are similar to proposals offered by some of the Progressives of the first decade of the twentieth century and by British Guild Socialists such as G. D. H. Cole.[25]

Winner's proposals, however, almost invariably involve small-scale, Jeffersonian-type efforts. In his essay "Citizen Virtues in a Technological Order," for example, he proposed reforms based on the successes of Scandinavian experiments in small-scale participatory democracy.[26] He has sharply criticized even medium-sized federal programs such as NASA's exploration of space, which he has labeled (apparently having a bit of fun with the title of Tom Wolfe's book) "the wrong stuff."

But it is possible to share Winner's enthusiasm for advancing the reform of technological culture by promoting small-scale democratic exercises and at the same time wonder how, short of their abolition, he would reform larger programs such as the U.S. military establishment. In his work as I know it, he does not provide an answer to this question. At least some of his readers are left with the impression that his proposal involves a kind of "trickle-up" strategy that says if the small, immediate technological-technical infrastructure is taken care of, then the larger one will take care of itself.

Dewey was acutely aware of this problem. Despite his enormous admiration for Jefferson, he argued that within technological societies Jefferson's ideas about liberty and equality can be brought to fruition only by also drawing on the ideas of Alexander Hamilton, namely, that common effort will be required on a much larger scale than Jefferson had ever imagined. If the Jeffersonian ideals that Winner applauds are threatened by big-scale technology at the national and international level, then they must be redefined and reconfigured by systematic efforts that are directed to national and international entities as well as to those that are small and local (LW.11.370–71).

Andrew Feenberg is for the purposes of this account an especially important representative of the later critical theorists. This is because his attempts to "update" the critique of technology advanced by his teacher Marcuse carry him a considerable distance down the road in the direction of Dewey's productive pragmatism. Although he briefly refers to Dewey's treatment of democratic deliberation in his 1999 book *Questioning Technology*, he seems for the most part unaware of this connection.[27]

Like Dewey, for example, Feenberg has argued that the role of technology is neither determining nor neutral.[28] Moreover, rejecting the technological determinism that lurks in the background of the work of Horkheimer and Marcuse, he has argued that "technology is not just the rational control of nature; both its development and impact are intrinsically social."[29] He has further insisted that "this view undermines the customary reliance on efficiency as a criterion of technological development . . . [which] opens broad possibilities of change foreclosed by the usual understanding of technology."[30] If one reads this statement in the light of the work of Horkheimer and Marcuse, "efficiency" should probably be understood as "instrumental reason" or "straight-line instrumentalism," and "the usual understanding of technology" should probably be read as the views espoused by the early critical theorists. With all of this Dewey would certainly have agreed.

Feenberg has posited two dimensions of what he calls "technical objects." The first is their social meaning, and the second is their cultural horizon. The point of the first dimension is that engineering goals hardly ever have the last word, even when successfully articulated. Although it may turn out to the disappointment of the engineers in question, social meanings, some of which are quite different from original engineering goals, also enter into the life of technical and technological objects. On this functionalist approach, straight-line instrumentalism gives way to the ramification of multiple possibilities. As Feenberg put the matter, "differences in the way social groups interpret and use technical objects are not merely extrinsic but make a difference in the nature of the objects themselves."[31] Again, Dewey would have applauded this conclusion.

The second hermeneutic dimension, cultural horizon, refers to cultural background assumptions. In the medieval period of the Latin West it involved a preoccupation with religious signs and symbols, and in our own period it involves "rationalization." Echoing remarks that Dewey made almost a century ago, Feenberg concluded that "technology is thus not merely a means to an end; technical design standards define major portions of the social environment."[32]

How would Feenberg reform technology? First, a Heideggerian type of reification of technology must be avoided, since it turns out to be similar with the "Prometheanism" that he himself criticized. As he put it in the preface to *Questioning Technology,* "The time has therefore come for an anti-essentialist philosophy of technology."[33] (This statement is particularly interesting in view of the fact that Dewey's philosophy of technology was anti-essentialist from at least the 1890s.) Second, technological design must be "de-hegemonized" within technology. Finally, technology will be democratized not solely, or even primarily, through the legal system, but through greater "initiative and participation" that would result in the "creation of a new public sphere embracing the technical back-ground of social life, and a new style of rationalization that internalizes unac-counted costs borne by 'nature.'"[34] One can almost hear Dewey cheering Feen-berg on.

Although I cannot go into greater detail in this chapter, it is worth emphasizing that Feenberg has moved perceptibly in the direction of Dewey's productive prag-matism, even if he does not recognize that he has done so. He has (a) moved from an essentialist to a functionalist understanding of technology; (b) developed a moderate form of social constructivism; (c) rejected a Heideggerian-type roman-ticism in favor of a naturalized technology; (d) rejected the critical theorists' notion of technology as ideology; (e) accepted the idea that the project of Enlight-enment rationality is not as much of a threat as the critical theorists had imag-ined; (f) proposed the idea that technical decisions are made within a network of competing factors in which one weighs various desired ends against one another; (g) warned against the reification of the results of inquiry as if they had existed prior to inquiry (Dewey's "philosopher's fallacy"); and (h) recast technology in a way that crosses the line between artifacts and social relations.[35]

Feenberg's examples, however, like Winner's, tend to remain small scale and local, focusing on what he terms "actor networks." Ultimately, his solutions look very much like the kind of Guild Socialism that Winner appears to recommend and that was a *part* of Dewey's program. Dewey's program, however, as I have indicated, included much more.

V. Phenomenology: Heidegger and Merleau-Ponty

Martin Heidegger, Maurice Merleau-Ponty, and many others have also substan-tially broadened the scope of philosophical discourse in ways that continue to en-rich our understanding of the technological dimensions of our environment. These philosophers have gone beyond the analysis of spoken and written language (and its putatively corresponding concepts) to consider the work of the gestalt psychologists, the role of the body in situating and anchoring human activity, and the function within human life-worlds of myriad instruments, from Heidegger's hammers to the hat feathers and canes of the blind investigated by Merleau-Ponty.

As admirable as their contributions have been, however, phenomenological ac-counts in themselves do not appear to contain the key to the reform of technology.

The work of Martin Heidegger richly illustrates this point. As is well known, Heidegger's critique of technology exhibited two quite distinct stages. In the first stage, represented by his 1927 *Being and Time (Sein und Zeit)*, Heidegger "existentialized" Husserlian phenomenology by jettisoning its foundationalism and its commitment to a transcendental ego, and by emphasizing and exploring the notion of human situatedness, or *Dasein*. Within this situatedness Heidegger provided a brilliant analysis of the deep fissure that divides two types of technological response to the world. On one side of the chasm there is a background of familiarity and competence, a background of tools and artifacts that have been assimilated to our quotidian lives in ways that have made them virtually transparent in use. As a part of the background, Heidegger's hammer is no longer consciously engaged, but just used. On the other side of the divide there are tools in use, that is, involved in activities that require conscious instrumental engagement and where intelligent, authentic work gets done. This is a matter that I discussed at some length in chapter 1. The early, phenomenological Heidegger thus masterfully undercut the traditional problems associated with skepticism and substance-accident metaphysics, and gave new urgency to analysis of the role of the body in human action. Here is Don Ihde's excellent gloss on the concept of *Dasein*, or human situatedness, in *Being and Time:* "The human being always finds himself or herself *already bodily in* a situation, *in* a World. Moreover, this existential 'in' becomes the primitive for all other 'ins' which could be abstracted or derived from it. The geometrical 'in' as a dot within a circle is a derivative 'in'. Heidegger's analysis is to be the explication of the dimensions of that being-in-a-situation."[36] So much for substance-accident metaphysics, disembodied egos, and the "problem of other minds," to boot.

Many of Heidegger's interpreters, including Ihde, have read the first, early Heidegger as inverting the traditional model according to which theory is treated as superior to practice, knowledge as superior to action, and science as antecedent to technology. I have no desire to quarrel with this reading, but rather to suggest that, although it is correct, it does not furnish the requisite conditions for the reform of technological culture.

Well-known difficulties arise when we come to the work of the second, or later Heidegger—the post-World War II Heidegger of the "Letter on Humanism," "The Question Concerning Technology," "The Turning," and most notably the notorious interview with *Der Spiegel*.

The second Heidegger seemed determined to reinvert his earlier inversion of Greek metaphysics by recourse to a romanticism in which all *technē* is reduced (or, perhaps more properly, arrogated) to poetry. In his hands, the nouns "essence," "accomplishment," and even the verb "to produce" take on meanings that are pri-

marily associated with thinking in almost a Parmenidean vein, and not with practice. In his "Letter on Humanism," for example, Heidegger wrote that

> the essence of action is accomplishment. To accomplish means to unfold some-
> thing into the fullness of its essence, to lead forth into this fullness—*producere.*
> Therefore only what already is can really be accomplished. But what "is" above
> all is Being. Thinking accomplishes the relation of Being to the essence of man.
> It does not make or cause the relation. Thinking brings this relation to Being
> solely as something handed over to it from Being. Such offering consists in the
> fact that in thinking Being comes to language. Language is the house of Being.
> In its home man dwells. Those who think and those who create with words are
> the guardians of this home. Their guardianship accomplishes the manifestation
> of Being insofar as they bring the manifestation of language and maintain it in
> language through their speech. Thinking does not become action only because
> some effect issues from it or because it is applied. Thinking acts insofar as it
> thinks. Such action is presumably the simplest and at the same time the highest,
> because it concerns the relation of Being to man.[37]

I am unable to find even a hint of a plan for the reform of technological culture
in this passage, which so finely distills the later Heidegger's view of technology.
As I have said, however, I do find evidence that Heidegger has reinverted what
he so skillfully inverted in the phenomenological accounts of his early work.
Some, including Richard Bernstein and George Steiner, have suggested that texts
such as this one offer a key to Heidegger's now notorious political and ethical
disasters—his anti-Semitism and his membership in the Nazi party. "Despite
Heidegger's own appreciation of Aristotle's *Ethics,*" wrote Bernstein, "he never
does justice to what distinguishes *praxis* from *poiēsis,* or *phronēsis* from *technē*—to
what Hannah Arendt calls the human condition of plurality—the basic condition
of both action and speech."[38]

Although I think that Bernstein's assessment is essentially correct, I would give
the matter a somewhat different spin. My own suggestion is that Heidegger's political and ethical failures were due to his peculiar failure of nerve. He thought he
saw the way to proceed beyond the threshold of technological revolution, and he
acted by focusing his hope on the "truth" of a totalizing political movement. But
in doing so, he failed in two important ways. First, he failed in his attempt to make
a clean break with the tradition of Western metaphysics. Seen in retrospect, his
early work now seems more an *analysis* of the notion of practical situatedness
than a *demonstration* or practical application of how practical situatedness can be
intelligent: more an *analysis* of authenticity than a *demonstration* or practical application of how claims to authenticity can be tested. At the very least, as Marcuse

observed, the treatment of situatedness and authenticity in *Being and Time* explicitly precludes any putative isolation of Heidegger the professor from Heidegger the morally accountable person.[39]

Second, Heidegger failed to realize the intrinsic connections between methods of technology and the methods of democracy, taking both terms in their most comprehensive and most honorific senses. Heidegger may well have attempted to politicize technology, but it is my hope that few of us would wish to follow the path he chose.

In short and in retrospect, the early Heidegger now seems to have treated the practical as a subject for analysis, for which he could find no appropriate outlet among existential, in his case political, concerns. In his later work, as I have argued, there seems to be a reinversion or restoration of what he had earlier inverted. Heidegger's technological malaise leads him during his later period to an almost pathological fear of technological nihilism and consequently to hold that thinking and poetizing are more than adequate substitutes for other types of concrete productive activities—and this because the former harbor the possibility of salvation from the unthinkable consequences of the latter. Heidegger seems to have had a troubled vision of the yawning maw of a nihilistic technological milieu and then to have retreated to a defensive position that eventually proved to be tragically vulnerable.

Some, of course, have claimed that what I have called the failure of the later Heidegger is not so much political failure as it is a retreat from political activity. Jean-Paul Sartre even went so far as to suggest that Heidegger's involvement with the Nazis was not the result of a character flaw, since Heidegger, he said, "has no character; there is the truth of the matter."[40] My own reaction to this type of argument is that there are at least some situations, among which is the public disappearance of tens of thousands of one's Jewish neighbors, in which to be apolitical is to be a moral failure. Dewey put this somewhat differently in 1922, when he wrote that "Non-resistance to evil which takes the form of paying no attention to it is a way of promoting it" (MW.14.17).

Seen in this light, there is deep irony in the work of the later Heidegger. Romanticism, as it is usually understood, involves a heightened sense of nature and emotion. But a full sensory involvement in inquiry is precisely what is lacking in Heidegger's later work. His romanticism remains internal, idealistic, and confessional in its approach to the problems of technology. It seems unencumbered by the dose of naturalism that is required if romanticism is to remain healthy. His romanticism involves the celebration of an aesthetic moment, but that moment never becomes fully cognitive and is therefore never able to make a fruitful entrance into the public sphere. If we learn anything from Heidegger, it is that the path to the reform of technological culture lies neither in the politicizing of technology with the help of anti-democratic totalizers, nor in the romantic hope that a god will come to save us.

Don Ihde has come to a similar conclusion from a slightly different direction. In his essay "Deromanticizing Heidegger," he quotes a passage from Heidegger's essay "The Origin of the Work of Art," in which he, Heidegger, contemplates a Greek temple. "Standing there, the [temple] rests on the rocky ground. This resting of the work draws up out of the rock the mystery of the rock's clumsy yet spontaneous support. Standing, there, the building holds its ground against the storm raging above it and so first makes the storm itself manifest in its violence. The luster and gleam of the stone, though itself apparently glowing only by the grace of the sun, yet first brings to light the light of the day, the breadth of the sky, the darkness of the night."[41]

Ihde's parodical response to this passage contains at once elements of both hilarity and tragedy. "Seen while sailing in Long Island Sound, on the horizon stands the stark super-silo, light green topped, of the Shoreham nuclear plant. Standing there, it brings to presence the very contrast between the seemingly featureless sandhill earth with the sky. It stands at and defines the contrast, too, between the sea and the shore, which without its focal presence would also be featureless along the horizon."[42]

The force of this passage goes beyond its obvious parody to insist that artifacts have politics and that Heidegger tragically misses that point. Standing in front of the Parthenon he misses the fact that the bare, deforested hills in the background are the result of the same sociopolitical system that constructed the temple. In short, Ihde's point is that Heidegger's post-war romantic turn was an abandonment of politics, and a willful blindness with respect to the possibilities of the reform of technological culture.

Even Maurice Merleau-Ponty, despite his brilliant analyses of perception and embodiment, spent years grappling with the problem of how to politicize technology, or what he called "work." More specifically, he characterized "work" as "the ensemble of activities by which man transforms physical and living nature."[43] But he thought it a part of work to transcend itself by means of dialectic. "Thus, the human dialectic is ambiguous: it is first manifested by the social or cultural structures, the appearance of which it brings about and in which it imprisons itself. *But its use-objects and its cultural objects would not be what they are if the activity which brings about their appearance did not also have as its meaning to reject them and to surpass them.*"[44] Merleau-Ponty thus rejected the type of "technology versus the human sciences" splits that seemed to infect much of the work of the early critical theorists.

Some of Merleau-Ponty's critics, however, thought that they saw a different type of split lurking beneath the surface of his phenomenology. They thought they could see a lingering Cartesian dualism of subject and object. Merleau-Ponty acknowledged as much in a passage in *The Visible and the Invisible,* where he wrote that "[t]he problems posed in *Ph.P.* [*Phenomenology of Perception*] are insoluble because I start there from the 'consciousness'-'object' distinction—."[45] He then went on to propose a solution that is in some ways reminiscent of passages of William James's *Principles of Psychology* or Dewey's essay "The Postulate of Immediate Empiricism."

Despite these insights, however, and despite his brilliant contributions to phenomenology, most of Merleau-Ponty's interpreters have viewed his attempts at politicizing technology—after his rejection of Marxism in the early 1950s—as ambiguous at best, and perhaps even thoroughly confused. Kerry H. Whiteside has done an admirable job of summarizing in a couple of paragraphs the views of a half dozen or so of Merleau-Ponty's interpreters regarding this matter.[46] Was it a complacent pluralism? Was it a kind of idealism that viewed all political practice as more or less equally valuable parts of "Being"? Was it a condemnation of activism? Was it a politics of hope? A part of the problem is that when Merleau-Ponty turned away from Marxism he turned to a weak form of liberalism in which the status of values was never resolved. As I have argued, this is one of the areas in which Dewey's program is the strongest.

Nevertheless, there is much to admire in Merleau-Ponty's work. Don Ihde's reconstructed and reinvigorated version of phenomenology, which he calls "postphenomenology," treats Merleau-Ponty's project as a bridge between classic phenomenologist and pragmatic philosophies.[47] This is also an argument that has been advanced by Joseph Margolis.[48] I for one find this move highly salutary.

The patrimony of the phenomenologists, then—or at least their representatives Heidegger and Merleau-Ponty—includes brilliant analyses of perception, of the embodied situatedness of human beings, of behavioral and gestalt psychology, and of the ways in which tools measure the contours of our life-worlds. They have explored the ways in which technique is embedded within technoscience as well as culture as a whole. On balance, however, their program remains primarily an analytic one that has not been able to produce workable political options. Some of their ideas—such as the embodied situatedness of human life—clearly provide important ingredients of the recipe for the reform of technological culture. But even taken together they are not sufficient. Perhaps Heidegger's retreat into romanticism and Merleau-Ponty's retreat into what was probably some sort of idealism signaled their frustration that despite their important contributions, they were unable to take the next move: to propose a viable program for productive engagement at the level of cultural reform and renewal.

VI. Pragmatic Paths to Technological Reform

I have argued that the proposals for the reform of technological culture advanced by three representative first-generation critical theorists were ultimately afflicted by pessimism, utopianism, or narrowness. Further, I have argued that the proposals of later critical theorist Habermas suffer from debilitating dualities such as the nature-as-constructed versus nature-as-noumenal split and the instrumental rationality versus communicative action split. Winner and Feenberg, both of whose work exhibits the influence of the critical theorists, have advanced programs that are in many ways quite appealing. At the end of the day, however, Winner's proposals may prove to be altogether too Jeffersonian, in the sense that he has made no provision for mid- to large-scale technoscientific projects such as NASA.

As for Feenberg, a productive pragmatist can only applaud his move away from technological determinism and toward anti-foundationalism, his de-linking of technology and straight-line instrumentalism, his treatment of ends and means as mutually informative, and his call for greater participatory democracy. These are also planks in the Deweyan platform for the reconstruction of technological culture, but of course Dewey succeeded in nailing them down long before the emergence of the critical theorists, to say nothing of Feenberg's "updating" or reform of their positions.

Finally, I have argued that the brilliant phenomenological accounts of Heidegger and Merleau-Ponty have advanced our understanding of human situatedness and embodiment but that they were not able to take the next step toward the reform of technological culture. If all this is true, then what does it portend for the "technological revolution" of the title of this chapter?

Is our best option now to turn to the various forms of idealism espoused by eastern Asian philosophies, as Michael Zimmerman has suggested?[49] If the central argument of Reinhard May's book *Heidegger's Hidden Sources* can be sustained, then it makes perfect sense for a philosopher such as Zimmerman, who has intimate knowledge of the Heideggerian texts, to make this move.[50] If May is correct, then that move would bring the serious Heideggerian full circle to the very sources of Heidegger's understanding of "Being," "clearing," and "openness" in eastern Asian thought. But eastern Asian idealism has not been known for notable successes in the field of social and political philosophy, not to mention the reform of technological culture.

It is the central argument of this book that Dewey's productive pragmatism offers a program for such reform. I am aware that some, including Don Ihde, have tended to view pragmatism as one of the praxis philosophies, along with Marxism and phenomenology. And it is apparent that there are remarkable similarities between the work of Dewey and George Herbert Mead on the one hand, and Heidegger and Merleau-Ponty on the other. The pragmatic instrumentalism of Dewey and Mead during the first decades of this century exhibited a number of ideas that would be taken up by Heidegger and Merleau-Ponty several decades hence.[51]

To name just a few of these similarities, there is a rejection of the metaphysics of the Western substance-accident tradition; there is a novel emphasis on the role of the body in human experience; there are discussions of the situatedness of human beings within their life-worlds; there is an appreciation of the role of non-linguistic tools in human life; there is a social behaviorism; and there is an appreciation for the temporal aspects of human existence. Further, Dewey even anticipated by several decades both Heidegger's discussion of tool-use with its background of "competence and familiarity" and Merleau-Ponty's treatment of instrumental space and knowing as prehensile rather than spectatorial.

Merely to stress the priority of these features of Dewey's work, however, would be to miss the larger point: some of his other insights push beyond the contributions of the praxis philosophers in ways that have still not been fully appropriated by many philosophers of technology. I shall limit my discussion to three of these features.

First, if praxis philosophies (with the possible exception of what I have called the "reinversions" of the later Heidegger and the later Merleau-Ponty) tend to invert the traditional relation between theory and praxis, raising praxis above theory, then Dewey's productive pragmatism recasts the relationship altogether. Since praxis philosophies tend to privilege practice over theory (thus reaching escape velocity from the gravitational pull of Cartesianism) and to demonstrate the ways in which theory derives from practice, praxis philosophies may be called philosophies of action.

Despite the claims of some of its critics, however, pragmatism is in the last analysis not a philosophy of action. In a richer sense even than has been developed by the critical theorists, pragmatism is a philosophy of *production*. To put the matter a bit differently, it is a philosophy of "warranted assertibility" in the broadest sense in which what is assertible with warrant is a part of art, historiography, and law, as well as the technosciences. Productive pragmatism is not interested in action for its own sake, but in action that operationalizes outcomes with a view to the production of tools and *habits* of action. Its concern focuses on the checks and cues that validate the results of the interactions of thinking and other types of behavior as such interactions come to be worked out in the realm of existential affairs. Productive pragmatism thus regards the question of primacy regarding theory and praxis as a false, or "chicken-and-egg" type question. Two of the three great pragmatists of the classical period—Peirce and Dewey—exhibit remarkable unanimity on this matter and James was moving toward their position at the end of his life: the goal of inquiry is not action, but the construction of new and more refined habits, tools, goals, and meanings, in short, new and more refined products. The term "more refined" is in their work *operationalized, contextualized,* and *provisionalized.*

Nowhere did Dewey express the matter of the pragmatic alternative to praxis philosophies more clearly than in his Gifford Lectures, published in 1929 as *The Quest for Certainty.* "In reaction against the age-long depreciation of practice in behalf of contemplative knowledge," he wrote, "there is a temptation simply to turn things upside down. But the essence of pragmatic instrumentalism [what I have called productive pragmatism] is to conceive of *both* knowledge [or theory] and practice as means of making goods—excellencies of all kinds—secure in experienced existence" (LW.4.30 n.1).

In the hands of the productive pragmatist, then, theory and practice become equal partners as phases of inquiry. Working together, they orient themselves not just to the analysis of the past or present, but to plans for the future. Like good business partners, they are always negotiating with one another about the feasibility, design, cost, and marketability of potential products. Theory keeps an eye on practice, making sure that options are kept open, that imagination enters into the design stage, and that potential products are coherent with the larger goals of the firm. Practice keeps an eye on theory, making sure that design and production goals are not too ambitious or too fanciful, that products correspond to the needs of the market, that inventories of products and spare parts are maintained, and that the cash flow is sufficient to start the next project. Together, theory and practice engage in a conversation that constantly adjusts means to ends-in-view, and ends-in-view to the means at hand. The goal of the partnership is not merely action, but production. The goal of the partnership is continual adjustment to changing situations by means of the development of enhanced tools and new products.

Second, in addition to recasting the relationship between theory and practice, Dewey's productive pragmatism offers an additional advance over the praxis philosophies that I have already discussed. Whereas a primary focus of phenomenology has been on analysis of situated perception, and whereas (at least until recently) critical theory has tended to lop off much of what happens in the technosciences as just unredeemable and outside the pale of communicative action or emancipatory action, Dewey's focus was on inquiry—or better put, on inquiry in its robust sense as technology. It is true that for the productive pragmatist technology embeds situated perception. But when there is technology there is something more. New ways of feeling and seeing are often the impetus of inquiry, and even more often its outcome. But they are only a part of its overall program. Technology also involves the active development of new and better tools for the articulation of problems, for the formulation and testing of ideas and other artifacts, and for the integration of results within the stable platforms that remain outside of a particular sequence of inquiry because they are behaviorally unproblematic.

In other words, productive pragmatism gives new emphasis to the time vector within inquiry. It is one thing for Marx to say that human beings are the makers of their world and to *predict* what kind of world they should make. It is one thing for Merleau-Ponty to tell us that human beings are "condemned to meaning" and to say that they adjust through time. But it is quite another, as Merleau-Ponty's critics[52] have pointed out, to go beyond the phenomenology, critique, and prophesy with respect to work and production—and then to advance concrete suggestions about how to test its outcomes. Productive pragmatism focuses on outcomes without suffering the defects of popular forms of consequentialism, and it advances the view, which it claims is derived from technological experience, that the norms of technology are produced as by-products of technological activities themselves, and not introduced from the outside.

Whence arise the norms by which we judge our technological and technical products, including those that are political? Dewey addressed this question in the introduction to his 1916 *Essays in Experimental Logic*. Just as in the case of agricultural practice, they are formed not *by* farming, but *from* farming. *Ceteris paribus,* the norms of politicizing technology are formed not *by* the process of politicizing technology, but arise *from* the process of politicizing technology. Norms arise neither from the iron laws of history nor even from the specific hardware or materials of technology. They arise through the interaction of theory and practice as it provides intelligent answers to perceived problems.

This leads to a third and final point of difference between productive pragmatism and the praxis philosophies that I have discussed. This point may also help to clarify the previous one. A central feature of Dewey's work—a feature that is noticeably missing from the praxis philosophies as I read them—is his philosophy of education. An outgrowth of his own groundbreaking work in psychology, Dewey's instrumental educational program was specifically designed to revolutionize technology by democratizing it, but in a different sense than I have discussed up to this point.

Specifically, Dewey defined democracy as "belief in the ability of human experience to generate the aims and methods by which further experience will grow in ordered richness" (LW. 14.229). Democracy is therefore not so much the maintenance of a historical institution, or even work toward a fixed goal, as it is a method of education. Dewey wanted to convince us that methods of democracy, like the methods of the technosciences in their broadest sense, involve "the faith that the process of experience is more important than any special result attained, so that special results achieved are of ultimate value only as they are used to enrich and order the ongoing process. Since the process of experience is capable of being educative, faith in democracy is all one with faith in experience and education" (LW.14.229).

What did Dewey mean by experience in this connection? He told us that it is "that free interaction of individual human beings with surrounding conditions, especially the human surroundings, which develops and satisfies need and desire by increasing knowledge of things as they are. . . . Need and desire—out of which grow purpose and direction of energy—go beyond what exists, and hence beyond knowledge, beyond science [as body of knowledge]. They continually open the way into the unexplored and unattained future" (LW.14.229).

In Dewey's view, then, there are many paths to technological revolution—a revolution that would democratize technology by introducing into political and social life the types of technologies and techniques that have proved so successful in the various technoscientific disciplines. These paths to the democratization of technology are not committed to any particular institution, to any particular historical practice, or to any particular set of beliefs. Nor are they committed to any predetermined goal. Because of their intimate relationship to technoscience and education, they do not seek any particular result. They consist instead of the application of methods of adjustive inquiry that have proven successful in the various technoscientific disciplines, and in education (insofar as they have been tried out), but that have yet to be applied in many areas of human life. Such methods are open ended in terms of their potential for their own (methodological) self-development and self-correction.

For Dewey, the type of education that is the consequence of productive pragmatism is neither indoctrination on the one side, nor haphazard self-expression on the other. It instead involves cooperation between teacher and learner—between expert and non-expert, if you will—in ways that alter and enrich the experience of both. It is this feature of education—not just in the schools but in a lifelong curriculum—that makes it potentially revolutionary.

In the broad sense in which Dewey uses the terms, therefore, there is ultimately no difference between technologizing politics and politicizing technology, since technology in its broadest sense is for him the name of the method of inquiry that, when applied to political association, enriches and makes worthwhile the life of each associated individual and therefore enriches the associated whole. And it is only as such political associations themselves become richer and more meaningful that other manifestations of technological culture will achieve balance.

For Dewey, the paths to technological revolution, and therefore both the politicizing of technology and the technologizing of politics, lead through the schoolhouse and the school board, through the local newspaper and the national journal of opinion, and through various levels of government. They lead through the workplace, through the places where religious and civic groups gather, and through the courts. They lead to more, not less technology, once technology is understood as the intelligent production of new tools, including conceptual and ideational ones, for dealing with problematic situations. They lead not to the cheap talk about individualism that is most often a cover for retreat from common action (as in some forms of libertarianism), but to a true commitment at every level of government to fostering a true individuality that enables children and adults alike to undertake a lifelong quest to develop their capacities to the fullest extent, whatever those capacities may be.

To politicize technology in Dewey's rich sense is thus to technologize politics in a richer sense than we have heretofore seen. For Dewey, technology is a rich blend of theory and practice that eventuates in new and improved tools for living and out of which new norms develop. It involves improved taxonomies of perception as inquirential skills are improved. Linguistic and other types of analysis, together with practice of all sorts, constitute *phases* of inquiry, but are neither separately nor conjointly its equivalent. For Dewey, technology has to do with ideals and goals and ends-in-view in so far as they are transformed by means of intelligence. For Dewey, differentiation between tangible and intangible tools is a functional, not an ontological matter. When such differentiation is required, it does not exist *in re* but in inquiry.

What I find so attractive in Dewey's work is his deep commitment to three ideas about technological revolution, or what in a 1939 essay he called "political technology." The first is that technological revolution is not a matter of distinguishing technological artifacts from the ways in which we use them, because our technological artifacts *are* the ways we use them. The second is that there are no recipes for technological reform, nor could there be. Technological reform is not a goal but a process that takes on new dimensions and new import at each stage of its development and whose outcome can therefore never be predicted. And the third is that talking about revolution is easy, but making one is probably the most difficult and necessary task before us.

What empirical method exacts of philosophy is two things: First, that refined methods and products be traced back to their origin in primary experience, in all its heterogeneity and fullness; so that the needs and problems out of which they arise and which they have to satisfy be acknowledged. Secondly, that the secondary methods and conclusions be brought back to the things of ordinary experience, in all their coarseness and crudity, for verification. In this way, the methods of analytic reflection yield material which form the ingredients of a method of designation, denotation, in philosophy. A scientific work in physics or astronomy gives a record of calculations and deductions that were derived from past observations and experiments. But it is more than a record; it is also an indication, an assignment, of further observations and experiments to be performed. No scientific report would get a hearing if it did not describe the apparatus by means of which experiments were carried on and results obtained; not that apparatus is worshipped, but because this procedure tells other inquirers how they are to go to work to get results which will agree or disagree in their experience with those previously arrived at, and thus confirm, modify and rectify the latter. The recorded scientific result is in effect a *designation* of a method to be followed and a *prediction* of what will be found when specified observations are set on foot. That is all a philosophy can be or do.

—John Dewey, *Experience and Nature* (LW.1.39)

When philosophy is looked upon as argument, numerous philosophical "problems" occur simply to keep the argument under way; but when we recognize philosophy as vision, it can possess both the values of art and the excitement of literature.

—John Dewey, "Three Contemporary Philosophers" (MW.12.206)

NOTES

1. Tuning Up Technology

1. Tamar Lewin, "Report Finds Girls Lagging Behind Boys in Technology," *New York Times,* 14 October 1998, p. B8.

2. Rachel P. Maines, *The Technology of Orgasm: "Hysteria," the Vibrator, and Women's Sexual Satisfaction* (Baltimore: Johns Hopkins University Press, 1999), 4.

3. One unfortunate example of this phenomenon is the so-called green revolution that took place in Mexico. Before the "green revolution" Mexico was agriculturally self-sufficient. Afterward, it became a net importer of food.

4. Jacques Ellul, *The Technological Society,* trans. John Wilkinson (New York: Vintage Books, 1964).

5. This matter was the subject of a "Morning Edition" report on National Public Radio on 8 December 1999. The report is available in the NPR archives on the Internet at www.npr.org. See also Charles Perrow, *Normal Accidents: Living with High-Risk Technologies* (Princeton, N.J.: Princeton University Press, 1984).

6. *The American Heritage Dictionary of the English Language,* 3d ed. (New York: Houghton Mifflin, 1992).

7. Robert Pool, *Beyond Engineering* (New York: Oxford University Press, 1997), ix.

8. I use the term "scientific revolution" advisedly. I take the tack of Steven Shapin in *The Scientific Revolution* (Chicago: University of Chicago Press, 1996). On page 1 he writes: "There was no such thing as the Scientific Revolution, and this is a book about it." What we call the scientific revolution of the seventeenth century is of course a construct, but one that is not made of nothing. The term signifies a period during which existing attitudes, procedures, and products were radically altered.

9. This definition is a gloss on John Dewey's instrumentalism. One of his clearest characterizations of technology occurs in the passage from "What I Believe" quoted as the epigraph to this chapter.

10. See Lynn White Jr., "The Act of Invention," in *Dynamo and Virgin Reconsidered* (Cambridge: MIT Press, 1968), 107–31. My point complements that of White. He argues that there is as much of the "spiritual" in the button-and-buttonhole as in the sonnet, provided one is interested in keeping one's children from the cold. On my reading, the sonnet, no less than the button-and-buttonhole, is a technological invention, although not one that falls under what we call the technosciences.

11. See Lionel Casson, *The Ancient Mariners: Seafarers and Sea Fighters of the Mediterranean in Ancient Times,* 2d ed. (Princeton, N.J.: Princeton University Press, 1991).

12. José Ortega y Gasset, "Man the Technician," in *History as a System and Other Essays Toward a Philosophy of History* (New York: W. W. Norton, 1962), 154.

13. David Pye, *The Nature and Art of Workmanship* (Cambridge: Cambridge University Press, 1968), 4–5.

14. Shoshana Zuboff, *In the Age of the Smart Machine: The Future of Work and Power* (New York: Basic Books, 1988).

15. Thomas S. Kuhn, *The Structure of Scientific Revolutions* (Chicago: University of Chicago Press, 1962).

16. Lewis Mumford, *Technics and Civilization* (New York: Harcourt, Brace and World, 1934).

17. Larry A. Hickman, *John Dewey's Pragmatic Technology* (Bloomington: Indiana University Press, 1990).

18. Carl Mitcham, *Thinking through Technology* (Chicago: University of Chicago Press, 1994), 74–75.

19. I use the qualifier "deliberate" here, even though it may appear redundant, out of respect for the claim made by C. S. Peirce that organic life also exhibits inference below the level of conscious awareness.

20. Charles Sanders Peirce, *The Collected Papers of Charles Sanders Peirce*, vol. 5, ed. Charles Hartshorne and Paul Weiss (Cambridge: Harvard University Press, 1934). Paragraph 263 (in its standard form, citation for this passage is CP 5.263).

21. Mitcham points out that two earlier works had "philosophy of technology" in their titles, but their aims were really quite restricted. These were Ernst Kapp's book *Grundlinien einer Philosophie der Technik* (1877) and Eberhard Zschimmer's *Philosophie der Technik* (1913). See *Philosophy and Technology*, ed. Carl Mitcham and Robert Mackey (New York: Free Press, 1972), 22.

22. Some very recent monographs on the philosophy of technology still ignore Dewey's contribution to the field. As I was writing this chapter, for example, I received a copy of Joseph C. Pitt's *Thinking about Technology: Foundations of the Philosophy of Technology* (New York: Seven Bridges Press, 2000), which contains no mention of Dewey.

23. Hickman, *Dewey's Pragmatic Technology*.

24. This characterization has certain advantages over some of its alternatives. In *Thinking about Technology*, for example, Joseph C. Pitt defines technology as "humanity at work." (p. xi) Pitt's definition does, of course, have the advantage of generality. Further, as he indicates, it also obviates the problems that Jacques Ellul generated when he treated technology as a thing with an essence. On the downside, however, Pitt's definition does not appear on its face to preserve the distinction that I established in the first section of this chapter, namely, the distinction between technology and technique. In other words, it does not preserve the distinction between cognitive and non-cognitive deployment of tools and other artifacts.

On pages 10 and 11, Pitt criticizes the definition advanced by Emmanuel Mesthene, whose work I will discuss in chapter 7, "Populism and the Cult of the Expert." Curiously, Pitt objects to Mesthene's notion that technology is "the organization of knowledge for the achievement of practical purposes" (Mesthene *Technological*, 25) on the grounds that the phrase "organized knowledge" is redundant. Given the fact that our culture is currently suffering the splintering effects of increased specialization, this is a remarkable claim. One of the great needs of our milieu is precisely that what currently counts as knowledge be not only expanded, but better organized as well. Pitt then repeats with emphasis his definition, *"technology is humanity at work"* (p. 11). The idea, he writes, is that technology must involve the activity of humans, as opposed to organisms such as beavers or aliens, and that it must also involve "their deliberate and purposeful use of tools, taken in the general sense" (p. 11).

Two things about Pitt's gloss on his own definition are striking. First, his gloss seems to amplify what is in the definition to the point of significant revision. It adds the terms "deliberate" and "purposeful," for example. Nevertheless, the amplified definition still fails to capture the distinction I made between what is technological (cognitive) and what is technical (habitual), since it is quite possible to work mechanically in ways that are both deliberate and purposeful. Assembly line workers and farm laborers must do this daily. Of course play can be purposeful and deliberate as well.

Second, there is no acknowledgment that technology is involved not just in the use of tools but also in their invention and development; that tools must be applied in certain ways and not others; and that the problem that initiates inquiry is a function of a situation that involves inquiry with a particular perspective.

David Rothenberg, in an interview published in *A Parliament of Minds: Philosophy for a New Millennium,* ed. Michael Tobias, J. Patrick Fitzgerald, and David Rothenberg (Albany: SUNY Press, 2000), does not provide much help in this regard. "What is technology? It's really the whole history of tools that human beings have used to live in the world." (p. 169). This definition, if it is intended to be one, provides scant guidance concerning how to sort out the underlying differences, for example, between Greek warships and contemporary spacecraft.

25. See Larry A. Hickman, "Making the Family Functional: The Case for Legalized Same-Sex Domestic Partnerships," *Philosophy of the Social Sciences* 29, no. 2 (June 1999): 231–47; a revised and enlarged version of "Making the Family Functional: The Case for Same-Sex Marriage," in *Same-Sex Marriage: The Moral and Legal Debate,* ed. Robert M. Baird and Stuart E. Rosenbaum (Amherst, N.Y.: Prometheus Books, 1997), 192–202.

26. C. P. Snow, *The Two Cultures* (Cambridge: Cambridge University Press, 1993).

27. Carl Mitcham has noted that one response to my interpretation of Dewey's critique of technology in *John Dewey's Pragmatic Technology* involved the claim of reductionism. He thinks that "[my] reply to one possible formulation of the charge of reductionism does not consider the possibility that if all life is technological then the concept of technology becomes vacuous." See Mitcham, *Thinking through Technology,* 75. I hope to have put that objection to rest with the fourfold taxonomy I have developed in this chapter.

28. Mathematical objects have been developed within the sphere of the philosophy of mathematics. See Philip J. Davis and Reuben Hersh, *The Mathematical Experience* (New York: Houghton Mifflin, 1981).

29. See John D. Barrow, *Pi in the Sky: Counting, Thinking, and Being* (Oxford: Clarendon Press, 1992). See especially chapter 2, "The Counter Culture." This is an excellent introduction to the history of counting.

30. James Moore, "The Creationist Cosmos of Protestant Fundamentalism," in *Fundamentalisms and Society: Reclaiming the Sciences, the Family, and Education,* ed. Martin E. Marty and R. Scott Appleby (Chicago: University of Chicago Press, 1993), 2:49.

31. See Eliot Wigginton, ed., *The Foxfire Book* (New York: Doubleday, 1972). This is a back-to-basics guide to making it on the land. See also David F. Noble, *The Religion of Technology* (New York: Knopf, 1997).

32. Don Ihde, *Postphenomenology: Essays in the Postmodern Context* (Evanston, Ill.: Northwestern University Press, 1993), 3.

33. Raphael Sassower, *Technoscientific Angst* (Minneapolis: University of Minnesota Press, 1997).

34. "In the present epoch, science and technology combine to form contemporary technoscience. In technoscience, technology plays the role of furnishing the proof of scientific arguments: it allows one to say of a scientific utterance that claims to be true, 'here is a case of it.' The result of this is a profound transformation in the nature of knowledge. Truth is subjected to more and more sophisticated means of 'falsifying' scientific utterances." Jean-François Lyotard, "New Technologies," in *Political Writings*, trans. Geoff Bennington and Brian Massumi (Minneapolis: University of Minnesota Press, 1979), 14–15.

35. Sassower, *Technoscientific*, 3.

2. Technology and Community Life

1. This position was a part of the program of the logical positivists during the 1930s and 1940s. Some of their followers continued to advance it well into the 1960s. As I write, there are still attempts to rehabilitate portions of the positivist program. See, for example, Michael Friedman, *Reconsidering Logical Positivism* (Cambridge: Cambridge University Press, 1999).

2. This view is usually attributed to neo-pragmatist Richard Rorty. See, for example, his essay "Private Irony and Liberal Hope," in *Contingency, Irony, and Solidarity* (New York: Cambridge University Press, 1989), 73–95.

3. Dewey in lecture notes for 10 April 1926, Special Collections at Morris Library, Southern Illinois University at Carbondale, John Dewey Papers, 65/1. I owe thanks to Dario Segato for drawing my attention to this reference.

4. Following up on the distinction I made in chapter 1, I want here to distinguish between technically produced artifacts and technologically produced artifacts. A technically produced artifact is one that is made with very little or no cognitive interaction with materials. A technologically produced artifact is accordingly one that is the result of deliberate cognitive intervention into materials. Although this distinction fuzzes at its borders, it is nevertheless helpful in meeting the types of objections to my general account of technology that I discussed in the first chapter. In *Art as Experience* (1934), Dewey made the point that even the most utilitarian of domestic objects often enjoy cognitive attention in the form of decorative elements added.

5. Dewey was attacked on just these grounds by Mortimer Adler during a speech in New York in 1940. Adler charged that Dewey, because of his claim that there are no absolute values, had become a "serious threat to Democracy" (*Vital Speeches*, 1 December 1940, p. 100). See Robert Westbrook, *John Dewey and American Democracy* (Ithaca, N.Y.: Cornell University Press, 1991), esp. pp. 519–20, for more on this subject.

6. Televangelist Pat Robertson has often repeated Adler's attack on Dewey, and school

board members across the country have joined the attack as well. Page 2 of the July-August issue of the *Illinois School Board Journal*, for example, contained a letter from the vice president of a suburban Chicago school district in which Dewey was blamed for the shootings at Columbine High School in Littleton, Colorado. According to the writer, "pragmatism proposes that there are no unchanging truths, no fixed standard of morality." From this the author concludes that "the seemingly mindless slaughter at Littleton was the acting out of the pragmatic view. If it works, if it feels good, do it. They did." The writer's primary fallacy lies in his essentialist coupling of absolute values, which for him are of supernatural origin, and morality. This is precisely what Dewey wanted to de-couple, since he thought that morality could flourish in a world without supernatural influences.

7. Max Horkheimer attacked Dewey as having abandoned the notion of "objective truth." See Horkheimer, *The Eclipse of Reason* (New York: Oxford University Press, 1947; reprint, New York: Seabury Press, 1974), 45.

8. Richard Rorty has claimed that there is no fundamental difference between his own view and that of Dewey (see Giovanna Borradori, *The American Philosopher* [Chicago: University of Chicago Press, 1994], 106). Some have claimed, however, that Rorty advances a "fuzzy" version of relativism that is not only at odds with Dewey's more objective relativism, but that serves as an implicit criticism of it (see Richard Bernstein, *The New Constellation* [Cambridge: MIT Press, 1992], 233 ff.). The problem, in the view of Bernstein and others, is Rorty's deep sympathy with deconstructionist philosophers such as Jacques Derrida, who is well known for his view that human beings are caught in an infinite regress of textual interpretations. See Derrida, *Of Grammatology*, trans. G. C. Spivak (Baltimore: Johns Hopkins University Press, 1976). Christopher Norris is one of the many critics of Derrida who see him as a kind of half-hearted pragmatist. "So Derrida becomes a kind of half-way honorary pragmatist, having deconstructed a great deal of surplus ontological baggage but then fallen victim to the lure of his own negative metaphysics or systematized anti-philosophy" (Norris, *Derrida* [Cambridge: Harvard University Press, 1987], 151).

9. See William Andrew Paringer, *John Dewey and the Paradox of Liberal Reform* (Albany: SUNY Press, 1990), 130.

10. Malcolm W. Browne, "She Puts the Brakes on Light," *New York Times*, 30 March 1999, p. D1.

11. Davis and Hersh, *Mathematical Experience*, 71.

12. Donald Koch has taken exception to this term. He thinks that Dewey avoided relativism altogether, since he thinks that the emphasis should be on the situation that is problematic. The situation, of course, includes the individual who is attempting to solve the problem, but much more as well. And it is not the satisfaction of the individual problem solver that interests Dewey, but the resolution of the objective situation. Of course Koch is correct in this assessment. I have used the term "objective relativism," however, as a way of accounting for what I take to be Dewey's emphasis on the perspectival nature of perception and his innocuous form of *cultural* relativism.

13. For a discussion of incommensurability in science, see Kuhn, *Structure*.

14. Max Scheler, for example, held the view that the big gap that separated humans from non-human animals was due to the addition of a human "soul."

15. Jeri Clausing, "A Push to Narrow Disparities in Training and Access to Web," *New York Times,* 10 December 1999, p. A25. The NPR/Kaiser/Kennedy School Survey found that the digital divide is the greatest between Americans over and under sixty years of age. The survey found a twenty-two-point gap, 73% to 51%, between blacks and whites who have a computer in the home. Perhaps even more importantly, however, its authors concluded that the schools appear to be a major factor in equalizing computer access for children of different economic and ethnic groups. The results of this poll were reported on NPR and obtained from their Internet site, at www.npr.org.

16. Zuboff, *Smart Machine.*

17. In the "Around Alone" event, a round-the-world race in which sailboat captains competed solo, schoolchildren followed the progress of the race on the event's Internet site. The sailors communicated with the children via e-mail, responding to their questions about geography, marine life, ocean currents, and so on. In another project, schoolchildren were sent out to find out about the "roadkill," or dead animals on the streets around their school. Using the Internet, they researched the habitats and feeding habits of the animals. They concluded that the number of squirrels run over by automobiles in the neighborhood of their school could be reduced if they stopped throwing apple cores out of the windows of the school bus. These are precisely the kind of activities that Dewey was undertaking at his laboratory school at the University of Chicago in the 1890s. Dewey would, I think, have loved the Internet.

3. Productive Pragmatism, Critical Theory, and *Agape*

1. I am using the term "technoscience" in this chapter as stipulated in the last section of chapter 1, to refer to disciplines such as the physical sciences, engineering, agriculture, and so on. In terms of the taxonomy I worked out in that chapter, it is a species of technology in the general sense of the term, which I defined as the *invention, development, and cognitive deployment of tools and other artifacts, brought to bear on raw materials and intermediate stock parts, to resolve perceived problems.*

2. Among those to whom I refer as creationists I include not only the so-called "scientific" creationists, but also the advocates of currently fashionable "intelligent design" arguments.

3. Charles Sanders Peirce, "The Fixation of Belief," in *The Essential Peirce,* vol. 1 (1867–1893), ed. Nathan Houser and Christian Kloesel (Bloomington: Indiana University Press, 1992), 109–23.

4. William James, *The Will to Believe and Other Essays in Popular Philosophy* (Cambridge: Harvard University Press, 1979), 27.

5. "Truth" was a term that Dewey reconstructed to the point that he eventually rejected it altogether. He argued that because of the absolutist sense traditionally carried by that term, the term "warranted assertibility" served his purposes better.

6. See, for example, Dewey's remarks in LW.12.489 ff.

7. Albert Borgmann, *Technology and the Character of Contemporary Life* (Chicago: University of Chicago Press, 1984), 28.

8. One example would be the experimentation on hyperthermia undertaken by Nazi researchers on concentration camp inmates. Another example would be the notorious syphilis studies done on Southern blacks in the 1930s and 1940s in this country, studies that became the basis for much important knowledge about that disease.

9. Horkheimer, *Eclipse,* 45 n. 29.

10. Ibid., 46.

11. Ibid., 48.

12. Ibid., 49.

13. Ibid., 50.

14. Langdon Winner, *Autonomous Technology* (Cambridge: MIT Press, 1977), 228.

15. Horkheimer, *Eclipse,* 45–46.

16. Ibid., 55.

17. Ibid.

18. Dewey, MW.10.48. Quoted in Horkheimer, p. 53.

19. Reinhold Niebuhr, *Moral Man and Immoral Society* (New York: Scribner's, 1932), xiii.

20. Ibid., xv.

21. Ibid., 71.

22. Paringer, *Dewey,* 42.

23. Ibid., 55.

24. Herbert Marcuse, *One-Dimensional Man* (Boston: Beacon Press, 1964), 158. Quoted in Paringer, p. 55.

25. Paringer, *Dewey,* 57–58.

4. Art, Technoscience, and Social Action

1. Fundamentalism, of course, refers to a religious view based on the 1910 tracts *The Fundamentals.* Nevertheless, each of the five items of the fundamentalist agenda had been around for some time before 1910. These included "the literal truth of the Bible, the authenticity of all its miracles, the Virgin Birth of Christ, His Resurrection, His substitutionary atonement for the sins of man." See Ray Ginger, *The Age of Excess* (New York: Macmillan, 1965), 283.

2. Richard Rorty, *The Consequences of Pragmatism* (Minneapolis: University of Minnesota Press, 1982), 51.

3. See Konstantin Kolenda, *Rorty's Humanistic Pragmatism* (Tampa: University of South Florida Press, 1990).

4. Richard Rorty, *Consequences,* 51.

5. Rorty, *Contingency,* 13.

6. Ibid., 83.

7. Ibid., 85.

8. Richard Rorty, *Achieving Our Country* (Cambridge: Harvard University Press, 1998), 91.

9. See John R. Wallach, "Liberals, Communitarians, and the Tasks of Political Theory," *Political Theory,* vol. 5, no. 4 (November 1987): 581–611. See also Richard J. Bernstein,

"One Step Forward, Two Steps Backward," *Political Theory,* vol. 5, no. 4 (November 1987): 538–63. See also Cornel West, *The American Evasion of Philosophy* (Madison: University of Wisconsin Press, 1989), esp. 194–209.

10. John Stuart Mill, *The Subjection of Women* (Buffalo, N.Y.: Prometheus Books, 1986).

11. Jacob A. Riis, *How the Other Half Lives: Studies among the Tenements of New York* (New York: Dover Publications, 1971).

12. Stephen Shames, *Outside the Dream* (Washington, D.C.: Children's Defense Fund and Aperture Foundation, 1991).

13. Kevin Phillips, *The Politics of Rich and Poor* (New York: Random House, 1990).

14. Paul Wallich and Elizabeth Corcoran, "The Discreet Disappearance of the Bourgeoisie," *Scientific American* 266, no. 2 (February 1992): 111.

15. See especially Andrew Hacker, *Money: Who Has How Much and Why* (New York: Simon & Schuster, 1997).

16. Janet Steele, *Enlisting Experts: Objectivity and the Operational Bias in Television News Analysis of the Persian Gulf War* (Washington, D.C.: Woodrow Wilson Center Media Studies Project, 1991).

17. See Doug Ireland, "Press Clips," in *Village Voice* 36 (24 December 1991): 8. The individual identified as a "university professor" was in fact an adjunct professor at Georgetown University. There is a crucial difference between a faculty member who teaches on a part-time basis and whose primary employment is as a member of a congressional staff, on the one hand, and a full-time faculty member who pursues research in a scientific and objective fashion. This is precisely the distinction that was obscured.

18. *Extra!* 4, no. 3 (May 1991): 5.

19. Ibid., 11.

20. Richard Rorty, "Religious Faith, Intellectual Responsibility, and Romance," in *The Cambridge Companion to William James,* ed. Ruth Anna Putnam (Cambridge: Cambridge University Press, 1997), 85.

21. Elizabeth Flower and Murray G. Murphey, *A History of Philosophy in America* (New York: Putnam's, 1977), 2:469.

22. Rorty, *Contingency,* 85.

23. Ralph Sleeper, *The Necessity of Pragmatism* (New Haven, Conn.: Yale University Press, 1986), 1.

24. Rorty, *Contingency,* 89.

5. Technoscience Education for a Lifelong Curriculum

1. Jean-François Lyotard, *The Postmodern Condition: A Report on Knowledge,* trans. Geoff Bennington and Brian Massumi (Minneapolis: University of Minnesota Press, 1984). See esp. sections 9 and 10.

2. Dewey developed his "post-Enlightenment" view of science in numerous works. Perhaps his clearest presentation is in *The Quest for Certainty* (LW.4.1–250).

3. See Phillips, *Politics of Rich and Poor.*

4. Marty and Appleby, eds., *Fundamentalisms.*

5. Seyyed Hossein Nasr, *Science and Civilization in Islam* (Cambridge: Harvard University Press, 1968), 27.

6. Everett Mendelsohn, "Religious Fundamentalism and the Sciences," in Marty and Appleby, eds., *Fundamentalisms,* 2:23–41.

7. Marc Cooper, "The Christian Right's Sex Machine: Public Schools Praise the Lord and Pass the Propaganda," *Village Voice* 39 (7 June 1994): 31–35.

8. Moore, "Creationist Cosmos," in Marty and Appleby, eds., *Fundamentalisms,* 2:42–72.

9. See Maitland A. Edey and Donald C. Johanson, *Blueprints: Solving the Mystery of Evolution* (New York: Penguin Books, 1989), 99–101, for an account of Lord Kelvin's attack on Darwin. For an account of the view espoused by Agassiz, see Robert V. Bruce, *The Launching of Modern American Science* (Ithaca, N.Y.: Cornell University Press, 1987), 29–30. According to Agassiz in 1849, "the characteristics of a species never changed. . . . God made each species separately out of nothing, discontinued it when he saw fit, and replaced it with a new line" (Bruce *Launching,* 29).

10. Northrop Frye, *The Great Code* (New York: Harcourt Brace Jovanovich, 1982), 28.

11. *Chronicle of Higher Education,* 19 November 1986, p. 37. Cited in Tim M. Berra, *Evolution and the Myth of Creationism* (Stanford, Calif.: Stanford University Press, 1990), 121.

12. This quotation is from Berra, *Evolution,* 122. His source is M. Zimmerman, "Ohio School Board Presidents' Views on the Evolution-Creation Controversy: Part 2," in *Newsletter of the Ohio Center for Technoscience Education,* January 1988.

13. See "Researchers Alarmed by Reports of Public's Lack of Scientific Knowledge," in *Scientist* 8, no. 13 (27 June 1994): 3.

14. Dewey insists that ideals are not *a priori,* but generated in use. Ends and means interact and are developed in relation to one another within inquiry.

15. Lyotard, *Postmodern.*

6. Literacy, Mediacy, and Technological Determinism

1. William James, *The Principles of Psychology* (New York: Holt, 1890; Cambridge: Harvard University Press, 1981), 961.

2. Joseph Margolis, "What Is a Literary Text?" in *At the Boundaries: Proceedings of the Northeastern University Center for Literary Studies,* ed. Herbert L. Sussman (Boston: Northeastern University Press, 1983), 1:47 ff.

3. Albert Borgmann, "Texts and Things: Holding on to Reality," a paper delivered at *Lifeworld and Technology,* a conference at Duquesne University, October 1987, and published in *Lifeworld and Technology,* ed. Timothy Casey and Lester Embree (Washington, D.C.: Center for Advanced Research in Phenomenology and University Press of America, 1990), 93–111. See also Borgmann's *Technology and the Character of Contemporary Life* (Chicago: University of Chicago Press, 1984).

4. See also Dewey's discussion of the function of language in his *Lectures on Psychological and Political Ethics,* ed. Donald F. Koch (New York: Hafner Press, 1976), 375 ff.

5. Albert Borgmann, *Holding on to Reality* (Chicago: University of Chicago Press, 1999).

6. Ibid., 33.

7. Ibid., 166.

8. Ibid., 167.

9. Borgmann, *Technology*, 97 ff.

10. Allan Bloom, *The Closing of the American Mind* (New York: Simon & Schuster, 1987), 64.

11. Borgmann, *Reality*, 49.

12. Although the prospect is a tempting one, I cannot here provide a taxonomy of forms of technological determinism. One indication of the size of such a project, however, is that Marx himself held several different and even conflicting varieties of the thesis during his lifetime.

13. Bloom at least allows that listening to recorded *classical* music may not be antagonistic to literacy.

14. Walter Benjamin, "The Work of Art in the Age of Mechanical Reproduction," in *Illuminations*, ed. Hannah Arendt (New York: Schocken Books, 1969), 217–51.

15. Richard Powers, *Three Farmers on Their Way to a Dance* (New York: McGraw-Hill, 1985), 331–32.

16. Sidney Hook, *The Metaphysics of Pragmatism* (Chicago: Open Court, 1927), 29.

17. Bloom, *Closing*, 63–64.

18. Sergei Eisenstein, "Dickens, Griffith, and the Film Today," in *Film Form: Essays in Film Theory*, ed. and trans. Jay Leyda (New York: Meridian Books, 1957), 208–9.

19. Ibid., 232.

7. Populism and the Cult of the Expert

1. Cecilia Tichi, *Shifting Gears: Technology, Literature, Culture in Modernist America* (Chapel Hill: University of North Carolina Press, 1987), 98.

2. Ibid., 99.

3. John M. Barry, *Rising Tide: The Great Mississippi Flood of 1927 and How It Changed America* (New York: Simon & Schuster, 1997), 264.

4. Ibid., 266 ff.

5. As late as 1948, Dewey's critics were still pointing to his attempts to treat moral problems as if they were "engineering issues." See Hans Morgenthau, *Scientific Man vs. Power Politics* (Chicago: University of Chicago Press, 1948), 36. For more on this matter see Gary Bullert, *The Politics of John Dewey* (Buffalo, N.Y.: Prometheus Books, 1983), 183.

6. Emmanuel G. Mesthene, *Technological Change: Its Impact on Man and Society* (New York: New American Library, 1970).

7. Ibid., 25.

8. Ibid., vii.

9. Ibid., 76.

10. Ibid., 77.

11. Ibid., 81.

12. John McDermott, "Technology: The Opiate of the Intellectuals," *New York Review of Books* 13, no. 2 (31 July 1969), 25–35. There is no anachronism in the fact that McDermott's 1969 article appeared before Mesthene's *Technological Change* in 1970. McDermott's re-

marks were based on a report published by Mesthene in 1968 and that formed the basis for his later book.

13. Ibid., 99.

14. Ibid.

15. Ibid., 111.

16. Ibid., 121.

17. Dewey probably has in mind the views of William Graham Sumner.

18. George Orwell, *1984* (New York: Signet Books, 1960).

19. Voltaire had already recognized this fact when he labeled his Dr. Pangloss a "professor of things in general."

20. Bruce Bimber, *The Politics of Expertise in Congress: The Rise and Fall of the Office of Technology Assessment* (Albany: SUNY Press, 1996).

21. Ibid., x.

22. Ibid., 8.

23. Ibid., 23–24. Emphasis in original.

24. Michael Eldridge, *Transforming Experience* (Nashville, Tenn.: Vanderbilt University Press, 1998)

25. Had this chapter provided more space, I would have liked to discuss three fine contributions to the issues that it addresses. They are Paul T. Durbin, *Social Responsibility in Science, Technology, and Medicine* (Bethlehem, Pa.: Lehigh University Press, 1992), Judith M. Green, *Deep Democracy: Community, Diversity, and Transformation* (Oxford: Rowman & Littlefield, 1999), and *Standing with the Public: The Humanities and Democratic Practice,* ed. James F. Veninga and Noëlle McAfee (Dayton, Ohio: Kettering Foundation Press, 1997).

8. Hope, Salvation, and Responsibility

1. An excellent account of the myth of nature as machine can be found in Paolo Rossi, *Philosophy, Technology, and the Arts in the Early Modern Era,* trans. Salvator Attanasio, ed. Benjamin Nelson (New York: Harper & Row, 1970).

2. Dava Sobel, *Longitude* (New York: Walker, 1995).

3. D. O. Edge, "Technological Metaphor as Social Control," *New Literary History* 6 (autumn 1974): 135–47.

4. Ellul, *Technological Society.*

5. Jacques Ellul, *The Technological System,* trans. Joachim Neugroschel (New York: Continuum, 1980); Jacques Ellul, *Perspectives on Our Age,* ed. William H. Vanderburg (New York: Seabury Press, 1981).

6. Jacques Ellul, *Hope in Time of Abandonment,* trans. C. Edward Hopkin (New York: Seabury Press, 1973), 176.

7. Ibid., 177.

8. Ibid., 179.

9. Ellul, *Perspectives,* 108.

10. George Steiner, *Martin Heidegger* (New York: Viking Press, 1978).

11. Martin Heidegger, "Only a God Can Save Us," *Der Spiegel's* Interview with Martin Heidegger, *Philosophy Today* 20, no. 4/4 (winter 1976): 277.

12. Ibid., 278.

13. Larry A. Hickman, "Nature as Culture: John Dewey's Pragmatic Naturalism," in *Environmental Pragmatism,* ed. Andrew Light and Eric Katz (London: Routledge, 1996), 50–72.

9. The Next Technological Revolution

1. Marx Wartofsky, "Technology, Power, and Truth: Political and Epistemological Reflections on the Fourth Revolution," in *Philosophy and Technology,* vol. 9, *Democracy in a Technological Society,* ed. Langdon Winner (Dordrecht: Kluwer, 1992), 15.

2. I use the term "scientific Marxists" in the sense that Alvin W. Gouldner employed it in his book *The Two Marxisms* (New York: Oxford University Press, 1980).

3. Winner, *Autonomous,* 228.

4. Max Horkheimer, "The Authoritarian State," *Telos* 10 (spring 1973): 11.

5. Wartofsky, "Technology," 18.

6. See Gerald W. Bracey, *Setting the Record Straight* (Alexandria, Va.: Association for Supervision and Curriculum Development, 1997).

7. Kuhn, *Structure.*

8. The work of Mario Bunge is interesting in this regard. Bunge is one of the few analytic philosophers of science who attempted to construct a philosophy of technology. On page 12 of his little book *Tecnología y Filosofía* (a 1976 publication of the Universidad Autonoma de Nuevo Leon, Mexico), Bunge defines "technology" as follows. "A body of knowledge is a technology if and only if (i) it is compatible with science and controllable by the scientific method, and (ii) it is employed to control, transform, or create things or processes, natural or social" (my translation). This definition has the advantage of treating social institutions and conceptual artifacts, including processes, as technological artifacts. From the point of view of the characterization of technology that I am developing, however, it has the disadvantage of treating technology as an application of science.

9. LW.1.134. "'Utensils' were discussed in the last chapter, in connection with the useful arts and knowledge, and their indispensable relation with science pointed out. But at every point appliances and application, utensils and uses, are bound up with directions, suggestions and records made possible by speech; what has been said about the role of tools is subject to a condition supplied by language, the tool of tools."

10. Jürgen Habermas, *The Past as Future,* ed. and trans. Max Pensky (Lincoln: University of Nebraska Press, 1994), 101.

11. John Rawls, *Political Liberalism* (New York: Columbia University Press, 1996), 383.

12. William James, *Pragmatism* (Cambridge: Harvard University Press, 1975), 63.

13. Thomas McCarthy, *The Critical Theory of Jürgen Habermas* (Cambridge: MIT Press, 1978), 265.

14. Max Horkheimer and Theodor W. Adorno, *Dialectic of Enlightenment* (New York: Continuum, 1987), 9.

15. Ibid., 41.

16. Ibid.

17. Marcuse, *One-Dimensional,* 228.

18. Ibid., 233.

19. Ibid., 167.

20. Steven Vogel, "New Science, New Nature: The Habermas-Marcuse Debate Revisited," in *Technology and the Politics of Knowledge,* ed. Andrew Feenberg and Alastair Hannay (Bloomington: Indiana University Press, 1995), 23–42.

21. Benjamin, *Illuminations,* 232.

22. Vogel, "New Science."

23. Langdon Winner, "Technē and Politeia," in *The Whale and the Reactor* (Chicago: University of Chicago Press, 1986), 52.

24. Ibid., 55.

25. Alan Ryan, *John Dewey and the High Tide of American Liberalism* (New York: W. W. Norton, 1995).

26. Langdon Winner, "Citizen Virtues in a Technological Order," in *Technology and the Politics of Knowledge,* ed. Feenberg and Hannay, 65–84.

27. Andrew Feenberg, *Questioning Technology* (London: Routledge, 1999), 136.

28. Ibid., xiii. See also Andrew Feenberg, "Subversive Rationalization: Technology, Power, and Democracy," in *Technology and the Politics of Knowledge,* ed. Feenberg and Hannay, 4.

29. Ibid.

30. Ibid.

31. Ibid., 10.

32. Ibid., 97.

33. Feenberg, *Questioning,* viii.

34. Feenberg, "Subversive Rationalization," 19.

35. Feenberg, *Questioning,* 201 ff.

36. Don Ihde, *Instrumental Realism* (Bloomington: Indiana University Press, 1991), 49.

37. Martin Heidegger, "Letter on Humanism," reprinted in *Martin Heidegger: Basic Writings,* ed. David F. Krell (New York: Harper, 1993), 217.

38. Bernstein, *New Constellation,* 124.

39. Victor Farías, *Heidegger and Nazism* (Philadelphia: Temple University Press, 1989), 283.

40. Jean-Paul Sartre, "A More Precise Characterization of Existentialism," in *The Writings of Jean-Paul Sartre,* trans. Richard C. McCleery, ed. Michel Contat and Michel Rybalka (Evanston, Ill.: Northwestern University Press, 1974), 2:156 (quoted in Elisabeth Roudinesco, *Jacques Lacan* [New York: Columbia University Press, 1997], 220).

41. Don Ihde, *Postphenomenology: Essays in the Postmodern Context* (Evanston, Ill.: Northwestern University Press, 1993), 103–4.

42. Ibid., 111.

43. Maurice Merleau-Ponty, *The Structure of Behavior* (Boston: Beacon Press, 1963), 162.

44. Ibid., 176.

45. Maurice Merleau-Ponty, *The Visible and the Invisible* (Evanston, Ill.: Northwestern University Press, 1968), 200.

46. Kerry H. Whiteside, *Merleau-Ponty and the Foundation of an Existential Politics* (Princeton, N.J.: Princeton University Press, 1988), 272–73.

47. Ihde, *Postphenomenology.*

48. Joseph Margolis, "Dewey in Dialogue with Continental Philosophy," in *Reading Dewey,* ed. Larry A. Hickman (Bloomington: Indiana University Press, 1998), 231–56.

49. Michael E. Zimmerman, "Quantum Theory, Intrinsic Value, and Panentheism," *Environmental Ethics* 10 (spring 1988): 3–30.

50. Reinhard May, *Heidegger's Hidden Sources,* trans. Graham Parkes (London: Routledge, 1996).

51. Patrick L. Bourgeois and Sandra B. Rosenthal, *Pragmatism and Phenomenology: A Philosophic Encounter* (Amsterdam: B. R. Grüner, 1980).

52. For a discussion of this point, see Sonia Kruks, *The Political Philosophy of Merleau-Ponty* (Atlantic Highlands, N.J.: Humanities Press, 1981), 57–58.

BIBLIOGRAPHY

References to Dewey's Work

References are given by series and volume number and, in the case of articles, page numbers to *The Collected Works of John Dewey*. The series is indicated as follows:

EW   *The Early Works, 1882–1898*
MW   *The Middle Works, 1899–1924*
LW   *The Later Works, 1925–1953*

EW.3.93–109   "Moral Theory and Practice"
EW.3.155–73   "Green's Theory of the Moral Motive"
EW.5.96–109   "The Reflex Arc Concept in Psychology"

MW.1.230–37   "The Place of Manual Training in the Elementary Course of Study"
MW.6.357–467   "Contributions to *Cyclopedia of Education*"
MW.9   *Democracy and Education*
MW.10.89–97   "Logical Objects"
MW.10.320–65   "Introduction to *Essays in Experimental Logic*"
MW.14   *Human Nature and Conduct*
MW.15.3–7   "Fundamentals"
MW.15.47–52   "Science, Belief and the Public"

LW.1   *Experience and Nature*
LW.2.3–21   "The Development of American Pragmatism"
LW.2.235–372   *The Public and Its Problems*
LW.3.55–72   "Appearing and Appearance"
LW.4   *The Quest for Certainty*
LW.5.41–123   *Individualism, Old and New*
LW.5.267–78   "What I Believe"
LW.6.49–52   "Science and Society"
LW.7   *Ethics*
LW.9.1–58   *A Common Faith*
LW.10   *Art as Experience*
LW.11.368–71   "Liberalism and Equality"
LW.11.454–63   "Religion, Science, and Philosophy"
LW.12   *Logic: The Theory of Inquiry*
LW.13.63–188   *Freedom and Culture*
LW.14.224–30   "Creative Democracy—The Task Before Us"
LW.15.97–100   "A Comment on the Foregoing Criticisms"

Other Sources

Barrow, John D. *Pi in the Sky: Counting, Thinking, and Being.* Oxford: Clarendon Press, 1992.

Barry, John M. *Rising Tide: The Great Mississippi Flood of 1927 and How It Changed America.* New York: Simon & Schuster, 1997.

Benjamin, Walter. "The Work of Art in the Age of Mechanical Reproduction." In *Illuminations,* edited by Hannah Arendt. New York: Schocken Books, 1969.

Bernstein, Richard. *The New Constellation.* Cambridge: MIT Press, 1992.

———. "One Step Forward, Two Steps Backward." *Political Theory* 5, no. 4 (November 1987): 538–63.

Berra, Tim M. *Evolution and the Myth of Creationism.* Stanford, Calif.: Stanford University Press, 1990.

Bimber, Bruce. *The Politics of Expertise in Congress: The Rise and Fall of the Office of Technology Assessment.* Albany: SUNY Press, 1996.

Bloom, Allan. *The Closing of the American Mind.* New York: Simon & Schuster, 1987.

Borgmann, Albert. *Holding on to Reality.* Chicago: University of Chicago Press, 1999.

———. *Technology and the Character of Contemporary Life.* Chicago: University of Chicago Press, 1984.

———. "Texts and Things: Holding on to Reality." In *Lifeworld and Technology,* edited by Timothy Casey and Lester Embree. Washington, D.C.: Center for Advanced Research in Phenomenology and University Press of America, 1990.

Borradori, Giovanna. *The American Philosopher.* Chicago: University of Chicago Press, 1994.

Bourgeois, Patrick L., and Sandra B. Rosenthal. *Pragmatism and Phenomenology: A Philosophic Encounter.* Amsterdam: B. R. Grüner, 1980.

Bracey, Gerald W. *Setting the Record Straight.* Alexandria, Va.: Association for Supervision and Curriculum Development, 1997.

Bruce, Robert V. *The Launching of Modern American Science.* Ithaca, N.Y.: Cornell University Press, 1987.

Bullert, Gary. *The Politics of John Dewey.* Buffalo, N.Y.: Prometheus Books, 1983.

Bunge, Mario. *Tecnología y Filosofía.* Nuevo Leon, Mexico: Universidad Autonoma de Nuevo Leon, 1976.

Casson, Lionel. *The Ancient Mariners: Seafarers and Sea Fighters of the Mediterranean in Ancient Times.* 2d ed. Princeton, N.J.: Princeton University Press, 1991.

Cooper, Marc. "The Christian Right's Sex Machine: Public Schools Praise the Lord and Pass the Propaganda." *Village Voice* 39 (7 June 1994): 31–35.

Davis, Philip J., and Reuben Hersh. *The Mathematical Experience.* New York: Houghton Mifflin, 1981.

Derrida, Jacques. *Of Grammatology.* Translated by G. C. Spivak. Baltimore: Johns Hopkins University Press, 1976.

Dewey, John. *The Collected Works of John Dewey, 1882–1953.* Edited by Jo Ann Boydston. Carbondale: Southern Illinois University Press, 1969–1991. Published as *The Early Works: 1882–1898* (EW), *The Middle Works: 1899–1924* (MW), and *The Later Works: 1925–1953* (LW).

———. *The Collected Works of John Dewey, 1882–1953: The Electronic Edition.* Edited by Larry A. Hickman. Charlottesville, Va.: InteLex Corporation, 1996.

———. *Lectures on Psychological and Political Ethics.* Edited by Donald F. Koch. New York: Hafner Press, 1976.

Edey, Maitland A., and Donald C. Johanson. *Blueprints: Solving the Mystery of Evolution.* New York: Penguin Books, 1989.

Edge, D. O. "Technological Metaphor as Social Control." *New Literary History* 6 (autumn 1974): 135–47.

Eisenstein, Sergei. "Dickens, Griffith, and the Film Today." In *Film Form: Essays in Film Theory,* edited and translated by Jay Leyda. New York: Meridian Books, 1957.

Eldridge, Michael. *Transforming Experience.* Nashville, Tenn.: Vanderbilt University Press, 1998.

Ellul, Jacques. *Hope in Time of Abandonment.* Translated by C. Edward Hopkin. New York: Seabury Press, 1973.

———. *Perspectives on Our Age.* Edited by William H. Vanderburg. New York: Seabury Press, 1981.

———. *The Technological Society.* Translated by John Wilkinson. New York: Vintage Books, 1964.

———. *The Technological System.* Translated by Joachim Neugroschel. New York: Continuum, 1980.

Extra! 4, no. 3 (May 1991).

Farias, Victor. *Heidegger and Nazism.* Philadelphia: Temple University Press, 1989.

Feenberg, Andrew. *Questioning Technology.* London: Routledge, 1999.

———. "Subversive Rationalization: Technology, Power, and Democracy." In *Technology and the Politics of Knowledge,* ed. Andrew Feenberg and Alastair Hannay (Bloomington: Indiana University Press, 1995).

Flower, Elizabeth, and Murray G. Murphey. *A History of Philosophy in America.* New York: Putnam's, 1977.

Friedman, Michael. *Reconsidering Logical Positivism.* Cambridge: Cambridge University Press, 1999.

Frye, Northrop. *The Great Code.* New York: Harcourt Brace Jovanovich, 1982.

Ginger, Ray. *The Age of Excess.* New York: Macmillan, 1965.

Gouldner, Alvin W. *The Two Marxisms.* New York: Oxford University Press, 1980.

Habermas, Jürgen. *The Past as Future.* Edited and translated by Max Pensky. Lincoln: University of Nebraska Press, 1994.

Hacker, Andrew. *Money: Who Has How Much and Why.* New York: Simon & Schuster, 1997.

Heidegger, Martin. "Only a God Can Save Us." *Der Spiegel's* Interview with Martin Heidegger. *Philosophy Today* 20, no. 4/4 (winter 1976): 277.

———. "Letter on Humanism." Reprinted in *Martin Heidegger: Basic Writings,* edited by David F. Krell. New York: Harper, 1993.

Hickman, Larry A. *John Dewey's Pragmatic Technology.* Bloomington: Indiana University Press, 1990.

———. "Making the Family Functional: The Case for Legalized Same-Sex Domestic Partnerships." *Philosophy of the Social Sciences* 29, no. 2 (June 1999): 231–47. A revised and enlarged version of "Making the Family Functional: The Case for Same-Sex Marriage." In *Same-Sex Marriage: The Moral and Legal Debate,* edited by Robert M. Baird and Stuart E. Rosenbaum. Amherst, N.Y.: Prometheus Books, 1997.

——. "Nature as Culture: John Dewey's Pragmatic Naturalism." In *Environmental Pragmatism,* edited by Andrew Light and Eric Katz. London: Routledge, 1996.

Hook, Sidney. *The Metaphysics of Pragmatism.* Chicago: Open Court, 1927.

Horkheimer, Max. *The Eclipse of Reason.* New York: Oxford University Press, 1947; reprint, New York: Seabury Press, 1974.

——. "The Authoritarian State." *Telos* 10 (spring 1973): 11.

Horkheimer, Max, and Theodor W. Adorno. *Dialectic of Enlightenment.* New York: Continuum, 1987.

Ihde, Don. *Instrumental Realism.* Bloomington: Indiana University Press, 1991.

——. *Postphenomenology: Essays in the Postmodern Context.* Evanston, Ill.: Northwestern University Press, 1993.

Ireland, Doug. "Press Clips." *Village Voice* 36 (24 December 1991): 8.

James, William. *Pragmatism.* Cambridge: Harvard University Press, 1975.

——. *The Principles of Psychology.* New York: Holt, 1890; Cambridge: Harvard University Press, 1981.

——. *The Will to Believe and Other Essays in Popular Philosophy.* Cambridge: Harvard University Press, 1979.

Kolenda, Konstantin. *Rorty's Humanistic Pragmatism.* Tampa: University of South Florida Press, 1990.

Kruks, Sonia. *The Political Philosophy of Merleau-Ponty.* Atlantic Highlands, N.J.: Humanities Press, 1981.

Kuhn, Thomas S. *The Structure of Scientific Revolutions.* Chicago: University of Chicago Press, 1962.

Lyotard, Jean-François. *The Postmodern Condition: A Report on Knowledge.* Translated by Geoff Bennington and Brian Massumi. Minneapolis: University of Minnesota Press, 1984.

——. "New Technologies." In *Political Writings.* Translated by Geoff Bennington and Brian Massumi. Minneapolis: University of Minnesota Press, 1979.

Maines, Rachel P. *The Technology of Orgasm: "Hysteria," the Vibrator, and Women's Sexual Satisfaction.* Baltimore: Johns Hopkins University Press, 1999.

Marcuse, Herbert. *One-Dimensional Man.* Boston: Beacon Press, 1964.

Margolis, Joseph. "What Is a Literary Text?" In *At the Boundaries: Proceedings of the Northeastern University Center for Literary Studies,* edited by Herbert L. Sussman. Boston: Northeastern University Press, 1983.

——. "Dewey in Dialogue with Continental Philosophy." In *Reading Dewey,* edited by Larry A. Hickman. Bloomington: Indiana University Press, 1998.

Marty, Martin E., and R. Scott Appleby, eds. *Fundamentalisms and Society: Reclaiming the Sciences, the Family, and Education.* Chicago: University of Chicago Press, 1993.

May, Reinhard. *Heidegger's Hidden Sources.* Translated by Graham Parkes. London: Routledge, 1996.

McCarthy, Thomas. *The Critical Theory of Jürgen Habermas.* Cambridge: MIT Press, 1978.

McDermott, John. "Technology: The Opiate of the Intellectuals." *New York Review of Books* 13, no. 2 (31 July 1969), 25–35.

Mendelsohn, Everett. "Religious Fundamentalism and the Sciences." In *Fundamentalisms and Society: Reclaiming the Sciences, the Family, and Education,* edited by Martin E. Marty and R. Scott Appleby. Vol. 2. Chicago: University of Chicago Press, 1993.

Merleau-Ponty, Maurice. *The Structure of Behavior.* Boston: Beacon Press, 1963.

———. *The Visible and the Invisible.* Evanston, Ill.: Northwestern University Press, 1968.

Mesthene, Emmanuel G. *Technological Change: Its Impact on Man and Society.* New York: New American Library, 1970.

Mill, John Stuart. *The Subjection of Women.* Buffalo, N.Y.: Prometheus Books, 1986.

Mitcham, Carl. *Thinking through Technology.* Chicago: University of Chicago Press, 1994.

Mitcham, Carl, and Robert Mackey, eds. *Philosophy and Technology.* New York: Free Press, 1972.

Moore, James. "The Creationist Cosmos of Protestant Fundamentalism." In *Fundamentalisms and Society: Reclaiming the Sciences, the Family, and Education,* edited by Martin E. Marty and R. Scott Appleby. Vol. 2. Chicago: University of Chicago Press, 1993.

Morgenthau, Hans. *Scientific Man vs. Power Politics.* Chicago: University of Chicago Press, 1948.

Mumford, Lewis. *Technics and Civilization.* New York: Harcourt, Brace and World, 1934.

Nasr, Seyyed Hossein. *Science and Civilization in Islam.* Cambridge: Harvard University Press, 1968.

Niebuhr, Reinhold. *Moral Man and Immoral Society.* New York: Scribner's, 1932.

Noble, David F. *The Religion of Technology.* New York: Knopf, 1997.

Norris, Christopher. *Derrida.* Cambridge: Harvard University Press, 1987.

Ortega y Gasset, José. "Man the Technician." In *History as a System and Other Essays Toward a Philosophy of History.* New York: W. W. Norton, 1962.

Orwell, George. *1984.* New York: Signet Books, 1960.

Paringer, William Andrew. *John Dewey and the Paradox of Liberal Reform.* Albany: SUNY Press, 1990.

Peirce, Charles Sanders. *The Collected Papers of Charles Sanders Peirce.* Vol. 5, edited by Charles Hartshorne and Paul Weiss. Cambridge: Harvard University Press, 1934.

———. "The Fixation of Belief." In *The Essential Peirce.* Vol. 1. Edited by Nathan Houser and Christian Kloesel. Bloomington: Indiana University Press, 1992.

Perrow, Charles. *Normal Accidents: Living with High-Risk Technologies.* Princeton, N.J.: Princeton University Press, 1984.

Phillips, Kevin. *The Politics of Rich and Poor.* New York: Random House, 1990.

Pitt, Joseph C. *Thinking about Technology: Foundations of the Philosophy of Technology.* New York: Seven Bridges Press, 2000.

Pool, Robert. *Beyond Engineering.* New York: Oxford University Press, 1997.

Powers, Richard. *Three Farmers on Their Way to a Dance.* New York: McGraw-Hill, 1985.

Pye, David. *The Nature and Art of Workmanship.* Cambridge: Cambridge University Press, 1968.

Rawls, John. *Political Liberalism.* New York: Columbia University Press, 1996.

Riis, Jacob A. *How the Other Half Lives: Studies among the Tenements of New York.* New York: Dover Publications, 1971.

Rorty, Richard. *Achieving Our Country.* Cambridge: Harvard University Press, 1998.

———. *The Consequences of Pragmatism.* Minneapolis: University of Minnesota Press, 1982.

———. *Contingency, Irony, and Solidarity.* Cambridge: Cambridge University Press, 1989.

——. "Private Irony and Liberal Hope." In *Contingency, Irony, and Solidarity*. New York: Cambridge University Press, 1989.

——. "Religious Faith, Intellectual Responsibility, and Romance." In *Cambridge Companion to William James*, edited by Ruth Anna Putnam. Cambridge: Cambridge University Press, 1997.

Rossi, Paolo. *Philosophy, Technology, and the Arts in the Early Modern Era*. Edited by Benjamin Nelson. Translated by Salvator Attanasio. New York: Harper & Row, 1970.

Roudinesco, Elisabeth. *Jacques Lacan*. New York: Columbia University Press, 1997.

Ryan, Alan. *John Dewey and the High Tide of American Liberalism*. New York: W. W. Norton, 1995.

Sartre, Jean-Paul. "A More Precise Characterization of Existentialism." In *The Writings of Jean-Paul Sartre*, edited by Michel Contat and Michel Rybalka, and translated by Richard C. McCleery. Evanston, Ill.: Northwestern University Press, 1974.

Sassower, Raphael. *Technoscientific Angst*. Minneapolis: University of Minnesota Press, 1997.

Shames, Stephen. *Outside the Dream*. Washington, D.C.: Children's Defense Fund and Aperture Foundation, 1991.

Shapin, Steven. *The Scientific Revolution*. Chicago: University of Chicago Press, 1996.

Sleeper, Ralph. *The Necessity of Pragmatism*. New Haven, Conn.: Yale University Press, 1986.

Snow, C. P. *The Two Cultures*. Cambridge: Cambridge University Press, 1993.

Sobel, Dava. *Longitude*. New York: Walker, 1995.

Steele, Janet. *Enlisting Experts: Objectivity and the Operational Bias in Television News Analysis of the Persian Gulf War*. Washington, D.C.: Woodrow Wilson Center Media Studies Project, 1991.

Steiner, George. *Martin Heidegger*. New York: Viking Press, 1978.

Tichi, Cecilia. *Shifting Gears: Technology, Literature, Culture in Modernist America*. Chapel Hill: University of North Carolina Press, 1987.

Tobias, Michael, J. Patrick Fitzgerald, and David Rothenberg, eds. *A Parliament of Minds: Philosophy for a New Millennium*. Albany: SUNY Press, 2000.

Vogel, Steven. "New Science, New Nature: The Habermas-Marcuse Debate Revisited." In *Technology and the Politics of Knowledge*, edited by Andrew Feenberg and Alastair Hannay. Bloomington: Indiana University Press, 1995.

Wallach, John R. "Liberals, Communitarians, and the Tasks of Political Theory." *Political Theory* 5, no. 4 (November 1987): 581–611.

Wallich, Paul, and Elizabeth Corcoran. "The Discreet Disappearance of the Bourgeoisie." *Scientific American* 226, no. 2 (February 1992): 111.

Wartofsky, Marx. "Technology, Power, and Truth: Political and Epistemological Reflections on the Fourth Revolution." In *Philosophy and Technology*. Vol. 9, *Democracy in a Technological Society*, edited by Langdon Winner. Dordrecht: Kluwer, 1992.

West, Cornel. *The American Evasion of Philosophy*. Madison: University of Wisconsin Press, 1989.

Westbrook, Robert. *John Dewey and American Democracy*. Ithaca, N.Y.: Cornell University Press, 1991.

White, Lynn, Jr. "The Act of Invention." In *Dynamo and Virgin Reconsidered*. Cambridge: MIT Press, 1968.

Whiteside, Kerry H. *Merleau-Ponty and the Foundation of an Existential Politics.* Princeton, N.J.: Princeton University Press, 1988.

Wigginton, Eliot, ed. *The Foxfire Book.* New York: Doubleday, 1972.

Winner, Langdon. *Autonomous Technology.* Cambridge: MIT Press, 1977.

———. "Citizen Virtues in a Technological Order." In *Technology and the Politics of Knowledge,* edited by Andrew Feenberg and Alastair Hannay. Bloomington: Indiana University Press, 1995.

———. "Technē and Politeia." In *The Whale and the Reactor.* Chicago: University of Chicago Press, 1986.

Zimmerman, Michael E. "Quantum Theory, Intrinsic Value, and Panentheism." *Environmental Ethics* 10 (spring 1988): 3–30.

Zuboff, Shoshana. *In the Age of the Smart Machine: The Future of Work and Power.* New York: Basic Books, 1988.

INDEX

LARRY A. HICKMAN is director of the Center for Dewey Studies and professor of philosophy at Southern Illinois University in Carbondale. He is author of *Modern Theories of Higher Level Predicates* and *John Dewey's Pragmatic Technology* (Indiana University Press). He has edited *Technology as a Human Affair* and *Reading Dewey* (Indiana University Press), and is co-editor (with Thomas Alexander) of the two-volume work *The Essential Dewey* (Indiana University Press). He is general editor of the electronic edition of *The Collected Works of John Dewey, 1882–1953* and *The Correspondence of John Dewey, Volume I: 1871–1918*.